Learning Three.js: The JavaScript 3D Library for WebGL

Create and animate stunning 3D graphics using the open source Three.js JavaScript library

Jos Dirksen

BIRMINGHAM - MUMBAI

Learning Three.js: The JavaScript 3D Library for WebGL

First published: October 2013

Production Reference: 1101013

Published by Packt Publishing Ltd.
Livery Place
35 Livery Street
Birmingham B3 2PB, UK.

ISBN 978-1-78216-628-3

www.packtpub.com

Cover Image by Asher Wishkerman (wishkerman@hotmail.com)

Credits

Author
Jos Dirksen

Reviewers
Andrea Barisone
Will Crichton
Yi-Fan Liao
Sebastian Poreba
I. Abiyasa Suhardi

Acquisition Editor
Kevin Colaco

Lead Technical Editor
Arun Nadar

Technical Editors
Anita Nayak
Ritika Singh

Project Coordinator
Leena Purkait

Proofreaders
Mario Cecere
Lawrence A. Herman

Indexer
Mariammal Chettiyar

Graphics
Abhinash Sahu

Production Coordinator
Arvindkumar Gupta

Cover Work
Arvindkumar Gupta

About the Author

Jos Dirksen has worked as a Software Developer and Architect for more than a decade. He has much experience in a large range of technologies ranging from backend technologies, such as Java and Scala, to frontend development using HTML5, CSS, and JavaScript. Besides working with these technologies, Jos also regularly speaks at conferences and likes to write about new and interesting technologies on his blog. He also likes to experiment with new technologies and see how they can best be used to create beautiful data visualizations, the results of which you can see on his blog at `http://www.smartjava.org/`.

Jos is currently working as an Enterprise Architect for Malmberg, a large Dutch publisher of educational material. He is helping to create a new digital platform for the creation and publishing of educational content for primary, secondary, and vocational education.

Previously, Jos has worked in many different roles in the private and public sectors, ranging from private companies such as Philips and ASML to organizations in the public sector, such as the Department of Defense.

Besides his interest in frontend JavaScript and HTML5 technologies, he is also interested in backend service development using REST and traditional web service technologies. Jos has already written two books on this subject. He is the coauthor of the *Open Source ESBs in action* book that was published in 2008, and in 2012 he published a book on how to apply SOA Governance in a practical manner. This book is titled *SOA Governance in Action*.

Acknowledgement

Writing books is a long and hard effort. I couldn't have done this without the support and hard work of many others. There are many people I'd like to thank.

First off, my project coordinator Leena Purkait, without whom I would never have finished all the chapters on time, for coordinating all the details and allowing me to focus on creating the content. I'd also like to thank Ritika Singh and Anita Nayak for all the time and effort they spent in finalizing the chapters.

All the other people from Packt Publishing who have helped me during the writing, reviewing, and laying out process. Great work, guys!

I, of course, have to thank Ricardo Cabello, also known as Mr.dò_ób, for creating the great Three.js library.

Much thanks go to the reviewers. You provided great feedback and comments that really helped improve the book. Your positive remarks really helped shape the book!

I haven't mentioned the most important persons yet. I'd like to thank my wife Brigitte, who once again had to endure me spending my weekends and evenings behind my laptop, my daughter Sophie for pulling me away from my keyboard and always making me laugh, and my daughter Amber, who, even though she is just a couple of weeks old, makes me appreciate the really important things and moments in life.

About the Reviewers

Andrea Barisone works for a leading Italian IT company and has over 13 years of experience in Information Technology, working on corporate projects as a Developer using different technologies. He has also strong experience in the ECM Systems, and several J2EE certifications. He has great ability to acquire new technologies and to exploit the knowledge acquired while working with different environments and technologies.

Andrea is a Technical Reviewer for *Agile Web Development with Rails 4* by Pragmatic Bookshelf, and also for *BPEL and Java Cookbook* by Packt Publishing (work in progress.)

> I would like to thank my parents, Renzo and Maria Carla, for the gift of life they gave me, my beloved wife Barbara, and my two wonderful little children, Gabriele and Aurora, for making my life wonderful every day.

Will Crichton has been a Web Developer for many years. He is currently studying Computer Science at the Carnegie Mellon University. Previously, he has worked with a web design company, Webspec Design, and a biotechnology company, Pioneer Hi-Bred. Beyond just work, Will loves creating web applications — many merely adopted JavaScript, but he was born to it. He has created several frameworks and applications by using HTML5 technologies and continues to do more every day.

> I'd like to thank my brother, Alex, for his excellent guidance as a brother and programming mentor, as well as my parents for supporting me throughout my coding endeavors!

Yi-Fan Liao is a Frontend Developer who is enthusiastic about exploring the possibilities of the web. He started programming with .NET for building an online medicine tutoring application in 2004 and is proficient in web application design, architecture design, and performance tuning. He has expertise in HTML5 multiplayer game development and extensive experience in JavaScript canvas animation. Yi-Fan loves widget-making and knowledge-sharing. He was a speaker for Begin Three.js at JSDC 2013 and is located in Taipei, Taiwan.

Sebastian Poreba is a JavaScript Developer with a game development background. At work, he uses the Google Closure tool chain for data analysis application. After hours, he plays with WebGL and physics, and blogs at `www.smashinglabs.pl`

I. Abiyasa Suhardi is an Indonesian guy living a double life in Berlin, Germany. His day job is as a Frontend Developer doing Flash/Flex, HTML5, and JavaScript programming. His passion is working on indie game projects in the evenings, weekends, or whenever he has free time. He is sort of like Batman, but instead of saving the city himself, he made his game characters the heroes.

He has a Bachelor's Degree in Informatics Engineering, a Master's Degree in Digital Media, and 9 years of experience working in the IT world, ranging from C/C++ for an intranet portal, teaching Macromedia Director, founding a J2ME game company, RIA Development using Flash/Flex, and mobile development with Android and Adobe AIR, to JavaScript development for backend and frontend.

Currently, he is working in a startup company, while backing up his partner-in-crime, his wife, in building their own startup.

You can follow his work at `http://www.abiyasa.com` and connect with him on Twitter (`@abiyasasuhardi`).

www.PacktPub.com

Support files, eBooks, discount offers and more

You might want to visit www.PacktPub.com for support files and downloads related to your book.

Did you know that Packt offers eBook versions of every book published, with PDF and ePub files available? You can upgrade to the eBook version at www.PacktPub.com and as a print book customer, you are entitled to a discount on the eBook copy. Get in touch with us at service@packtpub.com for more details.

At www.PacktPub.com, you can also read a collection of free technical articles, sign up for a range of free newsletters and receive exclusive discounts and offers on Packt books and eBooks.

http://PacktLib.PacktPub.com

Do you need instant solutions to your IT questions? PacktLib is Packt's online digital book library. Here, you can access, read and search across Packt's entire library of books.

Why Subscribe?

- Fully searchable across every book published by Packt
- Copy and paste, print and bookmark content
- On demand and accessible via web browser

Free Access for Packt account holders

If you have an account with Packt at www.PacktPub.com, you can use this to access PacktLib today and view nine entirely free books. Simply use your login credentials for immediate access.

Table of Contents

Preface	1
Chapter 1: Creating Your First 3D Scene with Three.js	**7**
Requirements for using Three.js	**11**
Getting the source code	**12**
Using Git to clone the repository	13
Downloading and extracting the archive	14
Testing the examples	14
Python-based approach should work on most Unix/Mac systems	15
NPM-based approach if you've got Node.js installed	15
Portable version of Mongoose for Mac/Windows	15
Creating an HTML skeleton page	**16**
Rendering and viewing a 3D object	**19**
Adding materials, lights, and shadows	**24**
Expanding your first scene with animations	**27**
Introducing the requestAnimationFrame() method	27
Animating the cube	30
Bouncing the ball	30
Using the dat.GUI library to make experimenting easier	**32**
Using the ASCII effect	**33**
Summary	**35**
Chapter 2: Working with the Basic Components That Make Up a Three.js Scene	**37**
Creating a scene	**37**
Basic functionality of the scene	38
Adding the fog effect to the scene	44
Using the overrideMaterial property	45
Working with the Geometry and Mesh objects	**46**
The properties and functions of a geometry	47

The functions and attributes for a mesh 52
Using the available cameras for different uses **57**
The orthographic camera versus the perspective camera 57
Focusing the camera on a specific point 62
Summary **64**

Chapter 3: Working with the Different Light Sources
Available in Three.js **65**
Exploring the lights provided by Three.js **66**
Learning about the basic lights **66**
AmbientLight – a globally applied light source 67
Using the THREE.Color() object 69
PointLight – the light that shines in all directions 71
SpotLight – the light with a cone effect 75
DirectionalLight – for a far away sun-like light source 80
Using special lights for advanced lighting 83
HemisphereLight 83
AreaLight 84
LensFlare 87
Summary **91**

Chapter 4: Working with the Three.js Materials **93**
Understanding the common material properties **94**
Basic properties 94
Blending properties 95
Advanced properties 96
Starting with the simple Mesh materials (basic, depth, and face) **97**
The MeshBasicMaterial for simple surfaces 97
The MeshDepthMaterial for depth-based coloring 100
Combining the materials 102
The MeshNormalMaterial for normal-based colors 104
The MeshFaceMaterial for assigning a material to each face 107
Learning about the advanced materials **110**
The MeshLambertMaterial for dull, non-shiny surfaces 110
The MeshPhongMaterial for shiny objects 112
Creating your own shaders with the ShaderMaterial 114
Using the materials for a line geometry **121**
The LineBasicMaterial 122
The LineDashedMaterial 124
Summary **125**

Chapter 5: Learning to Work with Geometries   127

The basic geometries provided by Three.js   128
Two-dimensional geometries   128
PlaneGeometry   128
CircleGeometry   130
ShapeGeometry   132
Three-dimensional geometries   137
CubeGeometry   138
SphereGeometry   139
CylinderGeometry   142
TorusGeometry   144
TorusKnotGeometry   145
PolyhedronGeometry   147
Summary   150

Chapter 6: Using Advanced Geometries and Binary Operations   153

ConvexGeometry   154
LatheGeometry   156
Create a geometry by extruding   158
ExtrudeGeometry   158
TubeGeometry   160
Extrude from SVG   162
ParametricGeometry   164
Creating 3D text   167
Rendering text   167
Adding custom fonts   170
Using binary operations to combine meshes   171
The subtract function   173
The intersect function   177
The union function   179
Summary   180

Chapter 7: Particles and the Particle System   181

Understanding particles   182
Particles, the particle system, and the BasicParticleMaterial   184
Styling particles with the HTML5 canvas   187
Using HTML5 canvas with the CanvasRenderer class   188
Using HTML5 canvas with the WebGLRenderer class   190
Using textures to style particles   192
Working with sprites   199
Creating a particle system from an advanced geometry   204
Summary   206

Chapter 8: Creating and Loading Advanced Meshes and Geometries — **207**

Geometry grouping and merging — **207**
Grouping objects together — 208
Merging multiple meshes into a single mesh — 210
Loading geometries from external resources — 212
Saving and loading in Three.js JSON format — 213
  Saving and loading a geometry — 213
  Saving and loading a scene — 216
Working with Blender — 218
  Installing the Three.js exporter in Blender — 219
  Loading and exporting a model from Blender — 221
Importing from 3D file formats — 224
  OBJ and MTL format — 224
  Loading a collada model — 228
  Loading STL, CTM, and VTK models — 229
  Showing proteins from the protein databank — 231
  Creating a particle system from a PLY model — 234

Summary — **235**

Chapter 9: Animations and Moving the Camera — **237**

Basic animations — **238**
Simple animations — 238
Selecting objects — 240
Animating with Tween.js — 242

Working with the camera — **245**
TrackballControls — 246
FlyControls — 248
RollControls — 250
FirstPersonControls — 250
OrbitControl — 252
PathControl — 254

Morphing and skeletal animation — **257**
Animation with morph targets — 258
  Animation with MorphAnimMesh — 259
  Creating an animation by setting the morphTargetInfluence property — 262
Animation using bones and skinning — 263

Creating animations using external models — **266**
Creating bones animation using Blender — 266
Loading an animation from a collada model — 270
Animation loaded from a Quake model — 272

Summary — **274**

Chapter 10: Loading and Working with Textures   277

Using textures in materials   278
   Loading a texture and applying it to mesh   278
   Using a bump map to create wrinkles   282
   Using more detailed bumps and wrinkles with a normal map   284
   Creating fake shadows using a light map   286
   Creating fake reflections using an environment map   288
   Specular map   292
Advanced usage of textures   294
   Custom UV mapping   294
   Repeat wrapping   297
   Rendering to canvas and using it as a texture   299
     Using canvas as a texture   300
     Using canvas as a bump map   301
     Using the output from a video as a texture   303
Summary   305

Chapter 11: Custom Shaders and Render Post Processing   307

Setting up the post processing   308
   Creating the EffectComposer object   309
     Configuring the EffectComposer object for post processing   310
     Updating the render loop   310
Post processing passes   311
   Simple post processing passes   312
     Using the FilmPass to create a TV-like effect   313
     Adding a bloom effect to the scene with the BloomPass   314
     Outputting the scene as a set of dots with the DotScreenPass   315
     Showing the output of multiple renderers on the same screen   317
   Advanced EffectComposer flows by using masks   318
   Using the ShaderPass for custom effects   323
     Simple shaders   324
     Blurring shaders   327
     Advanced shaders   329
Creating custom post processing shaders   330
   Custom grayscale shader   330
   Creating a custom bit shader   334
Summary   336

Chapter 12: Adding Physics to Your Scene with Physijs   339

Creating a basic Three.js scene ready for Physijs   340
Material properties   346
Basic supported shapes   348
Using constraints to limit movement of objects   354
   Using PointConstraint to limit movement between two points   355

Creating door-like constraints with a HingeConstraint   357
Limiting movement to a single axis with a SliderConstraint   359
Creating a ball joint-like constraint with the ConeTwist Constraint   361
Creating detailed control with the DOFConstraint   364
  Summary   **368**
Index   **371**

Preface

In the last couple of years, browsers have gotten more powerful and are capable platforms to deliver complex applications and graphics. Most of this, though, is standard 2D graphics. Most modern browsers have adopted WebGL, which allows you to not only create 2D applications and graphics in the browser, but also create beautiful and good performing 3D applications, using the capabilities of the GPU.

Programming WebGL directly, however, is very complex. You need to know the inner details of WebGL and learn a complex shader language to get the most out of WebGL. The Three.js library provides a very easy-to-use JavaScript API based on the features of WebGL, so that you can create beautiful 3D graphics, without having to learn the WebGL details.

The Three.js library provides a large number of features and APIs that you can use to create 3D scenes directly in your browser. In this book you'll learn all the different APIs that the Three.js library has to offer through lots of interactive examples and code samples.

What this book covers

Chapter 1, Creating Your First 3D Scene with Three.js, covers the basic steps that you need to take to get started with the Three.js library. You'll immediately create your first Three.js scene and at the end of this chapter, you'll be able to create and animate your first 3D scene directly in the browser.

Chapter 2, Working with the Basic Components That Make Up a Three.js Scene, explains the basic components that you need to understand while working with the Three.js library. You'll learn about lights, meshes, geometries, materials, and cameras. In this chapter you will also get an overview of the different lights that the Three.js library provides and the cameras you can use in your scene.

Chapter 3, Working with the Different Light Sources Available in Three.js, dives deeper into the different lights that you can use in your scene. It shows examples and explains how to use a SpotLight, DirectionLight, AmbientLight, PointLight, HemisphereLight, and AreaLight sources. Additionally, it also shows how to apply a LensFlare effect on your light source.

Chapter 4, Working with the Three.js Materials, talks about the materials available in the Three.js library that you can use in your meshes. It shows all the properties that you can set to configure the materials for your specific use and provides interactive examples to experiment with the materials that are available in the Three.js library.

Chapter 5, Learning to Work with Geometries, is the first of two chapters that explores all the geometries that are provided by the Three.js library. In this chapter you'll learn how to create and configure geometries in Three.js and you can experiment by using the provided interactive examples, with geometries such as plane, circle, shape, cube, sphere, cylinder, Torus, TorusKnot, and PolyHedron.

Chapter 6, Using Advanced Geometries and Binary Operations, continues where Chapter 5 left off. It shows you how to configure and use the more advanced geometries that are provided by the Three.js library such as Convex and Lathe. In this chapter you'll also learn how to extrude 3D geometries from the 2D shapes and how you can create new geometries by combining geometries using binary operations.

Chapter 7, Particles and the Particle System, explains how to use the particle system from the Three.js library. You'll learn how to create a particle system from scratch, and from the existing geometries. In this chapter you'll also learn how you can modify the way the particles look through the use of sprites and particle materials.

Chapter 8, Creating and Loading Advanced Meshes and Geometries, shows you how to import meshes and geometries from external sources. You'll learn how to use the Three.js library internal JSON format in order to save the geometries and scenes. This chapter also explains how to load models from formats like OBJ, DAE, STL, CTM, and PLY.

Chapter 9, Animations and Moving the Camera, explores the various types of animations that you can use to make your scene come to life. You'll learn how to use the Tween. js library together with Three.js, and you'll learn how to work with the animation models based on morphs and skeletons.

Chapter 10, Loading and Working with Textures, expands on Chapter 4 where materials were introduced. In this chapter we will dive into the details of textures. It introduces the various types of textures that are available and how you can control a texture that is applied to your mesh. Additionally in this chapter, you are shown how you can directly use the output from the HTML5 video and canvas elements as input for your textures.

Chapter 11, Custom Shaders and Render Post Processing, explores how you can use the Three.js library to apply the post processing effects to your rendered scene. With post processing you can apply effects, such as blur, tilt shift, and sepia to your rendered scene. Besides this, you'll also learn how to create your own post processing effect and create a custom vertex and fragment shader.

Chapter 12, Adding Physics to Your Scene with Physijs, explains how you can add physics to your Three.js scene. With physics, you can detect collisions between objects, make them respond to gravity, and apply friction. This chapter shows how to do so with the Physics JavaScript library.

What you need for this book

All that you need for this book is a text editor (for example, Sublime Text Editor) to play around with the examples and a modern web browser to access the examples. Some examples require a local web server, but you'll learn in Chapter 1 how to set up a very lightweight web server to use with the examples in this book.

Disclaimer:

Before we get started, a quick note on possible problems with the examples in this book. In Chapter 1 we give an overview of the browser support for WebGL, which is needed for Three.js. Modern browsers such as Chrome, Firefox, and Internet Explorer have good support for this standard. There is, however, something you need to take into account. When newer versions of browsers appear, they sometimes break support for specific features of WebGL. For instance, as of finalizing this book, Chrome and Firefox on Windows 7 have issues with the examples of Chapter 11. So make sure to upgrade to the latest versions of Chrome and Firefox before trying these examples.

Who this book is for

This book is great for everyone who already knows JavaScript and wants to start with creating 3D graphics that run in any browser. You don't need to know anything about advanced math or WebGL, all that is needed is a general knowledge of JavaScript and HTML. The required materials and examples can be freely downloaded and all the tools used in this book are open source. So if you've ever wanted to learn how to create beautiful, interactive 3D graphics that run in any modern browser, this is the book for you.

Conventions

In this book, you will find a number of styles of text that distinguish between different kinds of information. Here are some examples of these styles, and an explanation of their meaning.

Code words in text, database table names, folder names, filenames, file extensions, pathnames, dummy URLs, user input, and Twitter handles are shown as follows: "You can see in this code that besides setting the map property, we also set the bumpMap property to a texture."

A block of code is set as follows:

```
function createMesh(geom, texture, bump) {
    var texture = THREE.ImageUtils.loadTexture(
            "../assets/textures/general/" + texture)

    var mat = new THREE.MeshPhongMaterial();
    mat.map = texture;
    var bump = THREE.ImageUtils.loadTexture(
            "../assets/textures/general/" + bump)
    mat.bumpMap = bump;
    mat.bumpScale=0.2;
    var mesh = new THREE.Mesh(geom,mat);
    return mesh;
}
```

When we wish to draw your attention to a particular part of a code block, the relevant lines or items are set in bold as shown:

```
function createParticles() {
  var material = new THREE.ParticleBasicMaterial({size:4});

  var geom = new THREE.Geometry();
  for (var x = -5 ; x < 5 ; x++) {
    for (var y = -5 ; y < 5 ; y++) {
      var particle = new THREE.Vector3(x*10,y*10,0);
      geom.vertices.push(particle);
    }
  }

  var system = new THREE.ParticleSystem(geom,material);
  scene.add(system);
}
```

Any command-line input or output is written as follows:

```
#git clone https://github.com/josdirksen/learning-threejs
```

New terms and **important words** are shown in bold as follows: "The first one uses the **HTTP Server** module."

Words that you see on the screen, in menus or dialog boxes for example, appear in the text like this: "If you want to change this color, you can do so in the menu at the top-right corner, to a more prominent green color (**#007700**) and get the following result:".

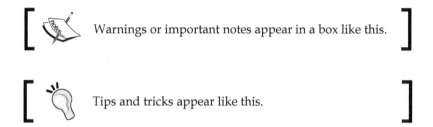

Warnings or important notes appear in a box like this.

Tips and tricks appear like this.

Reader feedback

Feedback from our readers is always welcome. Let us know what you think about this book—what you liked or may have disliked. Reader feedback is important for us to develop titles that you really get the most out of.

To send us general feedback, simply send an e-mail to feedback@packtpub.com, and mention the book title via the subject of your message.

If there is a topic that you have expertise in and you are interested in either writing or contributing to a book, see our author guide on www.packtpub.com/authors.

Customer support

Now that you are the proud owner of a Packt book, we have a number of things to help you to get the most from your purchase.

Downloading the example code

You can download the example code files for all Packt books you have purchased from your account at http://www.packtpub.com. If you purchased this book elsewhere, you can visit http://www.packtpub.com/support and register to have the files e-mailed directly to you.

Downloading the color images of this book

We also provide you a PDF file that has color images of the screenshots/diagrams used in this book. The color images will help you better understand the changes in the output. You can download this file from `http://www.packtpub.com/sites/default/files/downloads/6283OS_graphics.pdf`.

Errata

Although we have taken every care to ensure the accuracy of our content, mistakes do happen. If you find a mistake in one of our books — maybe a mistake in the text or the code — we would be grateful if you would report this to us. By doing so, you can save other readers from frustration and help us improve subsequent versions of this book. If you find any errata, please report them by visiting `http://www.packtpub.com/submit-errata`, selecting your book, clicking on the **errata submission form** link, and entering the details of your errata. Once your errata are verified, your submission will be accepted and the errata will be uploaded on our website, or added to any list of existing errata, under the Errata section of that title. Any existing errata can be viewed by selecting your title from `http://www.packtpub.com/support`.

Piracy

Piracy of copyright material on the Internet is an ongoing problem across all media. At Packt, we take the protection of our copyright and licenses very seriously. If you come across any illegal copies of our works, in any form, on the Internet, please provide us with the location address or website name immediately so that we can pursue a remedy.

Please contact us at `copyright@packtpub.com` with a link to the suspected pirated material.

We appreciate your help in protecting our authors, and our ability to bring you valuable content.

Questions

You can contact us at `questions@packtpub.com` if you are having a problem with any aspect of the book, and we will do our best to address it.

1
Creating Your First 3D Scene with Three.js

Modern browsers are slowly getting more powerful features that can be accessed directly from JavaScript. You can easily add video and audio with the new HTML5 tags and create interactive components through the use of the HTML5 canvas. A rather new addition to this feature set is the support of WebGL. With WebGL you can directly make use of the processing resources of your graphics card and create high-performance 2D and 3D computer graphics. Programming WebGL directly from JavaScript to create and animate 3D scenes is a very complex and error-prone process. Three.js is a library that makes this a lot easier. The following list shows some of the things that Three.js makes easy:

- Creating simple and complex 3D geometries
- Animating and moving objects through a 3D scene
- Applying textures and materials to your objects
- Loading objects from 3D modeling software
- Creating 2D sprite-based graphics

With a couple lines of JavaScript you can create anything from simple 3D models to photorealistic real-time scenes as shown:

In the first chapter, we'll directly dive into Three.js and create a couple of examples that show you how Three.js works and you can use them to play around with. We won't dive into all the technical details yet; that's something you'll learn in the later chapters. In this chapter we'll cover the following points:

- Tools required for working with Three.js
- Downloading the source code and examples used in this book
- Creating your first Three.js scene
- Improving the first scene with materials, lights, and animations
- Introducing a couple of helper libraries for statistics and controlling the scene

We'll start this book with a short introduction into Three.js and then quickly move on to the first examples and code samples. Before we get started, let's quickly look at the most important browsers out there and their support for WebGL.

At the moment Three.js works with the following browsers:

Browser	Support
Mozilla Firefox	Supported since Version 4.0.
Google Chrome	Supported since Version 9.
Safari	Supported since Version 5.1 and newly installed on Mac OS X Mountain Lion, Lion, and Snow Leopard. Make sure you enable WebGL in Safari. You can do this by navigating to **Preferences	Advanced** and checking the option **Show develop menu in menu bar**. After that navigate to **Develop	Enable WebGL**.
Opera	Supported since Version 12.00. You still have to enable this by opening the file opera:config and setting the value of **WebGL** and **Enable Hardware Acceleration** to 1. After that, restart the browser.
Internet Explorer	Internet Explorer had long been the only major player who didn't support WebGL. Starting with IE11, Microsoft has added WebGL support.

Basically, Three.js runs in any of the modern browsers, except most versions of IE. So if you want to use an older version of IE, you've got two options: you can get WebGL support through the use of Google Chrome Frame, which you can download from the following URL: https://developers.google.com/chrome/chrome-frame/. An alternative you can use instead of Google Chrome Frame is the iewebgl plugin, which you can get from http://iewebgl.com/. This installs inside IE and enables WebGL.

 Google has officially dropped support for Google Chrome Frame and it doesn't support IE10.

 Currently the guys behind Three.js are working on a renderer that uses the new CSS-3D specification, which is supported by a lot of browsers (even IE10). Besides desktop browsers, a number of mobile and tablet browsers also support CSS-3D.

In this chapter, you'll directly create your first 3D scene and will be able to run this in any of the mentioned browsers. We won't introduce too many complex Three.js features, but at the end of this chapter you'll have created the Three.js scene that you can see in the following screenshot:

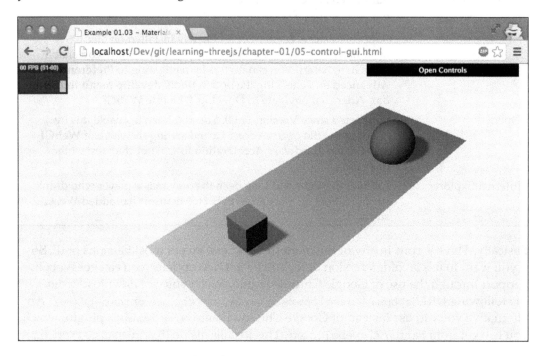

For this first scene you'll learn about the basics of Three.js and also create your first animation. Before you start your work on this example, in the next couple of sections we'll first look at the tools that you need to easily work with Three.js and how you can download the examples that are shown in this book.

Requirements for using Three.js

Three.js is a JavaScript library, so all that you need to create Three.js WebGL applications is a text editor and one of the supported browsers to render the results. I do like to recommend three JavaScript editors, which I've started using exclusively over the last couple of years:

- **WebStorm**: This editor from the JetBrains guides has great support for editing JavaScript. It supports code completion, automatic deployment, and JavaScript debugging directly from the editor. Besides this, WebStorm has excellent Git support (and other Version Control Systems). You can download a trial edition from http://www.jetbrains.com/webstorm/

- **Notepad++**: This is a general purpose editor that supports a wide range of programming languages. It can easily lay out and format JavaScript.

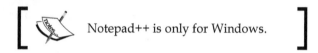 Notepad++ is only for Windows.

- **Sublime Text Editor**: This is a great little editor that has very good support for editing JavaScript. Besides this, it provides many very helpful selection and edit options, which once you get used to, provide a real good JavaScript editing environment. Sublime Text Editor can also be tested for free and can be downloaded from http://www.sublimetext.com/

Even if you don't use these three editors there are a lot of editors available, open source and commercial, which you can use to edit JavaScript and create your Three.js projects. An interesting project that you might want to look into is http://c9.io. This is a cloud-based JavaScript editor that can be connected to a GitHub account. This way you can directly access all the source code and examples from this book, and experiment with them.

I had mentioned that most modern web browsers support WebGL and can be used to run the Three.js examples. I usually run my code in Chrome. The reason is that, most often, Chrome has the best support and performance for WebGL and it has a really great JavaScript debugger. With this debugger you can quickly pinpoint problems, for instance, by using breakpoints and console output. Throughout this book I'll give you pointers on debugger usage and other debugging tips and tricks.

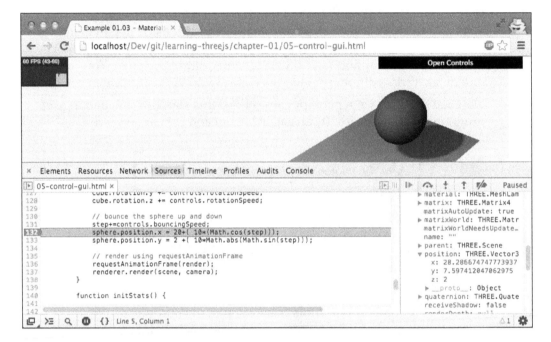

That's enough of an introduction for now; let's get the source code and start with the first scene.

Getting the source code

All the code for this book can be accessed from GitHub (`https://github.com/`). GitHub is an online Git-based repository that you can use to store, access, and version source code. There are a couple of ways you can get the sources for yourself:

- Clone the Git-based repository
- Download and extract the archive

In the following sections, we'll explore these options in more detail.

Using Git to clone the repository

Git is an open source distributed Version Control System that I have used to create and version all the examples in this book. For this I've used GitHub, a free, online Git-based repository. You can browse this repository by following this link:
`https://github.com/josdirksen/learning-threejs`

To get all the examples you can clone this repository using the `git` command line tool. To do this, you first need to download a Git client for your operating system. For most modern operating systems, a client can be downloaded from `http://git-scm.com` or you can use the one provided by GitHub itself (for Mac and Windows). After installing Git, you can use this to get a clone of this book's repository. Open a command prompt and go to the directory where you want to download the sources. In that directory, run the following command:

`git clone https://github.com/josdirksen/learning-threejs`

This will start downloading all the examples as shown in the following screenshot:

```
● ○ ○                                    Default
jos@Joss-MacBook-Pro.local:~/tmp$ git clone https://github.com/josdirksen/learning-threejs
Cloning into 'learning-threejs'...
remote: Counting objects: 729, done.
remote: Compressing objects: 100% (420/420), done.
remote: Total 729 (delta 317), reused 707 (delta 298)
Receiving objects: 100% (729/729), 85.93 MiB | 2.80 MiB/s, done.
Resolving deltas: 100% (317/317), done.
Checking out files: 100% (408/408), done.
jos@Joss-MacBook-Pro.local:~/tmp$ █
```

The directory `learning-three.js` will now contain all the examples that are used throughout this book.

Downloading and extracting the archive

If you don't want to use Git to download the sources directly from GitHub, you can also download an archive. Go to the URL `https://github.com/josdirksen/learning-threejs` and click on the download link as shown in the following screenshot:

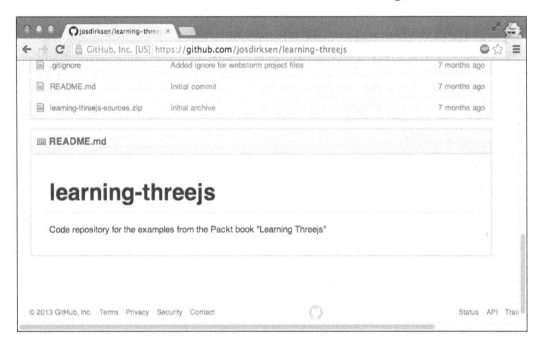

Extract this to a directory of your choice, and you'll have all the examples available.

Testing the examples

Now that you've downloaded or cloned the source code, let's do a quick check to see if everything is working and make you familiar with the directory structure. The code and examples are organized per chapter. There are two different ways of viewing the examples. You can either open the extracted or cloned directory in a browser directly and run a specific example, or you can install a local web server. The first approach will work for most of the basic examples, but when we start loading external resources such as models or texture images, just opening the HTML file isn't enough. In this case we need a local web server to make sure that the external resources are loaded correctly. In the following section, we will discuss a couple of different ways you can set up a simple local web server for testing.

Setting up a local web server is very easy, depending on what you've already got installed. We will list a couple of examples on how to do this.

Python-based approach should work on most Unix/Mac systems

Most Unix/Linux/Mac systems already have Python installed in them. On those systems you can very easily start a local web server:

```
> python -m SimpleHTTPServer
Serving HTTP on 0.0.0.0 port 8000 ...
```

Do this in the directory where you have checked out/downloaded the source code.

NPM-based approach if you've got Node.js installed

If you've already done some work with Node.js, there is a good chance that you've got NPM installed. With NPM you've got two simple options to set up a quick local web server for testing. The first one uses the **HTTP Server** module:

```
> npm install -g http-server
> http-server
Starting up http-server, serving ./ on port: 8080
Hit CTRL-C to stop the server
```

Alternatively you can also use the **Simple HTTP Server** option:

```
> npm install -g simple-http-server
> nserver
simple-http-server Now Serving: /Users/jos/git/Physijs at http://
localhost:8000/
```

A disadvantage of this second approach, however, is that it doesn't automatically show the directory listings, whereas the first approach does.

Portable version of Mongoose for Mac/Windows

If you haven't got Python or NPM installed, there is a simple, portable web server, named Mongoose, that you can use. First download the binaries for your specific platform from the following URL: https://code.google.com/p/mongoose/downloads/list. On the Windows platform, copy the downloaded file to the directory containing the examples and double-click on it to start a web browser showing the contents of the directory it is started in.

For other operating systems, you must also copy the executable to the target directory, but instead of double-clicking on the executable you have to launch it from the command line. In both cases, a local web server will be started on port 8080.

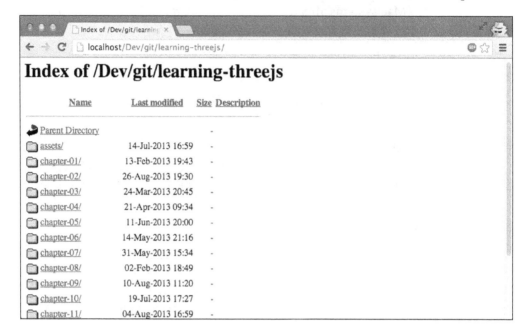

By just clicking on a chapter, we can show and access all the examples for that chapter. If I discuss an example in this book, I'll refer to the specific name and folder so that you can directly test and play around with the code.

At this point you should have an editor installed and have access to all the sources. Now it is time to start creating our first Three.js scene.

Creating an HTML skeleton page

The first thing we need to do is create an empty HTML skeleton page that we can use as the base for all our examples. This HTML skeleton is shown as follows:

```
<!DOCTYPE html>

<html>

  <head>
    <title>Example 01.01 - Basic skeleton</title>
    <script type="text/javascript"
```

```
            src="../libs/three.js"></script>
    <script type="text/javascript"
            src="../libs/jquery-1.9.0.js"></script>
    <style>
        body{
            /* set margin to 0 and overflow to hidden,
               to use the complete page */

            margin: 0;
            overflow: hidden;
        }
    </style>
  </head>
  <body>

<!-- Div which will hold the Output -->
<div id="WebGL-output">
</div>

<!-- Javascript code that runs our Three.js examples -->
    <script type="text/javascript">

    // once everything is loaded, we run our Three.js stuff.
    $(function () {
            // here we'll put the Three.js stuff
    });

    </script>
  </body>
</html>
```

Downloading the example code

You can download the example code files for all Packt books you have purchased from your account at http://www.packtpub.com. If you purchased this book elsewhere, you can visit http://www.packtpub.com/support and register to have the files e-mailed directly to you.

As you can see from this listing, the skeleton is a very simple HTML page, with only a couple of elements. In the <head> element, we will load the external JavaScript libraries that we'll use for the examples. For all the examples, we'll at least load the two mentioned in this listing: Three.js and jquery-1.9.0.js. In the <head> element, we also add a couple of lines of CSS. These style elements remove any scroll bars when we create a full page Three.js scene. In the <body> of this page you can see a single <div> element. When we write our Three.js code, we'll point the output of the Three.js renderer to that element. In the previous code snippet, you can already see a bit of JavaScript. That small piece of code uses jQuery to call an anonymous JavaScript function when the complete page is loaded. We'll put all the Three.js code inside this anonymous function.

Three.js comes in two versions:

- **Three.min.js**: This is the library you'd normally use when deploying Three.js sites on the internet. This is a minimized version of Three.js, created using **UglifyJS**, which is half the size of the normal Three.js library. All the examples and code used in this book are based on the Three.js r60 project, which was released in August 2013.

- **Three.js**: This is the normal Three.js library. We will use this library in our examples, since it makes debugging much easier when you can read and understand the Three.js source code.

If we view this page in our browser, the results aren't very shocking. As you'd expect, all that you would see is an empty page:

In the next section, you'll learn how to add the first couple of 3D objects and render those to the <div> element that we had defined in our HTML skeleton page.

Rendering and viewing a 3D object

In this step you'll create your first scene and add a couple of objects and a camera. Our first example will contain the following objects:

Object	Description
Plane	A two-dimensional rectangle that serves as our ground area. This is rendered as the gray rectangle in the middle of the scene.
Cube	A three-dimensional cube, which we'll render in red
Sphere	A three-dimensional sphere, which we'll render in blue
Camera	The camera determines what you'll see in the output
Axes	x, y, and z axes. This is a helpful debugging tool to see where the objects are rendered.

I'll first show you how this looks in code (the source file with comments can be found in the `chapter-01` folder and is labeled `02-first-scene.html`) and then I'll explain what's happening:

```
<script type="text/javascript">


    $(function () {
        var scene = new THREE.Scene();

        var camera = new THREE.PerspectiveCamera(45
                        , window.innerWidth / window.innerHeight
                        , 0.1, 1000);

        var renderer = new THREE.WebGLRenderer();
        renderer.setClearColorHex(0xEEEEEE);
        renderer.setSize(window.innerWidth, window.innerHeight);

        var axes = new THREE.AxisHelper( 20 );
        scene.add(axes);

        var planeGeometry = new THREE.PlaneGeometry(60,20,1,1);
        var planeMaterial = new THREE.MeshBasicMaterial(
                                    {color: 0xcccccc});
        var plane = new THREE.Mesh(planeGeometry,planeMaterial);

        plane.rotation.x=-0.5*Math.PI;
```

```
plane.position.x = 15;
plane.position.y = 0;
plane.position.z = 0;

scene.add(plane);

var cubeGeometry = new THREE.CubeGeometry(4,4,4);
var cubeMaterial = new THREE.MeshBasicMaterial(
                    {color: 0xff0000, wireframe: true});
var cube = new THREE.Mesh(cubeGeometry, cubeMaterial);

cube.position.x = -4;
cube.position.y = 3;
cube.position.z = 0;

scene.add(cube);

var sphereGeometry = new THREE.SphereGeometry(4,20,20);
var sphereMaterial = new THREE.MeshBasicMaterial(
                        {color: 0x7777ff, wireframe: true});
var sphere = new THREE.Mesh(sphereGeometry,sphereMaterial);

sphere.position.x = 20;
sphere.position.y = 4;
sphere.position.z = 2;

scene.add(sphere);

camera.position.x = -30;
camera.position.y = 40;
camera.position.z = 30;
camera.lookAt(scene.position);

$("#WebGL-output").append(renderer.domElement);
renderer.render(scene, camera);
});
```

If we open this example in the browser, we will see something that resembles what we're aiming for, but is still a long way off:

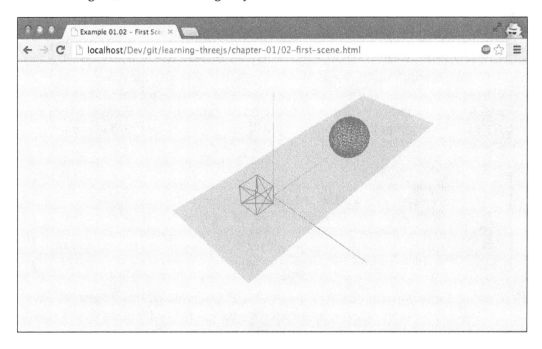

Before we start making this more beautiful, I'll first walk you through the code a step at a time so that you understand what the code does:

```
var scene = new THREE.Scene();

var camera = new THREE.PerspectiveCamera(45
                        , window.innerWidth / window.innerHeight
                        , 0.1, 1000);

var renderer = new THREE.WebGLRenderer();
renderer.setClearColorHex(0xEEEEEE);
renderer.setSize(window.innerWidth, window.innerHeight);
```

Prior to the given example we defined a scene, a camera, and a renderer. The scene variable is a container that is used to store and keep track of all the objects that we want to render. The sphere and the cube that we want to render will be added to this scene later on in the example. In this first fragment, we also create a camera variable. The camera variable defines what we'll see when we render the scene. In *Chapter 2, Working with the Basic Components That Make Up a Three.js Scene,* you will learn more about the arguments that you can pass into the camera. Next, we will define a renderer object. The renderer is responsible for calculating what the scene will look like in the browser based on the camera angle. We will create a WebGLRenderer object in this example that will use your graphics card to render the scene.

> If you look through the source code and the documentation of Three.js. you'll notice that there are different renderers available besides the WebGL-based one. There is a canvas-based renderer and even an SVG-based one. Even though they work and can render simple scenes, I wouldn't recommend using them. They're very CPU-intensive and lack features such as good material support and shadows.

Here we set the background color of the renderer to almost white (0XEEEEEE) with the setClearColorHex() function and tell the renderer how large the scene needs to be rendered by using the setSize() function.

So far, we've got a basic empty scene, a renderer, and a camera. There is, however, nothing yet to render. The following code adds the helper axes and the plane.

```
var axes = new THREE.AxisHelper( 20 );
scene.add(axes);

var planeGeometry = new THREE.PlaneGeometry(60,20);
var planeMaterial = new THREE.MeshBasicMaterial(
                                    {color: 0xcccccc});
var plane = new THREE.Mesh(planeGeometry,planeMaterial);

plane.rotation.x = -0.5*Math.PI;
plane.position.x = 15;
plane.position.y = 0;
plane.position.z = 0;
scene.add(plane);
```

As you can see, we have created an `axes` object and used the `scene.add()` function to add these axes to our scene. Now we will create the plane. This is done in two steps. First we define what the plane looks like using the new `THREE.PlaneGeometry(60,20)` code. In this case it has a width of `60` and a height of `20`. We also need to tell Three.js what this plane looks like (for example, its color and its transparency). In Three.js we do this by creating a material object. For this first example we'll create a basic material (by using the `MeshBasicMaterial()` method) with the color `0xcccccc`. Next we combine these two into a `Mesh` object with the name `plane`. Before we add this `plane` to the scene we need to put it in the correct position; we do this by first rotating it 90 degrees around the x axis and next we defining its position in the scene by using the `position` property. If you're already interested in the details of the `Mesh` object, look at example `06-mesh-properties.html` from *Chapter 2, Working with the Basic Components That Make Up a Three.js Scene*, which shows and explains rotation and positioning. The final step that we need to do is add this `plane` to the `scene`, just like we did with the `axes`.

The `cube` and `sphere` are added in the same manner, but with the `wireframe` property set to `true`, so let's move on to the final part of this example:

```
camera.position.x = -30;
camera.position.y = 40;
camera.position.z = 30;
camera.lookAt(scene.position);

$("#WebGL-output").append(renderer.domElement);
renderer.render(scene, camera);
```

At this point all the elements that we want to render are added to the scene at the correct positions. I've already mentioned that the camera defines what will be rendered. In this piece of code we position the camera using the x, y, and z `position` attributes to hover above our scene. To make sure that the camera is looking at our objects, we use the `lookAt()` function to point it at the center of our scene. All that is left to do is `append` the output from the `renderer` to the `<div>` element of our HTML skeleton; we use jQuery to select the correct output element, and tell the `renderer` to render the `scene` using the provided `camera`.

In the next couple of sections, we'll make this scene more pretty by adding lights, more materials, and even animations.

Adding materials, lights, and shadows

Adding new materials and lights in Three.js is very simple and is done in pretty much the same way as we explained in the previous section. We start by adding a light source to the scene (for the complete source, look at example 03-materials-light.html):

```
var spotLight = new THREE.SpotLight( 0xffffff );
spotLight.position.set( -40, 60, -10 );
scene.add( spotLight );
```

The SpotLight() method illuminates our scene from its position (spotLight. position.set(-40, 60, -10)). If we render the scene at this time, however, you won't see any difference with the previous one. The reason is that different materials respond differently to light. The basic material which we used in the previous example (by using the MeshBasicMaterial() method) doesn't do anything with the light sources in the scene. They just render the object in the specified color. So we have to change the materials for our plane, sphere, and cube as shown:

```
var planeGeometry = new THREE.PlaneGeometry(60,20);
var planeMaterial = new THREE.MeshLambertMaterial(
                                     {color: 0xffffff});
var plane = new THREE.Mesh(planeGeometry,planeMaterial);
...
var cubeGeometry = new THREE.CubeGeometry(4,4,4);
var cubeMaterial = new THREE.MeshLambertMaterial(
                                     {color: 0xff0000});
var cube = new THREE.Mesh(cubeGeometry, cubeMaterial);
...
var sphereGeometry = new THREE.SphereGeometry(4,20,20);
var sphereMaterial = new THREE.MeshLambertMaterial(
                                     {color: 0x7777ff});
var sphere = new THREE.Mesh(sphereGeometry,sphereMaterial);
```

In this piece of code, we have changed the material property for our objects to a MeshLambertMaterial. Three.js provides two materials that take light sources into account: MeshLambertMaterial and MeshPhongMaterial.

The result as shown in the following screenshot, however, still isn't what we're looking for:

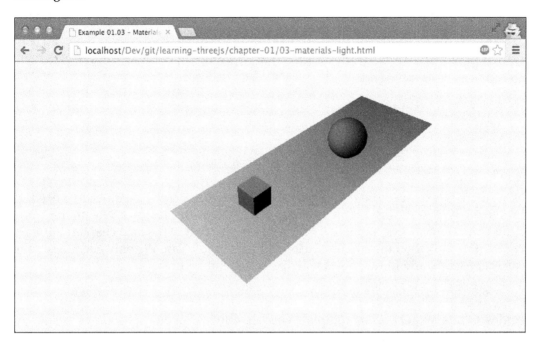

We're getting there, and the cube and sphere are looking a lot better. What is still missing though are the shadows.

Rendering shadows takes a lot of computing power and for that reason shadows are disabled by default in Three.js. Enabling them, though, is very easy. For shadows we have to change the source in a couple of places as shown in the following code snippet:

```
renderer.setClearColorHex(0xEEEEEE, 1.0);
renderer.setSize(window.innerWidth, window.innerHeight);
renderer.shadowMapEnabled = true;
```

The first change that we need to make is to tell the `renderer` that we want shadows. You can do this by setting the `shadowMapEnabled` property to `true`. If you look at the result from this change, you won't notice anything different yet. That is because we need to explicitly define which objects cast shadows and which objects receive shadows. In our example, we want the sphere and the cube to cast shadows on the ground plane. You can do this by setting the corresponding properties on those objects to `true` as follows:

```
plane.receiveShadow = true;
...
cube.castShadow = true;
...
sphere.castShadow = true;
```

Now, there is just one more thing that you need to do to get the shadows. We need to define which of the light sources in our scene will cause shadows. Not all the lights can cast shadows, and you'll learn more about that in the next chapter, but the `SpotLight()` method that we have used in this example can. We only need to set the correct property and the shadows will finally be rendered:

```
spotLight.castShadow = true;
```

And with this we get a scene complete with shadows from our light source as shown in the following screenshot:

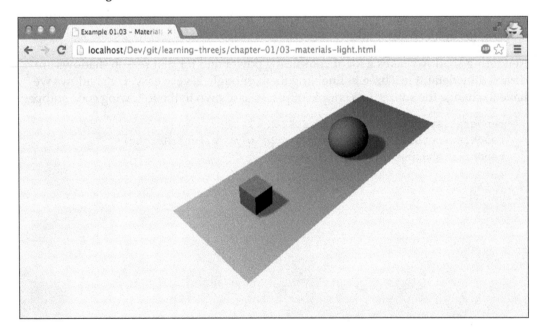

The last feature that we'll add to this first scene is some simple animation. In *Chapter 9, Animations and Moving the Camera*, you'll learn more advanced animation options.

Expanding your first scene with animations

If we want to animate the scene, the first thing that we need to do is find some way to rerender the scene at a specific interval. Before HTML5 and the related JavaScript APIs came along, the way to do this was by using the `setInterval(function,interval)` function. With the `setInterval()` method, we can specify a function that, for instance, would be called every 100 milliseconds. The problem with this function is that it doesn't take into account what is happening in the browser. If you were browsing another tab, this function would still be fired every couple of milliseconds. Besides that, the `setInterval()` method isn't synchronized with the redrawing of the screen. This could lead to higher CPU usage and bad performance.

Introducing the requestAnimationFrame() method

Modern browsers luckily have a solution for the problems associated with the `setInterval()` function: the `requestAnimationFrame()` function. With the `requestAnimationFrame()` function, you can specify a function that is called at an interval defined by the browser. You can do any drawing that you need to do in the supplied function and the browser will make sure it is painted as smoothly and efficiently as possible. Using this is really simple (the complete source can be found in the example, `04-materials-light-animation.html`); you just have to create a function that handles the rendering as shown:

```
function renderScene() {
  requestAnimationFrame(renderScene);
  renderer.render(scene, camera);
}
```

In the `renderScene()` function, we call the `requestAnimationFrame()` method again in order to keep the animation going. The only thing that we need to change in the code is that instead of calling the `renderer.render()` method after we've created the complete scene, we call the `renderScene()` function once to kick off the animation:

```
. . .
  $("#WebGL-output").append(renderer.domElement);
  renderScene();
```

If you run the given code snippet, you won't see any changes compared to the previous example, because we didn't animate anything yet. Before we add the animation, I want to introduce a small helper library that gives us information about the frame rate that the animation is running at. This library, which is from the same author as Three.js, renders a small graph that shows us the Frames Per Second (FPS) that we're getting for this animation.

To add this statistic, we first need to include the library in the HTML `<header>` tag:

```
<script type="text/javascript" src="../libs/stats.js"></script>
```

And we add a `<div>` element that will be used as output for the statistics graph:

```
<div id="Stats-output"></div>
```

The only thing left to do is initialize the statistics and add them to the `<div>` element as shown:

```
function initStats() {
            var stats = new Stats();
            stats.setMode(0);
            stats.domElement.style.position = 'absolute';
            stats.domElement.style.left = '0px';
            stats.domElement.style.top = '0px';
            $("#Stats-output").append( stats.domElement );
            return stats;
        }
```

This function initializes the statistics. The interesting part is the `setMode()` function. If we set it to `0` we'll measure the FPS, and if we set it to `1`, we can measure the rendering time. For this example we're interested in FPS, so `0` it is. At the beginning of our anonymous jQuery function, we'll call this function and we've got the statistics enabled:

```
$(function () {

        var stats = initStats();
        ...

}
```

The only thing left to do is tell the `stats` object when we're in a new rendering cycle. We can do this by adding a call to the `stats.update()` method and to the `render()` function as follows:

```
function render() {
        stats.update();

        ...
        requestAnimationFrame(render);
        renderer.render(scene, camera);
}
```

If you run the code with these additions, you'll see the statistics in the upper-left corner as shown in the following screenshot:

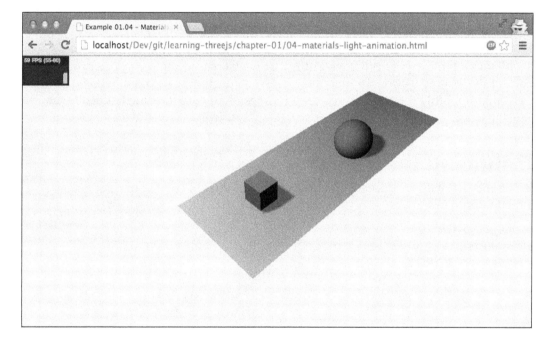

Animating the cube

With the `requestAnimationFrame()` method and the statistics configured, we've got a place to put our animation code. In this section we'll expand the `render()` function with code that will rotate our red cube around on all of its axes. Let's start by showing you the following code:

```
function render() {
        . . .
        cube.rotation.x += 0.02;
        cube.rotation.y += 0.02;
        cube.rotation.z += 0.02;
        . . .
        requestAnimationFrame(render);
        renderer.render(scene, camera);
    }
```

That looks simple, right? What we did is that we increased the `rotation` property of each of the axes by 0.02 every time the `render()` function was called, which showed as a cube smoothly rotating around all if its axes. Bouncing the blue ball isn't that much harder.

Bouncing the ball

To bounce the ball, we once again add a couple of lines of code to our `render()` function as follows:

```
var step=0;
function render() {
        . . .
        step+=0.04;
        sphere.position.x = 20+( 10*(Math.cos(step)));
        sphere.position.y = 2 +( 10*Math.abs(Math.sin(step)));
        . . .
        requestAnimationFrame(render);
        renderer.render(scene, camera);
    }
```

With the cube we changed the `rotation` property; for the sphere we're going to change its `position` in the scene. We want the sphere to bounce from one point in the scene to another with a nice, smooth curve.

For this we need to change its `position` on the x axis and its `position` on the y axis. The `Math.cos()` and `Math.sin()` functions help us in creating a smooth trajectory by using the `step` variable. I won't go into the details of how this works here. For now all that you need to know is that `step+=0.04` defines the speed of the bouncing sphere. In *Chapter 8, Creating and Loading Advanced Meshes and Geometries*, we'll go into more detail of how these functions can be used for animation, and I'll explain everything. The following screenshot shows the scene with the animation enabled:

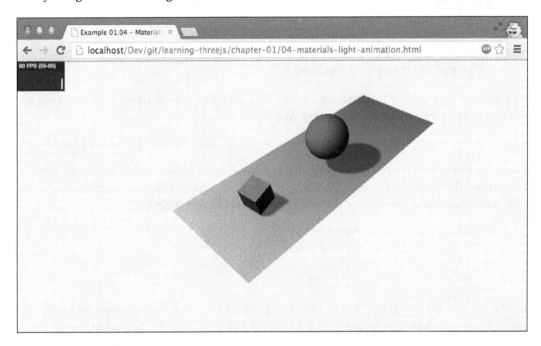

Before wrapping up this chapter, I want to add one more element to our basic scene. When working with 3D scenes, animations, colors, and properties like these, it often requires a bit of experimenting to get the correct color or speed. It would be very easy if you could just have a simple GUI that allows you to change these kind of properties on the fly. Luckily, there is one.

Using the dat.GUI library to make experimenting easier

A couple of guys from Google created a library called `dat.GUI` (you can find the documentation online at `http://code.google.com/p/dat-gui/`), which allows you to very easily create a simple user interface component that can change the variables in your code. In this part of the chapter, we'll use `dat.GUI` to add a user interface to our example that allows us to:

- Control the speed of the bouncing ball
- Control the rotation of the cube

Just like we had to do for the statistics, we will first add this library to the `<header>` of our HTML page by using the following code:

```
<script type="text/javascript" src="../libs/dat.gui.js"></script>
```

The next thing that we need to configure is a JavaScript object which will hold the properties that we want to change using the `dat.GUI` library. In the main part of our JavaScript code, we will add the following JavaScript object:

```
var controls = new function() {
        this.rotationSpeed = 0.02;
        this.bouncingSpeed = 0.03;
    }
```

In this JavaScript object we will define two properties: `this.rotationSpeed` and `this.bouncingSpeed` along with their default values. Next, we will pass this object into a new `dat.GUI` object and define the range for these two properties as shown:

```
var gui = new dat.GUI();
gui.add(controls, 'rotationSpeed',0,0.5);
gui.add(controls, 'bouncingSpeed',0,0.5);
```

The `rotationSpeed` and `bouncingSpeed` properties are both set to a range from `0` to `0.5`. All that we need to do now is make sure that in our `render` loop, we reference these two properties directly, so that when we make changes through the `dat.GUI` user interface, it immediately affects the rotation and bounce speed of our objects. This is shown as follows:

```
function render() {
        ...
        cube.rotation.x += controls.rotationSpeed;
        cube.rotation.y += controls.rotationSpeed;
        cube.rotation.z += controls.rotationSpeed;
```

```
step+=controls.bouncingSpeed;
sphere.position.x = 20+( 10*(Math.cos(step)));
sphere.position.y = 2 +( 10*Math.abs(Math.sin(step)));
...
}
```

Now when you run this example (`05-control-gui.html`), you'll see a simple user interface that you can use to control the bouncing and rotation speeds of the objects:

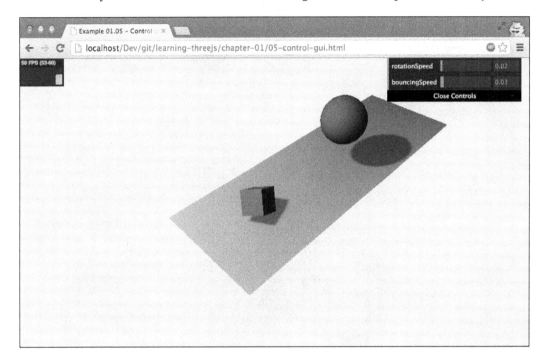

Using the ASCII effect

Throughout the chapter, we've worked at creating a pretty-looking 3D rendering by using the most modern browser features. Three.js also has a couple of interesting features that you can use to change the way the output is rendered. Before ending this chapter, I want to introduce you to one of these effects: the **ASCII Effect**. With the ASCII effect you can change our beautiful animation scene to a retro ASCII art-based animation, with a couple of lines of code. For this you have to change the last couple of lines of our main JavaScript loop from:

```
$("#WebGL-output").append(renderer.domElement);
```

To the following:

```
var effect = new THREE.AsciiEffect( renderer );
effect.setSize( window.innerWidth, window.innerHeight );
$("#WebGL-output").append(effect.domElement);
```

You also have to make a small change to the render loop. Instead of calling the `renderer.render(scene, camera)` method, you have to call the `effect.render(scene,camera)` method. The result of this effect is shown in the following screenshot:

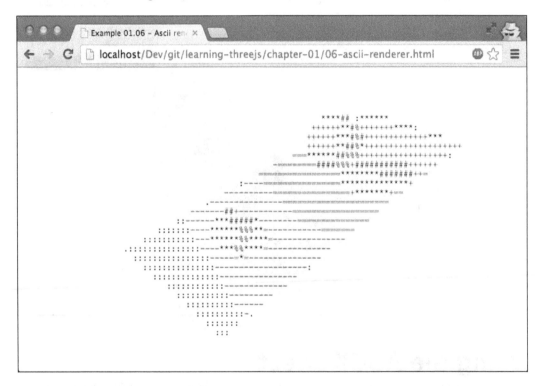

I have to admit that it isn't very useful, but it does nicely show you how easy it is to extend various parts of Three.js just because of its modularity.

Summary

That's it for the first chapter. In this chapter you've already learned a lot about the basic concepts that make up each Three.js scene and this should give you a good starting point for the next chapters. What you should remember from this chapter is the following:

- You can find all the source code for the examples in this and the other chapters online. The best way to learn is to play around and experiment with these examples

- In the Three.js project, you created a scene to which you added the objects (a geometry together with a material) that you wanted to render

- The materials that you used defined what the objects looked like. Each material reacted in a different way to light sources

- Rendering shadows is expensive and needs to be turned on for the renderer, for each object, and for each light

- You can do easy animations by just changing the `position` and the `rotation` properties of the objects in the scene

- Statistics and custom controls can be easily added with the two helper libraries and a couple of lines of JavaScript

In the next chapter we'll expand on the example that we've created here. You'll learn more about the most important building blocks that you can use in Three.js in the later chapters.

2

Working with the Basic Components That Make Up a Three.js Scene

In the previous chapter you learned the basics of a Three.js library. We saw a couple of examples and you created your first complete Three.js scene. In this chapter we'll dive a bit deeper into the Three.js library and explain the basic components that make up a Three.js scene. In this chapter you'll explore the following topics:

- Which components are used in a Three.js scene
- What you can do with the `THREE.Scene()` object
- How geometries and meshes are related
- The difference between the orthographic camera and the perspective camera

We will start by looking at how you can create a scene and add objects.

Creating a scene

In the previous chapter you've already created a `THREE.Scene()` object, so you already know the basics of the Three.js library. We've seen that for a scene to show anything, we need three types of components:

Component	Description
Camera	It determines what is rendered on the screen
Lights	They have an effect on how materials are shown and used when creating shadow effects (discussed in detail in *Chapter 3, Working with the Different Light Sources Available in Three.js*)

Component	Description
Objects	These are the main objects that are rendered from the perspective of the camera: cubes, spheres, and so on

The THREE.Scene() object serves as the container for all these different objects. This object itself doesn't have too many options and functions.

Basic functionality of the scene

The best way to explore the functionality of the scene is by looking at an example. In the source code for this chapter (chapter-02), you can find the 01-basic-scene. html example. I'll use this example to explain the various functions and options that a scene has. When we open this example in the browser, the output will look something like the following screenshot:

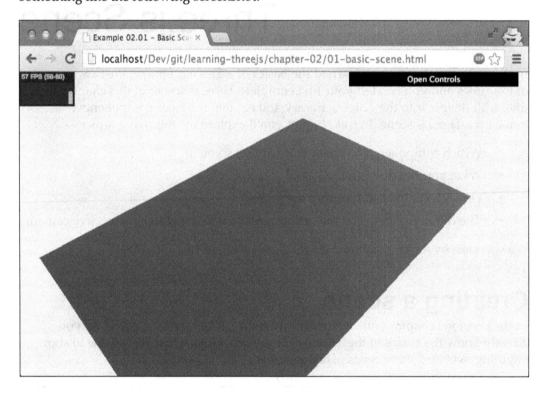

This looks pretty much like the examples that we've seen in the previous chapter. Even though the scene looks somewhat empty, it already contains a couple of objects. By looking at the following source code, we can see that we've used the Scene.add(object) function from the THREE.Scene() object to add a THREE.Mesh (the ground plane that you see), a THREE.SpotLight. and a THREE.AmbientLight object. The THREE.Camera object is added automatically by the Three.js library when you render the scene, but can also be added manually if you prefer.

```
var scene = new THREE.Scene();
var camera = new THREE.PerspectiveCamera(45,
window.innerWidth / window.innerHeight, 0.1, 1000);
...
var planeGeometry = new THREE.PlaneGeometry(60,40,1,1);
var planeMaterial = new THREE.MeshLambertMaterial({color: 0xffffff});
var plane = new THREE.Mesh(planeGeometry,planeMaterial);
...
scene.add(plane);
var ambientLight = new THREE.AmbientLight(0x0c0c0c);
scene.add(ambientLight);
...
var spotLight = new THREE.SpotLight( 0xffffff );
...
scene.add( spotLight );
```

Before we look deeper into the THREE.Scene() object, I'll first explain what you can do in the demonstration, and after that we'll look at some code. Open this example in your browser and look at the controls at the upper-right corner as you can see in the following screenshot:

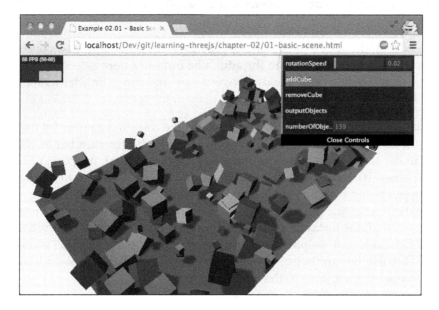

With these controls you can add a `cube` to the scene, remove the last added `cube` from the scene, and show all the current objects that the scene contains. The last entry in the control section shows the current number of objects in the scene. What you'll probably notice when you start up the scene is that there are already four objects in the scene. These are the ground plane, the ambient light, the spot light, and the camera that we had mentioned earlier. In the following code fragment, we'll look at each of the functions in the control section and start with the easiest one: the `addCube()` function:

```
this.addCube = function() {

    var cubeSize = Math.ceil((Math.random() * 3));
    var cubeGeometry = new
          THREE.CubeGeometry(cubeSize,cubeSize,cubeSize);
    var cubeMaterial = new THREE.MeshLambertMaterial(
          {color: Math.random() * 0xffffff });
    var cube = new THREE.Mesh(cubeGeometry, cubeMaterial);
    cube.castShadow = true;
    cube.name = "cube-" + scene.children.length;
    cube.position.x=-30 + Math.round(
              (Math.random() * planeGeometry.width));
    cube.position.y= Math.round((Math.random() * 5));
    cube.position.z=-20 + Math.round((Math.random() *
              planeGeometry.height));

    scene.add(cube);
    this.numberOfObjects = scene.children.length;
};
```

This piece of code should be pretty easy to read by now. Not many new concepts are introduced here. When you click on the **addCube** button, a new `THREE.CubeGeometry` instance is created with a random size between zero and three. Besides a random `size`, the cube also gets a random `color` and `position` in the scene.

A new thing in this piece of code is that we also give the `cube` a name by using the `name` attribute. Its name is set to `cube-` appended with the number of objects currently in the scene (shown by the `scene.children.length` property). So you'll get names like `cube-1`, `cube-2`, `cube-3`, and so on. A name can be useful for debugging purposes, but can also be used to directly find an object in your scene. If you use the `Scene.getChildByName(name)` function, you can directly retrieve a specific object and, for instance, change its location. You might wonder what the last line in the previous code snippet does. The `numberOfObjects` variable is used by our control GUI to list the number of objects in the scene. So whenever we add or remove an object, we set this variable to the updated count.

The next function that we can call from the control GUI is **removeCube** and, as the name implies, clicking on this button removes the last added `cube` from the scene. The following code snippet shows how this function is defined:

```
this.removeCube = function() {
  var allChildren = scene.children;
  var lastObject = allChildren[allChildren.length-1];
  if (lastObject instanceof THREE.Mesh) {
    scene.remove(lastObject);
    this.numberOfObjects = scene.children.length;
  }
}
```

To add an object to the scene we will use the `add()` function. To remove an object from the scene we use the not very surprising `remove()` function. In the given code fragment we have used the `children` property from the `THREE.Scene()` object to get the last object that was added. We also need to check whether that object is a `Mesh` object in order to avoid removing the camera and the lights. After we've removed the object, we will once again update the GUI property that holds the number of objects in the scene.

The final button on our GUI is labeled as **outputObjects**. You've probably already clicked on it and nothing seemed to happen. What this button does is print out all the objects that are currently in our scene and will output them to the web browser **Console** as shown in the following screenshot:

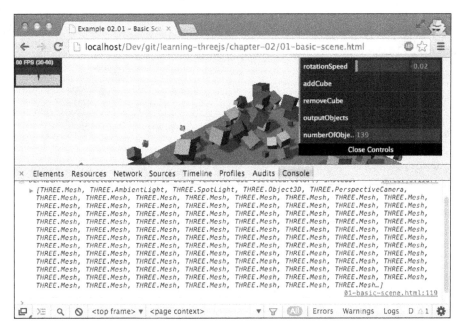

The code to output information to the **Console** log makes use of the built-in console object as shown:

```
this.outputObjects = function() {
  console.log(scene.children);
}
```

This is great for debugging purposes; especially when you name your objects, it's very useful for finding issues and problems with a specific object in your scene. For instance, the properties of the cube-17 object will look like the following code snippet:

```
__webglActive: true
__webglInit: true
_modelViewMatrix: THREE.Matrix4
_normalMatrix: THREE.Matrix3
_vector: THREE.Vector3
castShadow: true
children: Array[0]
eulerOrder: "XYZ"
frustumCulled: true
geometry: THREE.CubeGeometry
id: 20
material: THREE.MeshLambertMaterial
matrix: THREE.Matrix4
matrixAutoUpdate: true
matrixRotationWorld: THREE.Matrix4
matrixWorld: THREE.Matrix4
matrixWorldNeedsUpdate: false
name: "cube-17"
parent: THREE.Scene
position: THREE.Vector3
properties: Object
quaternion: THREE.Quaternion
receiveShadow: false
renderDepth: null
rotation: THREE.Vector3
rotationAutoUpdate: true
scale: THREE.Vector3
up: THREE.Vector3
useQuaternion: false
visible: true
__proto__: Object
```

So far we've seen the following scene-related functionality:

- `Scene.Add()`: This method adds an object to the scene
- `Scene.Remove()`: This removes an object from the scene
- `Scene.children()`: This method gets a list of all the children in the scene
- `Scene.getChildByName()`: This gets a specific object from the scene by using the `name` attribute

These are the most important scene-related functions, and most often you won't need any more. There are, however, a couple of helper functions that could come in handy, and I'd like to show them based on the code that handles the `cube` rotation.

As you've already seen in the previous chapter, we had used a `render` loop to render the scene. Let's look at the same code snippet for this example:

```
function render() {
    stats.update();
        scene.traverse(function(e) {
            if (e instanceof THREE.Mesh && e != plane ) {
                e.rotation.x+=controls.rotationSpeed;
                e.rotation.y+=controls.rotationSpeed;
                e.rotation.z+=controls.rotationSpeed;
            }
        });

    requestAnimationFrame(render);
    renderer.render(scene, camera);
}
```

Here we can see that the `THREE.Scene.traverse()` function is being used. We can pass a function as an argument to the `traverse()` function. This passed in function will be called for each child of the scene. In the `render()` function, we will use the `traverse()` function to update the rotation for each of the `cube` instances (we will explicitly ignore the ground `plane`). We could also have done this by iterating over the `children` property array by using a `for` loop.

Before we dive into the `Mesh` and `Geometry` object details, I'd like to show you two interesting properties that you can set on the `Scene` object: `fog` and `overrideMaterial`.

Adding the fog effect to the scene

The `fog` property let's you add a fog effect to the complete scene. The farther an object is, the more it will be hidden from sight. The following screenshot shows how the `fog` property is enabled:

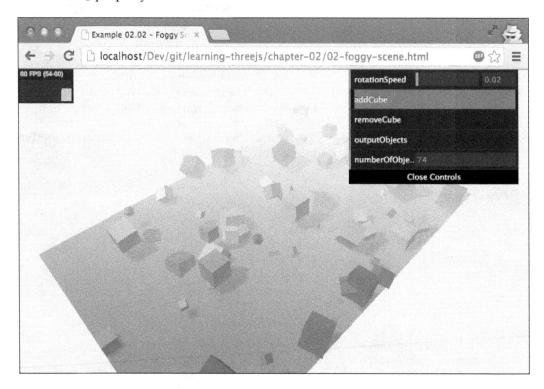

Enabling the `fog` property is really easy to do in the Three.js library. Just add the following line of code after you've defined your scene:

```
scene.fog=new THREE.Fog( 0xffffff, 0.015, 100 );
```

Here we are defining a white fog (`0xffffff`). The last two properties can be used to tune how the mist will appear. The `0.015` value sets the `near` property and the `100` value sets the `far` property. With these properties you can determine where the mist will start and how fast it will get denser. There is also a different way to set the mist for the scene; for this you will have to use the following definition:

```
scene.fog=new THREE.FogExp2( 0xffffff, 0.015 );
```

This time we don't specify the `near` and `far` properties, but just the color and the mist density. It's best to experiment a bit with these properties in order to get the effect that you want.

Using the overrideMaterial property

The last property that we will discuss for the scene is the `overrideMaterial` property, which is used to fix the materials of all the objects. When you use this property as shown in the following code snippet, all the objects that you add to the scene will make use of the same material:

```
scene.overrideMaterial = new
        THREE.MeshLambertMaterial({color: 0xffffff});
```

The scene will be rendered as shown in the following screenshot:

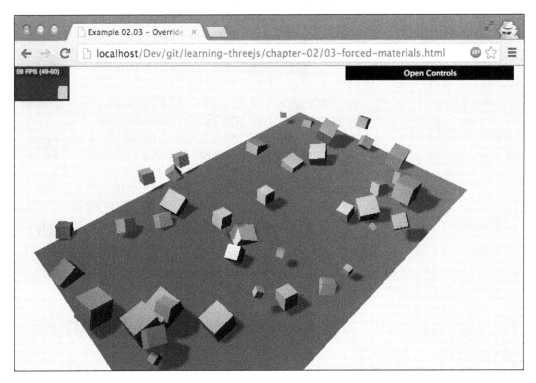

In the earlier screenshot, you can see that all the `cube` instances are rendered by using the same material and color. In this example we've used a `MeshLambertMaterial` object as the material. With this material type, you can create non-shiny looking objects which will respond to the lights that you add to the scene. In *Chapter 4, Working with the Three.js Materials*, you'll learn more about this material.

In this section we've looked at the first of the core concepts of the Three.js library: the scene. The most important thing to remember about the scene is that it is basically a container for all the objects, lights, and cameras that you want to use while rendering. The following table summarizes the most important functions and attributes of the `Scene` object:

Function/Property	Description
add(object)	Adds an object to the scene. You can also use this function, as we'll see later, to create groups of objects.
children	Returns a list of all the objects that have been added to the scene, including the camera and lights.
getChildByName(name)	When you create an object, you can give it a distinct name by using the name attribute. The Scene object has a function that you can use to directly return an object with a specific name.
remove(object)	If you've got a reference to an object in the scene, you can also remove it from the scene by using this function.
traverse(function)	The children attribute returns a list of all the children in the scene. With the traverse() function we can also access these children by passing in a callback function.
fog	This property allows you to set the fog for the scene. It will render a haze that hides the objects that are far away.
overrideMaterial	With this property you can force all the objects in the scene to use the same material.

In the next section we'll look closely at the objects that you can add to the scene.

Working with the Geometry and Mesh objects

In each of the examples so far you've already seen the geometries and meshes that are being used. For instance, to add a sphere object to the scene we did the following:

```
var sphereGeometry = new THREE.SphereGeometry(4,20,20);
var sphereMaterial = new THREE.MeshBasicMaterial({color: 0x7777ff});
var sphere = new THREE.Mesh(sphereGeometry,sphereMaterial);
```

We have defined the shape of the object, its geometry, what this object looks like, its material, and combined all of these in a mesh that can be added to a scene. In this section we'll look a bit closely at what the Geometry and Mesh objects are. We'll start with the geometry.

The properties and functions of a geometry

The Three.js library comes with a large set of out-of-the-box geometries that you can use in your 3D scene. Just add a material, create a `mesh` variable, and you're pretty much done. The following screenshot, from example `04-geometries.html`, shows a couple of the standard geometries available in the Three.js library:

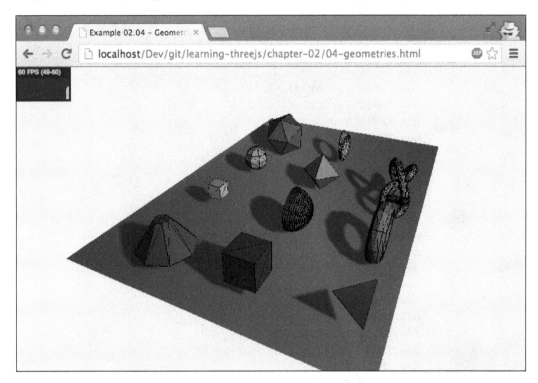

In *Chapter 5*, *Learning to Work with Geometries*, and *Chapter 6*, *Using Advanced Geometries and Binary Operations*, we'll explore all the basic and advanced geometries that the Three.js library has to offer. For now, we'll go into more detail on what the `geometry` variable actually is.

A `geometry` in Three.js, and in most other 3D libraries, is basically a collection of points in a 3D space and a number of faces connecting all those points together. Take, for example, a `cube`:

- A `cube` has eight corners. Each of these corners can be defined as a combination of x, y, and z coordinates. So, each cube has eight points in a 3D space. In the Three.js library, these points are called **vertices**.

- A `cube` has six sides, with one vertex at each corner. In the Three.js library, each of these sides is called a **face**.

When you use one of the Three.js library-provided geometries, you don't have to define all the vertices and faces yourself. For a `cube` you only need to define the width, height, and depth. The Three.js library uses that information and creates a geometry with eight vertices at the correct position and the correct face. Even though you'd normally use the Three.js library-provided geometries, or generate them automatically, you can still create geometries completely by hand by defining the vertices and faces. This is shown in the following code snippet:

```
var vertices = [
            new THREE.Vector3(1,3,1),
            new THREE.Vector3(1,3,-1),
            new THREE.Vector3(1,-1,1),
            new THREE.Vector3(1,-1,-1),
            new THREE.Vector3(-1,3,-1),
            new THREE.Vector3(-1,3,1),
            new THREE.Vector3(-1,-1,-1),
            new THREE.Vector3(-1,-1,1)
        ];

var faces = [
            new THREE.Face3(0,2,1),
            new THREE.Face3(2,3,1),
            new THREE.Face3(4,6,5),
            new THREE.Face3(6,7,5),
            new THREE.Face3(4,5,1),
            new THREE.Face3(5,0,1),
            new THREE.Face3(7,6,2),
            new THREE.Face3(6,3,2),
            new THREE.Face3(5,7,0),
            new THREE.Face3(7,2,0),
            new THREE.Face3(1,3,4),
            new THREE.Face3(3,6,4),
        ];

var geom = new THREE.Geometry();
geom.vertices = vertices;
geom.faces = faces;
geom.computeCentroids();
geom.mergeVertices();
```

This code shows you how to create a simple `cube`. We have defined the points that make up this `cube` in the `vertices` array. These points are connected to create triangular faces and are stored in the `faces` array. For instance, the `new THREE.Face3(0,2,1)` element creates a triangular face by using the points 0, 2, and 1 from the `vertices` array.

In this example we have used a THREE.Face3 element to define the six sides of the cube, that is, two triangles for each face. In the previous versions of the Three.js library, you could also use a quad instead of a triangle. A quad uses four vertices instead of three to define the face. Whether using quads or triangles is better is a much-heated debate in the 3D modeling world. Basically, using quads is often preferred during modeling, since they can be more easily enhanced and smoothed much easier than triangles. For rendering and game engines, though, working with triangles is easier since every shape can be rendered as a triangle.

Using these vertices and faces, we can now create our custom geometry, and use it to create a mesh. I've created an example that you can use to play around with the position of the vertices. In example 05-custom-geometry.html, you can change the position of all the vertices of a cube. This is shown in the following screenshot:

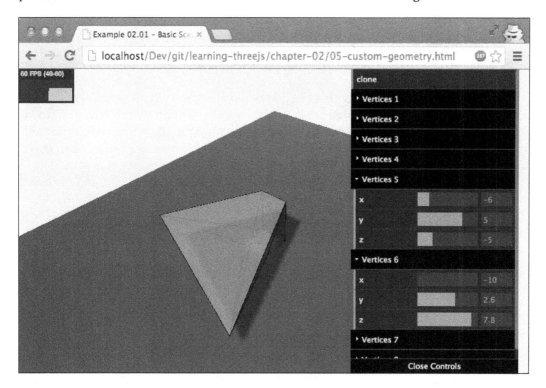

This example, which uses the same setup as all our other examples, has a `render` loop. Whenever you change one of the properties in the drop-down control box, the `cube` is rendered correctly based on the changed position of one of the vertices. This isn't something that works out-of-the-box. For performance reasons, the Three.js library assumes that the geometry of a mesh won't change during its lifetime. To get our example to work we need to make sure that the following is added to the code in the `render` loop:

```
mesh.geometry.vertices=vertices;
mesh.geometry.verticesNeedUpdate=true;
mesh.geometry.computeFaceNormals();
```

In the first line of the given code snippet, we point the vertices of the `mesh` that you see on the screen to an array of the updated vertices. We don't need to reconfigure the faces, since they are still connected to the same points as they were before. After we've set the updated vertices, we need to tell the `geometry` that the vertices need to be updated. We can do this by setting the `verticesNeedUpdate` property of the `geometry` to `true`. Finally we will do a recalculation of the faces to update the complete model by using the `computeFaceNormals()` function.

The last `geometry` functionality that we'll look at is the `clone()` function. We had mentioned that the `geometry` defines the form, the shape of an object, and combined with a material we can create an object that can be added to the scene to be rendered by the Three.js library. With the `clone()` function, as the name implies, we can make a copy of the `geometry` and, for instance, use it to create a different `mesh` with a different material. In the same example, that is, `05-custom-geometry.html`, you can see a **clone** button at the top of the control GUI, as seen in the following screenshot:

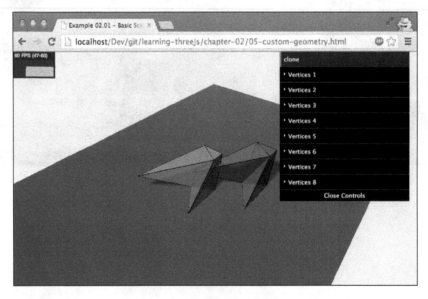

If you click on this button, a clone will be made of the `geometry` as it currently is, and a new object is created with a different material and is added to the scene. The code for this is rather trivial, but is made a bit more complex because of the materials that I have used. Let's take a step back and first look at the code that was used to create the green material for the `cube`:

```
var materials = [
  new THREE.MeshLambertMaterial( { opacity:0.6,
                                    color: 0x44ff44,
                                    transparent:true } ),
  new THREE.MeshBasicMaterial( { color: 0x000000,
                                  wireframe: true } )
];
```

As you can see, I didn't use a single material, but an array of two materials. The reason is that besides showing a transparent green `cube`, I also wanted to show you the wireframe, since that shows very clearly where the vertices and faces are located. The Three.js library, of course, supports the use of multiple materials when creating a `mesh`. You can use the `SceneUtils.createMultiMaterialObject()` function for this as shown:

```
var mesh = THREE.SceneUtils.createMultiMaterialObject(
              geom,materials);
```

What the Three.js library does in this function is that it doesn't create one `THREE.Mesh` instance, but it creates one for each material that you have specified, and puts all of these meshes in a group. This group can be used in the same manner that you've used for the `Scene` object. You can add meshes, get meshes by name, and so on. For instance, to add shadows to all the children in this group, we will do the following:

```
mesh.children.forEach(function(e) {e.castShadow=true});
```

Now back to the `clone()` function that we were discussing earlier:

```
this.clone = function() {

  var cloned = mesh.children[0].geometry.clone();
  var materials = [
    new THREE.MeshLambertMaterial( { opacity:0.6,
                                      color: 0xff44ff,
                                      transparent:true } ),
    new THREE.MeshBasicMaterial({ color: 0x000000,
                                  wireframe: true } )
              ];

  var mesh2 =
```

```
        THREE.SceneUtils.createMultiMaterialObject(cloned,materials);
    mesh2.children.forEach(function(e) {e.castShadow=true});
    mesh2.translateX(5);
    mesh2.translateZ(5);
    mesh2.name="clone";
    scene.remove(scene.getChildByName("clone"));
    scene.add(mesh2);
}
```

This piece of JavaScript is called when the **clone** button is clicked on. Here we clone the geometry of the first child of the cube. Remember, the mesh variable contains two children: a mesh that uses the MeshLambertMaterial and a mesh that uses the MeshBasicMaterial. Based on this cloned geometry, we will create a new mesh, aptly named mesh2. We can move this new mesh by using the translate() function (more on this in *Chapter 5, Learning to Work with Geometries*), remove the previous clone (if present), and add the clone to the scene.

That's enough on geometries for now.

The functions and attributes for a mesh

We've already learned that, in order to create a mesh, we need a geometry and one or more materials. Once we have a mesh, we can add it to the scene, and it is rendered. There are a couple of properties that you can use to change where and how this mesh appears in the scene. In the first example, we'll look at the following set of properties and functions:

Function/Property	Description
position	Determines the position of this object relative to the position of its parent. Most often the parent of an object is a THREE.Scene() object.
rotation	With this property you can set the rotation of an object around any of its axes.
scale	This property allows you to scale the object around its x, y, and z axes.
translateX(amount)	Moves the object through the specified amount over the x axis.
translateY(amount)	Moves the object through the specified amount over the y axis.
translateZ(amount)	Moves the object through the specified amount over the z axis.

As always, we have an example ready for you that'll allow you to play around with these properties. If you open up the `06-mesh-properties.html` example in your browser, you will get a drop-down menu where you can alter all these properties and directly see the result, as shown in the following screenshot:

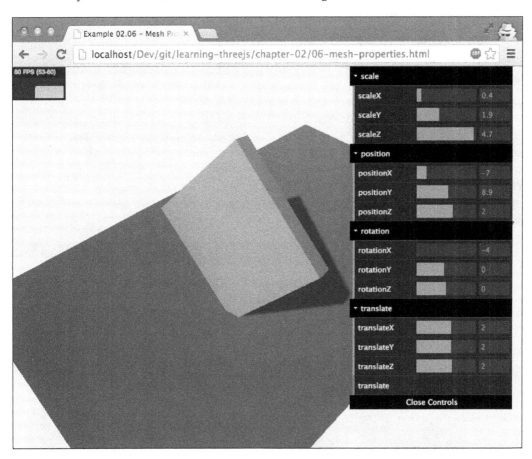

Let me walk you through them; I'll start with the `position` property. We've already seen this property a couple of times, so let's quickly address it. With this property you can set the x, y, and z coordinates of the object. The position of an object is relative to its parent object, which usually is the scene that you have added the object to. We'll get back to this in *Chapter 5, Learning to Work with Geometries*, when we will look at grouping objects. We can set an object's `position` property in three different ways; each coordinate can be set directly as follows:

```
cube.position.x=10;
cube.position.y=3;
cube.position.z=1;
```

But we can also set all of them at once:

```
cube.position.set(10,3,1);
```

There is also a third option. The `position` property is a `THREE.Vector3` object. This means that we can also do the following to set this object:

```
cube.postion=new THREE.Vector3(10,3,1)
```

I want to make a quick sidestep before looking at the other properties of this `mesh`. I had mentioned that this position is set relative to the position of its parent. In the previous section on `THREE.Geometry`, we made use of the `THREE.SceneUtils.createMultiMaterialObject` object to create a multimaterial object. I had explained that this doesn't really return a single mesh, but a group that contains a mesh based on the same geometry for each material. In our case, it is a group that contains two meshes. If we change the position of one of the meshes that is created, you can clearly see that there really are two distinct objects. However, if we now move the created group around, the offset will remain the same. These two meshes are shown in the following screenshot:

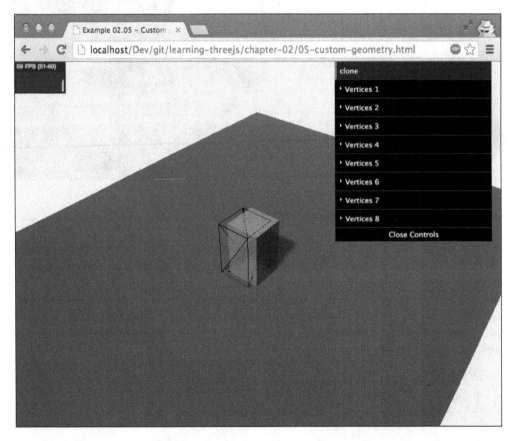

In *Chapter 8, Creating and Loading Advanced Meshes and Geometries*, we will look deeper into the parent-child relations and how grouping affects transformation, such as scaling, rotation, and translation. Ok, the next one on the list is the `rotation` property. You've already seen this property being used a couple of times in this as well as the previous chapter. With this property, you can set the rotation of the object around one of its axes. You can set this value in the same manner as we did the for the `position` property. A complete rotation, as you might remember from math class, is two pi. The following code snippet shows how to configure this:

```
cube.rotation.x=0.5*Math.PI;
cube.rotation.set(0.5*Math.PI,0,0);
cube.rotation = new THREE.Vector3(0.5*Math.PI,0,0);
```

You can play around with this property by using the `06-mesh-properties.html` example.

The next property on our list is one that we haven't talked about: `scale`. The name pretty much sums up what you can do with this property. You can scale the object along a specific axis. If you set the scale to values smaller than one, the object will shrink as shown:

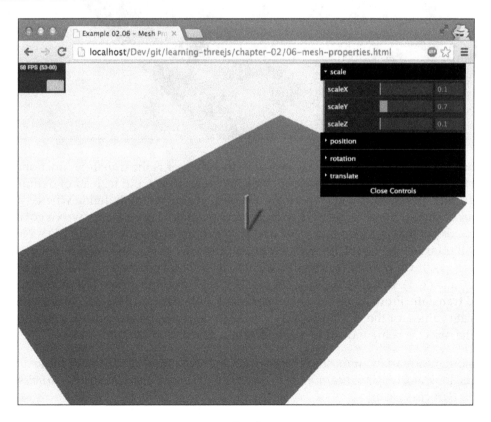

When you use values larger than one, the object will become larger as shown in the screenshot that follows:

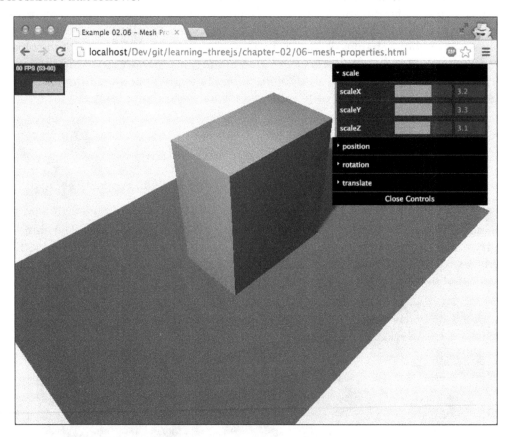

The last part of the mesh that we'll look at in this chapter is the **translate** functionality. With translate, you can also change the position of an object, but instead of defining the absolute position of where you want the object to be, you will define where the object should move to, relative to its current position. For instance, we've got a sphere object that is added to a scene and its position has been set to (1,2,3). Next, we will translate the object along its x axis by translateX(4). Its position will now be (5,2,3). If we want to restore the object to its original position we will set it to translateX(-4). In the 06-mesh-properties.html example, there is a menu tab called **translate**. From there you can experiment with this functionality. Just set the translate values for the x, y, and z axes, and click on the **translate** button. You'll see that the object is being moved to a new position based on these three values.

For more information on meshes, geometries, and what you can do with these objects, look at *Chapter 5, Learning to Work with Geometries*, and *Chapter 7, Particles and the Particle System*.

Using the available cameras for different uses

There are two different camera types in the Three.js library: the orthographic camera and the perspective camera. In *Chapter 3*, *Working with the Different Light Sources Available in Three.js*, we'll have a more detailed look at how to work with these cameras, so for this chapter I'll stick to the basics. The best way to explain the difference between these cameras is by looking at a couple of examples.

The orthographic camera versus the perspective camera

In the examples for this chapter you can find an example called `07-both-cameras.html`. When you open this example, you'll see something like the following screenshot:

This is called a perspective view and is the most natural view. As you can see from this screenshot, the further away the cubes are from the camera, the smaller they are rendered.

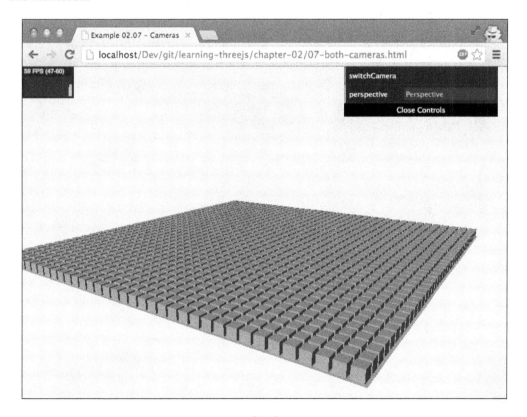

If we change the camera to the other type supported by the Three.js library, which is the orthographic camera, you'll see the following view of the same scene:

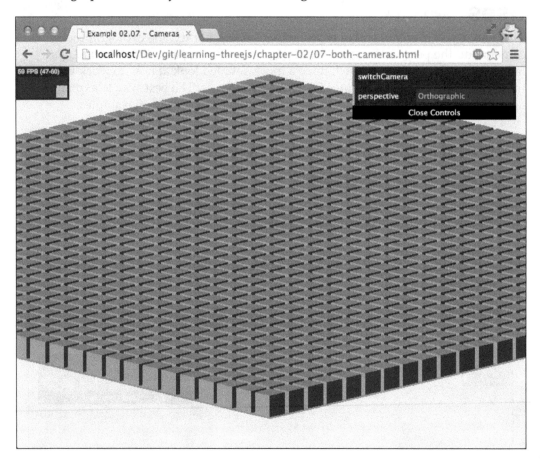

With the orthographic camera, all the cubes are rendered at the same size; the distance between an object and the camera doesn't matter. This is often used in 2D games such as SimCity 4 and older versions of Civilization as shown in the following screenshot:

In our examples we'll be using the perspective camera the most, since it best resembles the real world. Switching cameras is really very easy. The following piece of code is called whenever you click on the **switchCamera** button in the 07-both-cameras.html example:

```
this.switchCamera = function() {
  if (camera instanceof THREE.PerspectiveCamera) {
    camera = new THREE.OrthographicCamera(
        window.innerWidth / - 16, window.innerWidth / 16,
```

```
                    window.innerHeight / 16, window.innerHeight / - 16,
                    -200, 500 );
        camera.position.x = 2;
        camera.position.y = 1;
        camera.position.z = 3;
        camera.lookAt(scene.position);
        this.perspective = "Orthographic";
    } else {
        camera = new THREE.PerspectiveCamera(45,
                window.innerWidth / window.innerHeight, 0.1, 1000);
        camera.position.x = 120;
        camera.position.y = 60;
        camera.position.z = 180;

        camera.lookAt(scene.position);
        this.perspective = "Perspective";
    }
};
```

In this listing you can see that there is a difference in the way we create the `THREE.PerspectiveCamera` as opposed to the `THREE.OrthographicCamera` object. Let's look at the `THREE.PerspectiveCamera` object first. It takes the following arguments:

Argument	Description
fov	fov stands for **field of view**. This is the part of the scene that can be seen from the position of the camera. Humans, for instance, have an almost 180-degree field of view, while some birds might even have a complete 360-degree field of view.
	But since a normal computer screen doesn't completely fill our vision, normally a smaller value is chosen. Most often, for games, a field of view between 60 and 90 degrees is chosen.
	Good default: 45
aspect	This is the aspect ratio between the horizontal and vertical size of the area where we'll render the output. In our case, since we will use the entire window, we will just use that ratio. The aspect ratio determines the difference between the horizontal field of view and the vertical field of view as you can see in the figure on the following page.
	Good default: window.innerWidth/window.innerHeight
near	The near property defines from how close to the camera the Three.js library should render the scene. Normally we set this to a very small value to directly render everything from the position of the camera.
	Good default: 0.1

Argument	Description
far	The far property defines how far the camera can see from the position of the camera. If we set this as too low, a part of our scene might not be rendered; if we set it as too high, in some cases, it might affect the rendering performance. Good default: 1000

The following figure gives a good overview of how these properties work together to determine what you will see:

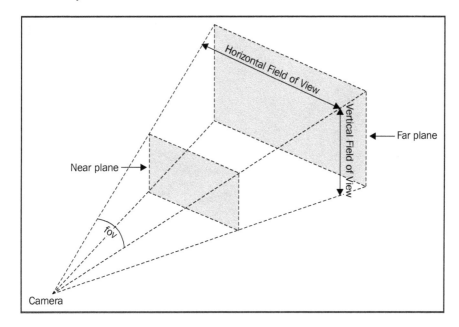

To configure the orthographic camera, we need to use other properties. The orthographic projection isn't interested in the aspect ratio to use, or with what field of view we look at the scene. All the objects are rendered at the same size. For an orthographic camera, you need to define the cube that needs to be rendered. The properties for the OrthographicCamera object reflect this in the following table:

Argument	Description
left	This is described in the Three.js documentation as Camera frustum left plane. You should see this as what is the left border of what will be rendered. If we set this value to -100, you won't see any objects that are farther to the left.
right	The same as for the left property, but this time it is to the other side of the screen. Anything farther to the right won't be rendered.

Argument	Description
top	The top position to be rendered.
bottom	The bottom position to be rendered.
near	From this point, based on the position of the camera, the scene will be rendered.
far	To this point, based on the position of the camera, the scene will be rendered.

All of these properties can be summarized in the following figure:

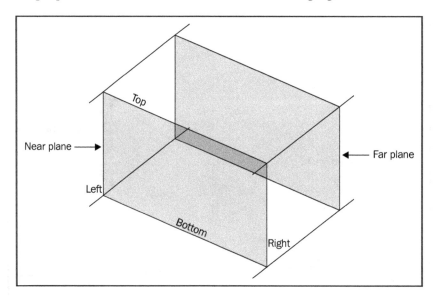

Focusing the camera on a specific point

So far we've seen how to create a camera and what the various arguments mean.
In the previous chapter, we've also seen that you need to position your camera
somewhere in the scene and that the view from that camera to the center of the scene
is rendered. Normally the camera is pointed to the center of the scene by using the
coordinates: position (0,0,0). We can, however, easily change what the camera is
looking at as shown:

```
camera.lookAt(new THREE.Vector3(x,y,z));
```

I've added an example where the camera moves and the point it is looking at is marked with a red dot, as you can see in the following screenshot:

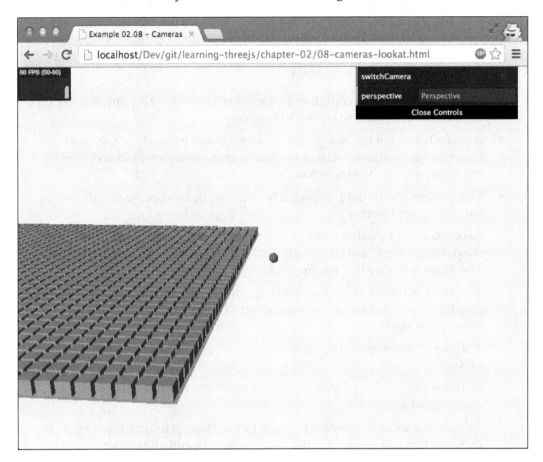

If you open the example `08-cameras-lookat.html`, you'll see that the scene is moving from left to right. The scene isn't really moving. The camera is looking at different points (see the red dot in the center), which gives the effect that the scene is moving from left to right. In this example you can also switch the camera to the orthographic one. There you will see that changing where the camera looks at has a different effect than it does on the perspective camera.

Summary

We've discussed a lot of items in this second introduction chapter and this should give you a good overview of what a scene is and what the most important components of a scene are. In the next couple of chapters we'll dive a lot deeper into the details of the Three.js library. The following are a few of the points that you should remember from this chapter:

- The scene is the main container in the Three.js library. You can add the objects that you want to render to a scene.

- A scene hasn't got too many specific options and properties. The most important ones allow you to add objects, remove objects, and work on the `children` attribute of the scene.

- You can easily add the `fog` property to the scene by configuring one of the supplied `Fog` objects.

- Geometries and meshes work closely together. A `geometry` defines the shape of an object, and combined with a material you can create a `mesh`. The Three.js library can render the `mesh`.

- The Three.js library comes with a large number of standard geometries. You can, however, create your own ones, but that is a lot of work if not done through an algorithm.

- You can programmatically control the `position`, `rotation`, and `scale` of a `mesh`.

- With the `translate` property, you can move the mesh relative to its current position.

- To render a scene, we need a camera. In the Three.js library there are two different types of cameras: a perspective camera and an orthographic camera.

- The perspective camera renders the scene in a real world-like perspective.

- The orthographic camera renders all objects of the same size and doesn't take the distance to the camera into account. Use this for SimCity-like effects.

In the next chapter we'll look at the various light sources that are available in the Three.js library. You'll learn how the various light sources behave, how to create and configure them, and the effect that they'll have on specific materials.

3

Working with the Different Light Sources Available in Three.js

In the first chapter you learned about the basics of the Three.js library, and in the previous chapter we looked a bit deeper into the most important parts of the scene: the geometries, meshes, and cameras. You might have noticed that we skipped lights in that chapter even though they make up an important part of every Three.js scene. Without lights, we won't see anything that is rendered. Since the Three.js library contains a large number of lights, each of which has a specific use, we'll use this whole chapter to explain the various details of the lights and prepare you for the next chapter on material usage. In this chapter you'll learn about the following topics:

- Which light sources are available in the Three.js library
- When you should use a specific light source
- How you can tune and configure the behavior of all these light sources
- As a bonus, we'll also quickly look at how you can create lens flares

As with all the chapters, we've got a lot of examples that you can use to experiment with the lights' behavior. The examples shown in this chapter can be found in the `chapter-03` folder of the supplied sources.

Exploring the lights provided by Three.js

There are a number of different lights available in the Three.js library that have specific behavior and usage. In this chapter we'll discuss the following set of lights:

Name	Description
AmbientLight	This is the basic light whose color is added to the current color of the complete scene and objects.
PointLight	A single point in space that emanates light in all directions.
SpotLight	This light source has a cone effect like a desk lamp, a spot in the ceiling, or a torch.
DirectionalLight	Also called as an infinite light. The light rays from this light can be seen as parallel. For instance, light from the sun.
HemisphereLight	This is a special light and can be used to create more natural-looking outdoor lighting by simulating a reflective surface and a faintly emanating sky.
AreaLight	With this light source you can specify an area that emanates light, instead of a single point in space.
LensFlare	Not a light source, but with a lens flare you can add a LensFlare effect to the lights in your scene.

This chapter is divided into two main parts. First we'll look at the basic lights: AmbientLight, PointLight, SpotLight, and DirectionalLight. These are simple lights that require little setup, and can be used to recreate most of the required lighting scenarios. In the second part, we will look at a couple of special purpose lights and effects: HemisphereLight, AreaLight, and the LensFlare effect. You'll probably only need these lights in very specific cases.

Learning about the basic lights

We'll start with the most basic of the lights: the AmbientLight.

AmbientLight – a globally applied light source

When you create an AmbientLight source, the color is applied globally. There isn't a specific direction that this light comes from and the AmbientLight source doesn't contribute to any shadows. You don't use an AmbientLight as the single source of light in a scene. You will use it together with the other light sources, such as a SpotLight or a DirectionalLight, to soften the shadows or add some color to the scene. The easiest way to understand this is by looking at the 01-ambient-light.html example in the chapter-03 folder. In this example you will get a simple user interface that can be used to modify the AmbientLight source that is added to the scene.

 In this scene, we have a SpotLight source that handles the lighting of the objects and provides shadows.

In the following screenshot, you can see that we've used the scene from the first chapter and made the color of the AmbientLight source configurable:

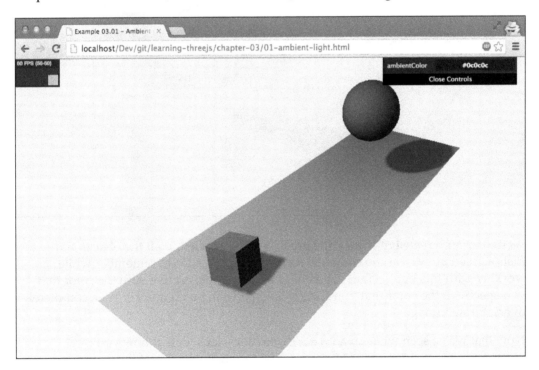

The standard color that we will use in this scene is `#0c0c0c`. This is a hexadecimal representation of the color; if you're not familiar with specifying colors in hexadecimal, you can find more information in Wikipedia: `http://en.wikipedia.org/wiki/Web_colors#Hex_triplet`. In this example we will use a very dimmed light gray color that will smoothen the hard shadows that our meshes cast on the ground `plane`. If you want to change this color to a more prominent green color (`#007700`), you can do so in the menu at the top-right corner; the objects will then have a light green glow over them. This is shown in the following screenshot:

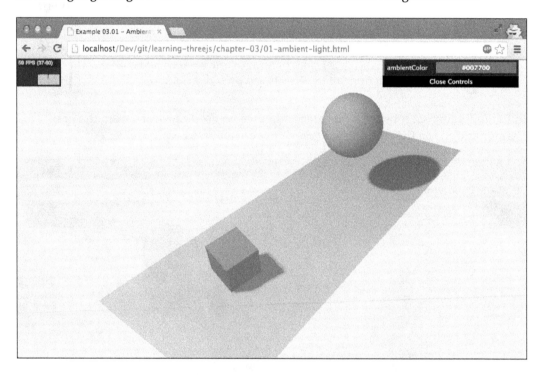

As the earlier screenshot shows, the green color is applied to all the objects and casts a green glow over the complete scene. What you should remember while working with this light is that you should be very conservative with the color that you specify. If the color that you specify is too bright, you'll quickly get a completely oversaturated image.

Now that we've seen what an `AmbientLight` does, let's look at how you can create and use an `AmbientLight` source. The following couple of lines of code will show you how to create an `AmbientLight` source and also how to connect it to the `dat.GUI` control menu:

```
var ambiColor = "#0c0c0c";
var ambientLight = new THREE.AmbientLight(ambiColor);
```

```
    scene.add(ambientLight);
    ...

    var controls = new function() {
        this.ambientColor = ambiColor  ;
    }

    var gui = new dat.GUI();
    gui.addColor(controls, 'ambientColor').onChange(function(e) {
        ambientLight.color = new THREE.Color(e);
    });
```

Creating an `AmbientLight` source is very trivial. Since an `AmbientLight` source doesn't have a position, we only need to specify the color (in hex) by using `new THREE.AmbientLight(ambiColor);`. Add this light to the scene and you're done. In the example we have bound the color of the `AmbientLight` source to the control menu. To do this, you can use the same kind of configuration that we've used in the previous chapters. The only change is that instead of using the `gui.add(...)` function, we will use the `gui.addColor(...)` function. This will create an option in the control menu, with which we can directly change the color of the passed in variable. In the code you can see that we have used the `onChange` feature of the `dat.GUI` control menu as `gui.addColor(...).onChange(function(e){...})`. With this function we will tell the `dat.GUI` control menu to call the passed in function each time the color changes. In this specific case we will set the color of our `AmbientLight` source to a new value.

Using the THREE.Color() object

Before we move on to the next light, a quick note on using the `THREE.Color()` object. In the Three.js library, when you construct an object, you can (usually) specify the color as either a hex string (`#0c0c0c`) or a hex value (`0x0c0c0c`). The Three.js library, internally, will convert this to a `THREE.Color()` object. If you want to change the color after construction, you'll have to create a new `THREE.Color()` object (once again by using a hex string or value) or modify the internal properties of the current `THREE.Color()` object. This object comes with the following functions to set and get information about the current object:

Name	Description
`set(value)`	Sets the value of this color to the supplied hex value. This hex value may either be a string or number.
`setHex(value)`	Sets the value of this color to the supplied numeric hex value.

Name	Description
setRGB(r,g,b)	Sets the value of this color based on the supplied RGB values. The values range from 0 to 1.
setHSV(h,s,v)	Sets the value of this color based on the supplied HSV values. The values range from 0 to 1.
setStyle(style)	Sets the value of this color based on a CSS color.
copy(color)	Copies the color values from the provided color to this color.
copyGammaToLinear(color)	Mostly used internally:
	Sets the color of this object based on the supplied color. The color is first converted from the gamma color space to the linear color space. The gamma color space also uses RGB values, but uses an exponential scale instead of a linear one.
copyLinearToGamma(color)	Mostly used internally:
	Sets the color of this object based on the supplied color. The color is first converted from the linear color space to the gamma color space.
convertGammaToLinear()	Converts the current color from the gamma color space to the linear color space.
convertLinearToGamma()	Converts the current color from the linear color space to the gamma color space.
getHex()	Returns the value from this color object as a number.
getHexString()	Returns the value from this color object as a hex string.
getStyle()	Returns the value from this color object as a CSS-based value.
getHSV()	Returns the value from this color object as a HSV value.
add(color)	Adds the supplied color to the current color.
addColors(color1, color2)	Mostly used internally:
	Adds the supplied colors to the current color.
addScalar(s)	Mostly used internally:
	Adds a value to the RGB components of the current color.
multiply(color)	Mostly used internally:
	Multiplies the current color by the supplied color.
multiplyScalar(s)	Mostly used internally:
	Multiplies the light by the supplied value.

Name	Description
lerp(color, alpha)	Mostly used internally:
	Finds the color that is between the color of this object and the supplied color. The resulting color is multiplied by the supplied alpha value.
clone()	Creates an exact copy of this color.

In this table you can see that there are many ways you can change the current color. A lot of these functions are used internally by the Three.js library, but they also provide a good way to easily change the color of the lights and materials.

The next light that we will look at is the PointLight.

PointLight – the light that shines in all directions

A PointLight in the Three.js library is a light source that shines light in all directions, emanating from a single point. A good example of a point light is a signal flare fired in the night sky. Just as with all the lights, we've got a specific example that you can use to play around with a PointLight. If you look at 02-point-light.html in the chapter-03 folder, you can find an example where a PointLight source is moving around a simple Three.js scene. The following screenshot shows this example:

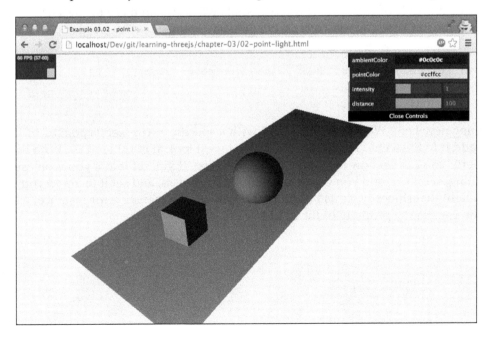

In this example from *Chapter 1, Creating Your First 3D Scene with Three.js*, a PointLight source moves around the scene. To make it more clear where the PointLight source is, we will move a small orange sphere along the same path. As the light source will move around, you'll see the red cube and blue sphere being illuminated from this light.

 You might have noticed that we don't see any shadows in this example. In the Three.js library, a PointLight source doesn't cast shadows. Since a PointLight source emits light in all directions, calculating shadows would be too heavy for the GPU.

With the AmbientLight source that we saw earlier, all you had to do was set the color and add the light to the scene. With the PointLight source, however, we've got a couple of additional options as shown:

Property	Description
color	The color of the light.
intensity	The intensity that the light shines with. Defaults to 1.
distance	The distance to which the light shines.
position	The position of the light.
visible	If set to true, the light is turned on; if set to false, the light is turned off.

In the next couple of examples and screenshots we'll explain these properties. First off, let's look at how you can create a PointLight source:

```
var pointColor = "#ccffcc";
var pointLight = new THREE.PointLight(pointColor);
pointLight.distance = 100;
scene.add(pointLight);
```

Nothing new here. We will create a light with a specific color, set its position, and add it to the scene. The first property that we'll look at is intensity. With this property you can set how bright the light will shine. If you set it to 0 you won't see anything, set it to 1 and you've got the default brightness, and set it to 2 and you will get a light that shines twice as bright. In the following screenshot, for instance, we've set the intensity property of the light to 2.4:

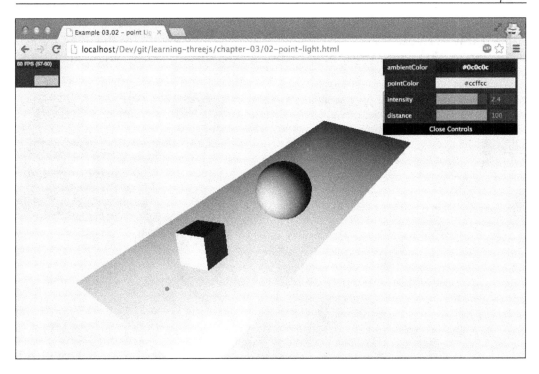

All that you have to do to change the `intensity` property of the light is the following:

```
pointLight.intensity = 2.4;
```

You can also use the `dat.GUI` listener as in the following code snippet:

```
var controls = new function() {
  this.intensity = 1;
}
var gui = new dat.GUI();
  gui.add(controls, 'intensity', 0, 3).onChange(function (e) {
    pointLight.intensity = e;
  });
```

The final property of the PointLight source is a very interesting one, and best explained with an example. In the following screenshot you will see the same scene again, but this time with a very high intensity (as we have a very bright light), but with a small distance:

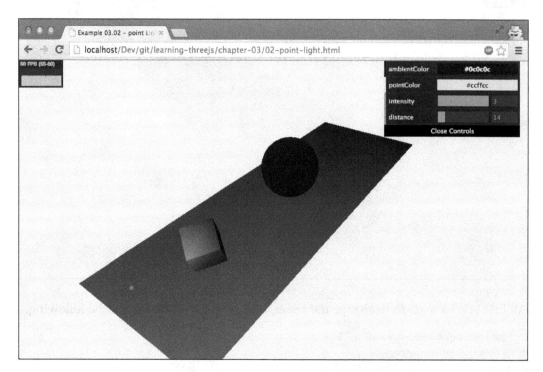

The distance property of the SpotLight source determines how far the light will travel from the source. You can set the property like this: pointLight.distance = 4;. In our example, the light's brightness (intensity) will slowly decrease to 0 at a distance of 14. That's why you can still see a brightly-lit cube in the example, but the light won't reach the blue sphere, as you can see in the earlier screenshot. The default value for the distance property is 0, which means that the light won't decay over a distance.

SpotLight – the light with a cone effect

A SpotLight is probably one of the lights that you'll use most often (especially if you want a shadow). A SpotLight is a light source that has a cone effect. You can compare this with a flashlight, or a lantern. This light has a direction and an angle at which it produces light. The properties that we've seen for the PointLight source also apply to the SpotLight. A SpotLight source also has a number of additional properties:

Property	Description
castShadow	If set to true, this light will cast shadows.
shadowCameraNear	From what point from the light the shadows should be created.
shadowCameraFar	To what point from the light should the shadows be created.
shadowCameraFov	How large is the field of view that is used to create the shadows (see the section on the perspective camera in *Chapter 2, Working with the Basic Components That Make Up a Three.js Scene.*)
target	Determines where the light is aimed.
shadowBias	Can be used to offset the position of the rendered shadow.
angle	How wide the beam is from this light source. It is measured in radians. Defaults to Math.PI/3.
exponent	A light is aimed at a specific target. The farther away the light source is from this direction, the more the light's intensity will decrease. This value determines how fast the light's intensity decreases.
onlyShadow	If set to true, this light will only cast a shadow and won't add any light to the scene.
shadowCameraVisible	If set to true, you can see how and where this light source casts a shadow (see the example in the following section).
shadowDarkness	Defaults to 0.5. Defines how dark the shadow is rendered. Can't be changed after the scene is rendered.
shadowMapWidth	Determines how many pixels are used to create the shadow. It can be increased when the shadow has jagged edges or doesn't look smooth. Can't be changed after the scene is rendered.
shadowMapHeight	Determines how many pixels are used to create the shadow. It can be increased when the shadow has jagged edges or doesn't look smooth. Can't be changed after the scene is rendered.

Creating a `SpotLight` source is very easy. Just specify the color, set the properties you want, and add it to the scene as shown:

```
var pointColor = "#ffffff";
var spotLight = new THREE.SpotLight(pointColor);
spotLight.position.set(-40, 60, -10);
spotLight.castShadow = true;
spotLight.target = plane;
scene.add(spotLight);
```

Not that different from the `PointLight` source. The only difference is that we will set the `castShadow` property to `true` because we want shadows, and we need to set the `target` for the `SpotLight` source. The target determines where the light is aimed at. In this case we will point it at the center of the ground `plane`. When you run the `03-spot-light.html` example, you'll see a scene like the following screenshot:

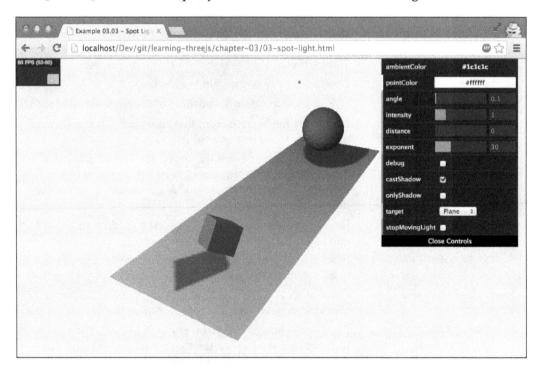

In this example you can set a number of SpotLight-specific properties. One of them is the target property. If we set this property to the blue sphere, the light will stay aimed at the center of the sphere, even if it moves around the scene. When we created the light source, we aimed it at the ground plane, and in our example we can also aim it at the other two objects. But what if you don't want to aim the light at a specific object, but at an arbitrary point in space? You can do that by creating an empty THREE.Object3D() instance as follows:

```
var target = new THREE.Object3D();
target.position = new THREE.Vector3(5, 0, 0);
```

And set the target property of the SpotLight source as shown:

```
spotlight.target = target
```

In the table earlier in this section, we showed a couple of properties that can be used to control how the light emanates from the SpotLight source. The distance and angle properties define the shape of the cone. The angle property defines the width of the cone and, with the distance property, we can set the length of the cone. If we dive into the Three.js source code, we can find exactly how this is defined:

```
var coneLength = light.distance ? light.distance : 10000;
var coneWidth = coneLength * Math.tan( light.angle * 0.5 ) * 2;
```

Without diving too deep into trigonometry, let's have a quick look at the second statement. The tangent function (Math.tan()) can be used to determine the ratio of the opposite side (the cone width) to the length of the adjacent side (the cone length). The following figure shows how the angle and cone length determine the cone width:

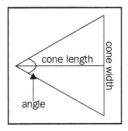

In the Three.js code, the light source angle is first divided by two (see the earlier figure), since the tangent function should be used on right-angled triangles. To get the cone width, the result from the Math.tan() function, the ratio, is multiplied by the cone length. This gives us half the cone width, which we will multiply by two to get the final cone width.

Usually you won't have to set these values, since they come with reasonable defaults, but you can use these properties, for instance, to create SpotLight sources that have a very narrow beam, or quickly decrease in light intensity. The last property that you can use to change the way a SpotLight light is perceived is the exponent property. With this property, you can set how fast the light intensity will decrease from the center of the light cone, as shown in the following screenshot:

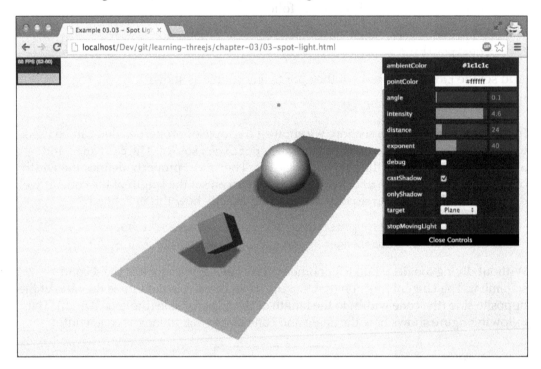

We've got a very bright light (high intensity) that rapidly decreases in intensity (high exponent) as it moves away from the center. We could also have created the same focused beam effect by using a small exponent value, and a small angle.

 A very small angle can quickly lead to **artifacts** (this is a term used in graphics for unwanted distortions and strangely-rendered parts of the screen) in the way that the light is rendered.

Before moving on to the next light, we'll quickly look at the shadow-related properties that are available to the SpotLight source. We've already learned that we can get shadows by setting the castShadow property of the SpotLight source to true. The Three.js library also allows you very fine-grained control on how the shadow is rendered. This is done by a couple of properties that we explained in the table earlier in this section. With the shadowCameraNear, shadowCameraFar, and shadowCameraFov properties, you can control how and where this light will cast a shadow. This works in the same way as the perspective camera field of view that we explained in the previous chapter. The easiest way to see this in action is by setting the shadowCameraVisible property to true; you can do this by checking the menu's **debug** checkbox. This shows the area that is used to determine the shadows for this light, as you can see in the following screenshot:

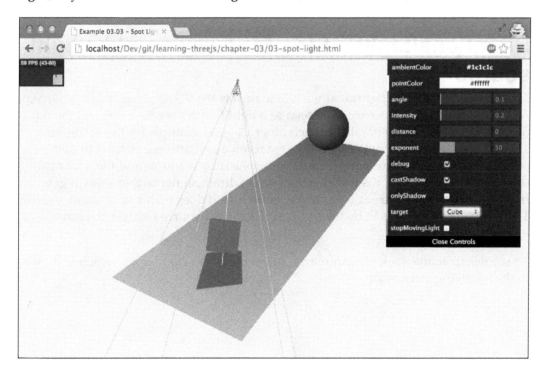

I'll end this section with a couple of pointers should you run into issues with shadows:

- Enable the `shadowCameraVisible` property. This shows the area that is affected by this light for shadow purposes.

- If the shadow looks blocky, you can either increase the `shadowMapWidth` and `shadowMapHeight` properties, or make sure that the area that is used to calculate the shadow tightly wraps your object. You can use the `shadowCameraNear`, `shadowCameraFar`, and `shadowCameraFov` properties to configure this area.

- Remember that you not only have to tell the light to cast shadows, you also have to tell each geometry whether it will receive and/or cast shadows, by setting the `castShadow` and `receiveShadow` properties.

DirectionalLight – for a far away sun-like light source

The last one of the basic lights that we will look at is the `DirectionalLight` source. A `DirectionalLight` source can be seen as a light that is very far away. All the light rays that it sends out are parallel to each other. A good example for this is the sun. The sun is so far away that the light rays we receive on Earth are parallel to each other. The main difference between a `DirectionalLight` source and the `SpotLight` source that we saw earlier is that this light won't diminish the farther away it gets from the target of the `DirectionalLight` source, as it does with a `SpotLight` source. The complete area that is lit by the `DirectionalLight` source receives the same intensity of light.

To see this in action, look at example `04-directional-light.html`, which is shown in the following screenshot:

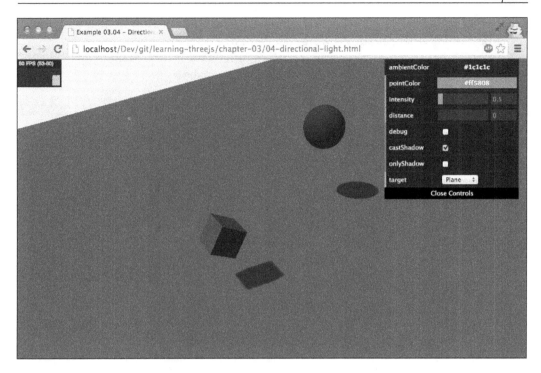

As you can see, there isn't a cone of light that is applied to the scene. Everything receives the same intensity of light. Only the direction, the color, and the intensity of the load is used to calculate the colors and shadows.

Just as with the SpotLight source, there are a couple of properties that you can set to control the intensity of the light and the way it casts shadows. A DirectionalLight source has a lot of properties that are the same as those of a SpotLight: position, target, intensity, distance, castShadow, onlyShadow, shadowCameraNear, shadowCameraFar, shadowDarkness, shadowCameraVisible, shadowMapWidth, shadowMapHeight, and shadowBias. For more information on these properties, you can look at the earlier section on the SpotLight source. Only the additional properties are discussed in the following couple of paragraphs.

If you look at the SpotLight source examples, you would see that we had to define the cone of light where shadows were applied. For a DirectionalLight source, since all the rays are parallel to each other, we don't have a cone of light; instead, we have a cube, as you can see in the following screenshot:

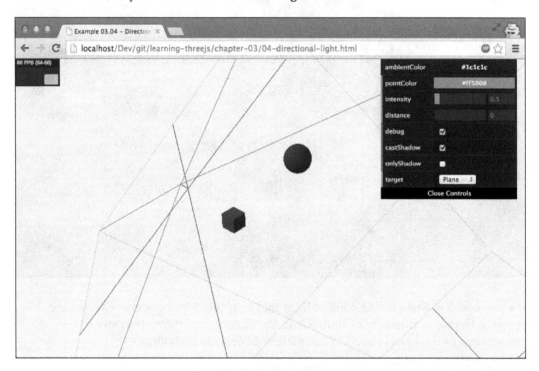

Everything that falls within the cube can cast and receive shadows from the light. Just as for the SpotLight source, the tighter you define the area around the objects, the better your shadows will look. You can define the cube instance by using the following properties:

```
directionalLight.shadowCameraNear = 2;
directionalLight.shadowCameraFar = 200;
directionalLight.shadowCameraLeft = -50;
directionalLight.shadowCameraRight = 50;
directionalLight.shadowCameraTop = 50;
directionalLight.shadowCameraBottom = -50;
```

You can compare this with the way that we configured the orthographic camera in the *Using the available cameras for different uses*, section in *Chapter 2, Working with the Basic Components That Make Up a Three.js Scene*.

Using special lights for advanced lighting

In this section on special lights we'll discuss two additional lights provided by the Three.js library. First we'll discuss the `HemisphereLight` source that helps to create more natural lighting for outdoor scenes, then we'll look at an `AreaLight` source that emits light from a large area instead of a single point, and finally we'll show you how you can add a `LensFlare` effect to your scene.

HemisphereLight

The first special light that we're going to look at is the `THREE.HemisphereLight`. With a `HemisphereLight` source, we can create a more natural-looking outdoor lighting. Without this light we could simulate the outdoors by creating a `DirectionalLight` source emulating the sun, and maybe add an `AmbientLight` source to provide some general color to the scene. This, however, won't look really natural. When you're outdoors, not all the light comes directly from above; much is diffused by the atmosphere, reflected by the ground, and reflected by other objects. The `HemisphereLight` source in the Three.js library is created for this scenario. It provides an easy way to get more natural-looking outdoor lighting. To see an example, look at `05-hemisphere-light.html`. This is the first example that requires a local web server. If you haven't done so, look at *Chapter 1*, *Creating Your First 3D Scene with Three.js*, and set up a local web server. The following screenshot shows a scene where a `HemisphereLight` source is used:

In this example, you can turn the `HemisphereLight` source on and off, and set the `color` and `intensity`. Creating a `HemisphereLight` source is very easy, as shown in the following code snippet:

```
var hemiLight = new THREE.HemisphereLight(0x0000ff, 0x00ff00, 0.6);
hemiLight.position.set(0, 500, 0);
scene.add(hemiLight);
```

You just have to specify the color from the top, the color received from the sky, the color received from the ground, and the intensity with which they shine. If you want to change these properties later on, you can use the following properties:

Property	Description
groundColor	The color that is emitted from the ground
Color	The color that is emitted from the sky
intensity	The intensity with which the light shines

AreaLight

The last real light source that we'll look at is the `AreaLight` source. With the `AreaLight` source, we can define a rectangular area that emits light. The `AreaLight` source isn't included in the standard Three.js library, but in its extensions, so we have to take a couple of additional steps before we can use this light source. Before we look at the details, let's first look at the result that we're aiming for (`06-area-light.html` opens this example):

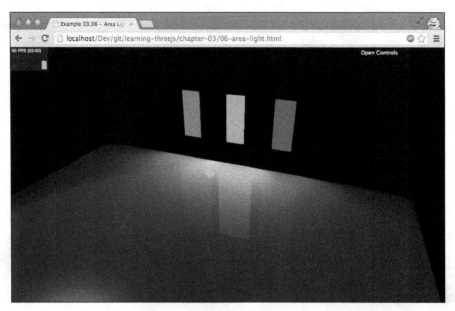

When you want to use an `AreaLight` source, we can't use the `THREE.WebGLRenderer` object that we've used in our examples so far. The reason is that an `AreaLight` source is a very complex light source; this would cause a very serious performance penalty in the normal `THREE.WebGLRenderer` object. The `THREE.WebGLDeferredRenderer` object uses a different approach when rendering a scene and can handle complex lights (or a very high number of light sources for that matter.)

To use the `THREE.WebGLDeferredRenderer` object, we have to include a couple of additional Three.js-provided JavaScript sources. In the head of your HTML skeleton, make sure that you've got the following set of `<script/>` sources defined:

```
<head>
    <title>Example 03.07 - Area Light</title>
    <script type="text/javascript" src="../libs/three.js"></script>
    <script type="text/javascript"
        src="../libs/jquery-1.9.0.js"></script>
    <script type="text/javascript" src="../libs/stats.js"></script>
    <script type="text/javascript" src="../libs/dat.gui.js"></script>
    <script type="text/javascript"
        src="../libs/WebGLDeferredRenderer.js"></script>
    <script type="text/javascript"
        src="../libs/ShaderDeferred.js"></script>
    <script type="text/javascript"
        src="../libs/RenderPass.js"></script>
    <script type="text/javascript"
        src="../libs/EffectComposer.js"></script>
    <script type="text/javascript"
        src="../libs/CopyShader.js"></script>
    <script type="text/javascript"
        src="../libs/ShaderPass.js"></script>
    <script type="text/javascript"
        src="../libs/FXAAShader.js"></script>
    <script type="text/javascript"
        src="../libs/MaskPass.js"></script>
</head>
```

With these libraries included, we can use the `THREE.WebGLDeferredRenderer` object; you can use this renderer in pretty much the same way as the one that we have used in the other examples. It just takes a couple of extra arguments, as shown in the following code snippet:

```
var renderer = new THREE.WebGLDeferredRenderer({
    width: window.innerWidth,
    height: window.innerHeight,
    scale: 1, antialias: true,
    tonemapping: THREE.FilmicOperator, brightness: 2.5 });
```

Don't worry too much at the moment about what all these properties mean. In *Chapter 10, Loading and Working with Textures*, we'll dive deeper into the THREE.WebGLDeferredRenderer object and explain it to you. With the correct JavaScript libraries and a different renderer, we can start adding the Three.AreaLight object properties.

You can do this in pretty much the same way as all the other lights:

```
var areaLight1 = new THREE.AreaLight(0xff0000, 3);
areaLight1.position.set(-10, 10, -35);
areaLight1.rotation.set(-Math.PI / 2, 0, 0);
areaLight1.width = 4;
areaLight1.height = 9.9;
scene.add(areaLight1);
```

In this example, we have created a new THREE.AreaLight instance. This light has a color of value 0xff0000 and an intensity of 3. Just like the other lights, we can use the position attribute to set its location in the scene. When you create a THREE.AreaLight instance, it will be created as a horizontal plane. In our example, we've created three AreaLight sources that are positioned vertically, so we need to rotate our lights by -Math.PI/2 around their x axes. Finally we will set the size of the AreaLight source by using the width and height properties and add them to the scene. If you try this by yourself for the first time, you might wonder why you don't see anything where you positioned your light. This is because you can't see the light source itself but the light that it emits, which you can only see when it touches an object. If you want to recreate what I've shown in the example, you can add a plane or cube at the same position to simulate the area emitting the light as follows:

```
var planeGeometry1 = new THREE.CubeGeometry(4, 10, 0);
var planeGeometry1Mat = new THREE.MeshBasicMaterial({color: 0xff0000})
var plane1 = new THREE.Mesh(planeGeometry1, planeGeometry1Mat);
plane1.position = areaLight1.position;
scene.add(plane1);
```

You can create really beautiful effects with a THREE.AreaLight instance, but you'll probably have to experiment a bit to get the desired effect. If you pull down the dat. GUI control panel at the top-right corner, you've got some controls that you can play around with to set the color and intensity of the three lights from this scene, as shown in the following screenshot:

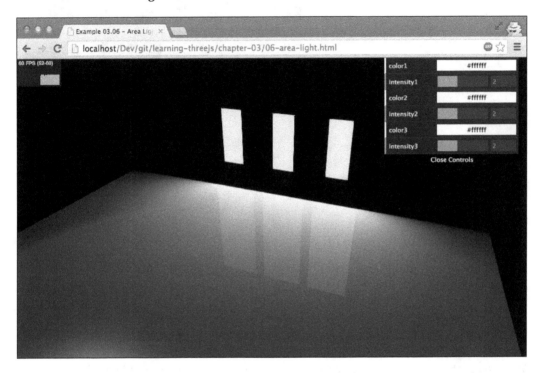

LensFlare

The last subject that we'll explore in this chapter deals with **lens flares**. You are probably already familiar with lens flares. For instance, they appear when you take a photograph directly towards the sun. In most cases you want to avoid this, but for games and 3D-generated images, it provides a nice effect that makes the scenes look a bit more realistic.

The Three.js library also has support for lens flares, and makes it very easy to add them to your scene. In this section we're going to add a lens flare to a scene and create the output you can see in the following screenshot. You can see this for yourself by opening the 07-lensflares.html example.

We can create a lens flare by instantiating the THREE.LensFlare object. The first thing that we need to do is create this object. The THREE.LensFlare object takes the following arguments:

```
THREE.LensFlare=function(texture, size, distance, blending,
color);
```

These arguments are explained in the following table:

Argument	Description
texture	A texture argument is used as the material for the flare. This determines what the flare looks like.
size	We can specify how large the flare should be. This is the size in pixels. If you specify -1, the size of the texture itself is used.
distance	This is the distance from the light source (0) to the camera (1).

Argument	Description
blending	We can specify multiple `texture` arguments for the flares. The `blending` mode determines how these are blended together. The default to use with the `LensFlare` is `THREE.AdditiveBlending`, which provides a nice semitransparent flare. More on this in the next chapter.
color	The color of the flare.

Let's look at the code that is used to create this object (see example `07-lensflares.html`):

```
var textureFlare0 = THREE.ImageUtils.loadTexture
        ("../assets/textures/lensflare/lensflare0.png");

var flareColor = new THREE.Color(0xffaacc);
var lensFlare = new THREE.LensFlare(textureFlare0, 350, 0.0, THREE.
AdditiveBlending, flareColor);

lensFlare.position = spotLight.position;
scene.add(lensFlare);
```

We will first load a texture. For this example I've used the `LensFlare` texture provided in the Three.js library examples, as shown in the screenshot that follows:

If you compare this texture with the screenshot that is present earlier in this section, you can see that it defines what the lens flare looks like. Next, we will define the color of the lens flare by using new THREE.Color(0xffaacc);. This will give the lens flare a red glow. With these two objects, we can create the THREE.LensFlare object. For this example we've set the size of the flare to 350 and the distance to 0.0 (directly at the light source.)

After we've created the THREE.LensFlare object, we will position it at the location of our light and add it to the scene, as shown in the following screenshot:

It already looks nice, but if you compare this with the screenshot from earlier in the chapter, you'll notice that we're missing the small round artifacts in the middle of the page. We will create these in pretty much the same way as we did the main flare:

```
var textureFlare3 = THREE.ImageUtils.loadTexture
        ("../assets/textures/lensflare/lensflare3.png");

lensFlare.add(textureFlare3, 60, 0.6, THREE.AdditiveBlending);
lensFlare.add(textureFlare3, 70, 0.7, THREE.AdditiveBlending);
lensFlare.add(textureFlare3, 120, 0.9, THREE.AdditiveBlending);
lensFlare.add(textureFlare3, 70, 1.0, THREE.AdditiveBlending);
```

This time, though, we don't create a new `THREE.LensFlare` object, but use the `add()` function provided by the `THREE.LensFlare` object that we just created. In this method we need to specify the `texture`, `size`, `distance`, `blending` mode, and that's it. The texture that we will use for these flares is a very light circle as shown:

If you look at the scene again, you'll see the artifacts appearing at the positions that you've specified with the `distance` argument.

Summary

That was a lot of information about the different kinds of lights that are available in the Three.js library. The most important things to remember from this chapter are the following:

- Configuring the lights, colors, and shadows is not an exact science. Experiment with it; use a `dat.GUI` control to fine-tune your configuration.

- An `AmbientLight` source color is added to each and every color in the scene. It has no position. Usually this light is used to smooth hard colors and shadows.

- A `PointLight` source doesn't create shadows and emits light in all directions. You can compare this light with a flare in the night sky.

- A `SpotLight` is a light that resembles a flash light. It has a conical shape and can be configured to fade over distance. A `SpotLight` source can be configured to cast shadows.

- A `SpotLight`, just like a `DirectionalLight`, has a **debug** flag that you can use to fine-tune the shadow camera configuration.

- A `DirectionalLight` source can be compared with a far away light, such as the sun, whose light rays travel parallel to each other. The farther away it gets from the configured `target`, the more the `intensity` of the light decreases.

- If you want a more natural outdoor effect, you can use the `HemisphereLight`, which takes into account the ground and sky reflections.

- When you want to use an `AreaLight` source, you have to remember to use the `WebGLDeferredRenderer` object. If you have a large number of lights, and performance becomes an issue, you should consider using the `WebGLDeferredRenderer` object instead of the `WebGLRenderer`.

- For a photographic-like lens flare, you can use the `LensFlare` component from the Three.js library to add this effect to the light sources in your scene.

In the chapters so far, we've already introduced a couple of different materials, and in this chapter you've seen that not all materials respond in the same manner to the available lights. In the next chapter, we'll give an overview of the materials that are available in the Three.js library.

4
Working with the Three.js Materials

In the previous chapters we've already talked a bit about materials. You've learned that a material, together with a geometry, forms a mesh. The material is like the skin of the object, which defines what the outside of a geometry looks like. For example, a skin defines whether a geometry is metallic-looking, transparent, or shown as a wireframe. This mesh can then be added to the scene to be rendered by the Three.js library. So far we haven't really looked at the materials in much detail. In this chapter, we'll dive into all the materials that the Three.js library has to offer and you'll learn how you can use these materials to create good-looking 3D objects. The materials that we'll explore in this chapter are shown in the following table:

Name	Description
MeshBasicMaterial	The basic material that you can use to give your geometries a simple color or show the wireframe of your geometries
MeshDepthMaterial	A material that uses the distance from the camera to determine how to color your mesh
MeshNormalMaterial	A simple material that bases the color of a face on its normal vector
MeshFaceMaterial	A container that allows you to specify a unique material for each face of the geometry
MeshLambertMaterial	A material that takes lighting into effect and is used to create dull, non-shiny looking objects
MeshPhongMaterial	A material that also takes lighting into effect and can be used to create shiny objects
ShaderMaterial	This material allows you to specify your own shader programs to directly control how vertices are positioned and pixels are colored

Name	Description
LineBasicMaterial	A material that can be used on the THREE.Line geometry to create colored lines
LineDashedMaterial	This is the same as the LineBasicMaterial, but this one also allows you to create a dash effect

Materials have a number of common properties, so before we look at the first material, that is, the MeshBasicMaterial, we'll look at the properties that are shared by all the materials.

Understanding the common material properties

You can quickly see for yourself which properties are shared between all the materials. The Three.js library provides a material base class, THREE.Material, that lists all the properties. We've divided these common material properties into three categories as shown:

- **Basic properties**: These are the properties that you'll use most often. With these properties you can, for instance, control the opacity of the object, whether it is visible or how it is referenced (by the ID or custom name).

- **Blending properties**: Every object has a set of blending properties. These properties define how the object is combined with its background.

- **Advanced properties**: There are a number of advanced properties that control how the low-level WebGL-context renders objects. In most cases you won't need to mess with these properties.

We start with the first one from the list: the basic properties.

Basic properties

The basic properties from the THREE.Material class are listed in the following table. You can see these properties in action in the section on MeshBasicMaterial.

Property	Description
ID	This is used to identify a material, and is assigned when you create a material.
name	You can assign a name to a material with this property.
opacity	It defines how transparent an object is. Use this together with the transparent property. The range of this property is from 0 to 1.

Property	Description
transparent	If set to `true`, the Three.js library will render this object with the set `opacity`. If `false`, the object won't be transparent; just more lightly colored.
overdraw	When you use the `THREE.CanvasRenderer` object, the polygons will be rendered a bit bigger. Set this to `true` when you see gaps while using this renderer.
visible	Defines whether this material is visible. If you set this to `false`, you won't be able to see the object in the scene.
side	With this property you can define to which side of the geometry a material is applied. The default is `THREE.FrontSide`, which applies the material to the front (outside) of an object. You can also set this to `THREE.BackSide`, which applies the material to the back (inside) or `THREE.DoubleSide`, which applies it to both sides.
needsUpdate	For some updates to the material, you need to tell the Three.js library that the material has changed. If this property is set to `true`, Three.js will update its cache with the new material properties.

For each material you can also set a number of blending properties.

Blending properties

Materials have a couple of generic blending-related properties. We'll touch this subject in a little while, when we will talk about combining materials, but we won't go into much detail.

Name	Description
blending	It determines how the material on this object blends with the background. The normal mode is `NormalBlending`, which only shows the top layer.
blendsrc	Besides using the standard blending modes, you can also create custom blend modes by setting the `blendsrc`, `blenddst`, and `blendequation` properties. This property defines how the object (the source) is blended into the background (the destination). The default, `SrcAlphaFactor`, uses the alpha (transparency) channel for blending.
blenddst	This property defines how the background (the destination) is used in blending and defaults to `OneMinusSrcAlphaFactor`, which means that it also uses the alpha channel of the source for blending but as value uses 1 – (alpha channel of the source).

Name	Description
blendequation	This defines how the blendsrc and blenddst values are used. The default is to add the two color values by using the AddEquation property. With these three properties, you can create your own custom blend modes.

The last set of properties is mostly used internally and controls the specifics of how WebGL is used to render the scene.

Advanced properties

We won't go into detail on these properties. These are related to how WebGL works internally. If you do want to know more about these properties, the OpenGL specification is a good starting point. You can find this specification at the following address: http://www.khronos.org/registry/gles/specs/2.0/es_full_spec_2.0.25.pdf

Name	Description
depthTest	This is an advanced WebGL property. With this property you can enable or disable the GL_DEPTH_TEST parameter. This parameter controls whether the depth of a pixel is used to determine a new pixel's value. Normally you wouldn't need to change this. More information can be found in the OpenGL specification that we mentioned earlier.
depthWrite	This is another internal property. It can be used to determine whether this material affects the WebGL depth buffer. When you will use an object for a 2D overlay (for example, a hub), you should set this property to false. Usually, though, you shouldn't need to change this property.
polygonOffset, polygonOffsetFactor, and polygonOffsetUnits	With these properties you can control the POLYGON_OFFSET_FILL WebGL feature. It is normally not needed. For an explanation of what this does, you can look at the OpenGL specification.
alphaTest	This property can be set to a specific value (from 0 to 1). Whenever a pixel has an alpha value smaller than this value, it won't be drawn.

Now let's look at all the available materials, so you can see the effects that these properties will have on the rendered output.

Starting with the simple Mesh materials (basic, depth, and face)

In this section we'll look at a couple of simple Mesh materials: `MeshBasicMaterial`, `MeshDepthMaterial`, `MeshNormalMaterial`, and `MeshFaceMaterial`. We will start with the `MeshBasicMaterial`.

The MeshBasicMaterial for simple surfaces

The `MeshBasicMaterial` is a very simple material that doesn't take lighting into account. Meshes with this material will be rendered as simple flat polygons, and you've also got the option to show the geometry's wireframe. Besides the common properties that we saw in the earlier section on this material, we can set the following properties:

Name	Description
color	This sets the color of the material.
wireframe	This property renders the material as a wireframe. It is great for debugging purposes.
wireframeLinewidth	If you enable the `wireframe`, this property will define the width of the wires from the wireframe.
wireframeLinecap	This property defines how the end of a line between the two vertices will look in the `wireframe` mode. Possible values are `butt`, `round`, and `square`. The default is `round`. In practice, the results from changing this property are very difficult to see. This property isn't supported by the `WebGLRenderer` object.
wireframeLinejoin	This defines how the line joins are visualized. Possible values are `round`, `bevel`, and `miter`. Default is `round`. If you look very closely you can see this in the example using a low `opacity` and a very large `wireframeLinewidth`. This property isn't supported by the `WebGLRenderer` object.
shading	This property defines how shading is applied. Possible values are `THREE.SmoothShading` and `THREE.FlatShading`. This property isn't enabled in the example for this material. For an example, look at the section on the `MeshNormalMaterial`.
vertexColors	You can define individual colors to be applied to each vertex with this property. It doesn't work on the `CanvasRenderer`, but works on the `WebGLRenderer`. For an example, look at the section on the `LineBasicMaterial`, where we will use this property to color the various parts of a line.

Name	Description
fog	This defines whether this material is affected by the global fog settings. It is not shown in action, but if set to `false` the global `fog` property that we saw in *Chapter 2, Working with the Basic Components That Make Up a Three.js Scene*, doesn't affect how this object is rendered.

In the previous chapters we've already seen how to create materials and assign them to objects. We will set the `MeshBasicMaterial` as follows:

```
var meshMaterial = new THREE.MeshBasicMaterial({color: 0x7777ff});
```

This will create a new material and initialize the `color` property to `0x7777ff`. All the properties can either be passed into the constructor as shown, or you can set them after the material is created:

```
var meshMaterial = new THREE.MeshBasicMaterial({color: 0x7777ff});
meshMaterial.visible = false;
```

I've added an example that you can use to play around with the `MeshBasicMaterial` properties and the basic properties that we discussed in the previous section. If you open example `01-basic-mesh-material.html` in the `chapter-04` folder, you'll see a rotating cube as in the following screenshot:

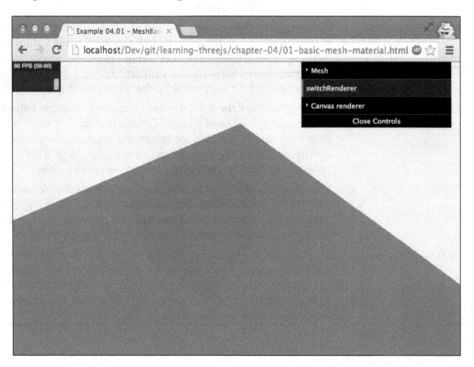

This is a very simple object. You can play around with the properties in the menu at the upper-right corner and select different meshes (and even change the renderer). For instance, let us consider a `sphere`. Suppose it has an `opacity` of 0.2, `transparent` is set to `true`, `wireframe` is set to `true`, `wireframeLinewidth` is 9, and it uses the `CanvasRenderer` object; then it is rendered as follows:

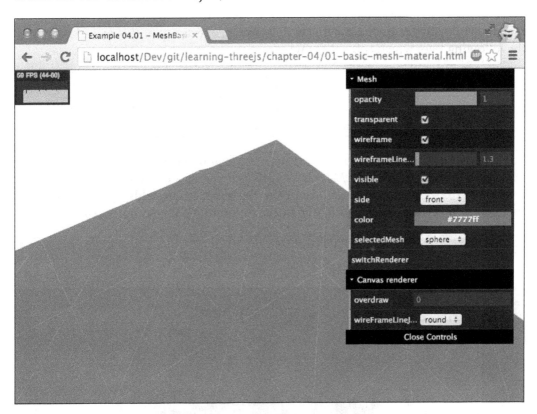

One of the properties that you can set in this example is the `side` property. With this property, you can define to which side of a geometry the material is applied. You can test how this property works when you select the `plane` mesh. Since a material is normally only applied to the front side of an object, the rotating plane will be invisible half the time (that is, when it shows its back to you). If you set the `side` property to `double`, the plane will be visible the whole time, since the material is applied to both sides of the geometry.

The MeshDepthMaterial for depth-based coloring

The next material on the list is the `MeshDepthMaterial`. With this material, the way an object looks isn't defined by the lights or a specific material property; it is defined by the distance from the object to the camera. You can combine this with the other materials to easily create fading effects. The only properties that this material has are the following two, which control the wireframe:

Name	Description
wireframe	This defines whether to show the wireframe
wireframeLinewidth	This defines the width of the wireframe

To demonstrate this, we have modified the cube example from *Chapter 2, Working with the Basic Components That Make Up a Three.js Scene*, as shown in the following screenshot (`02-depth-material.html` from the `chapter-04` folder). Remember that you have to click on the **addCube** button to populate the scene.

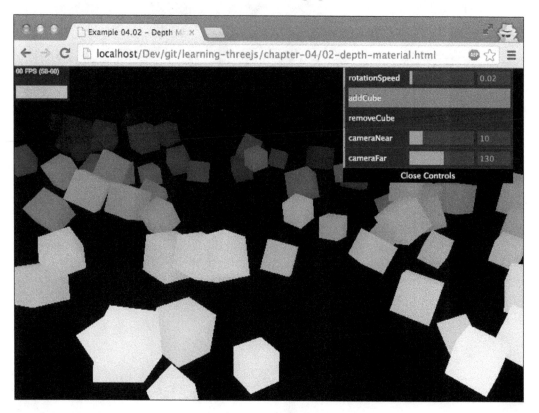

Even though the material doesn't have many additional properties to control how an object is rendered, we can still control how fast the object's color fades out. In this example, we've exposed the `near` and `far` properties of the camera. As you probably remember from *Chapter 2, Working with the Basic Components That Make Up a Three.js Scene*, we set the visible area for the camera with these two properties. Any objects that are nearer to the camera than the `near` property aren't shown, and any objects that are farther than the `far` property also fall outside the camera's visible area.

The distance between the `near` and `far` properties of the camera defines the brightness and the rate at which the objects will fade out. If the distance is very large, the objects will only fade out a little as they move away from the camera. If the distance is small, the fade out will be much more notable, as you can see in the following screenshot:

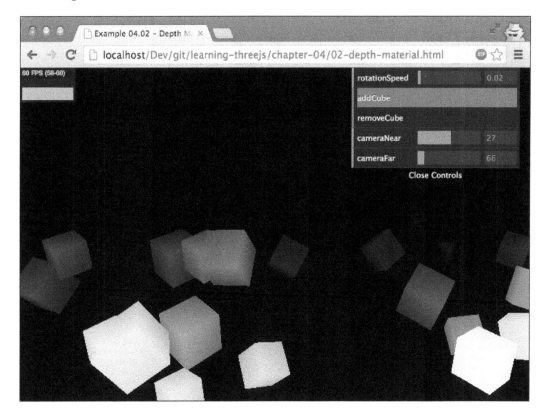

Creating the `MeshDepthMaterial` is very easy. The object doesn't take any arguments. For this example, we've used the `scene.overrideMaterial` property to make sure that all the objects in the scene reuse this material, as shown in the following code snippet:

```
var scene = new THREE.Scene();
scene.overrideMaterial = new THREE.MeshDepthMaterial();
```

The next subject that we'll discuss in this section isn't really a material, but a way in which you can combine all the materials together.

Combining the materials

If you will look back at the `MeshDepthMaterial`, you can see that there wasn't an option to set the color of the cubes. Everything was decided for you by the default properties of the material. The Three.js library, however, has the option to combine the materials together to create new effects (this is also where blending comes into play). If we use the following code, we can assign materials to the cubes in the `MeshDepthMaterial`:

```
var cubeMaterial = new THREE.MeshDepthMaterial();
var colorMaterial = new THREE.MeshBasicMaterial({color: 0x00ff00,
            transparent: true, blending: THREE.MultiplyBlending})
var cube = new THREE.SceneUtils.createMultiMaterialObject(
            cubeGeometry, [colorMaterial, cubeMaterial]);
cube.children[1].scale.set(0.99, 0.99, 0.99);
```

We will then get the following green colored cubes, which will use the shading from the `MeshDepthMaterial` object and the color from the `MeshBasicMaterial` object (open `08-combined-material.html` for this example).

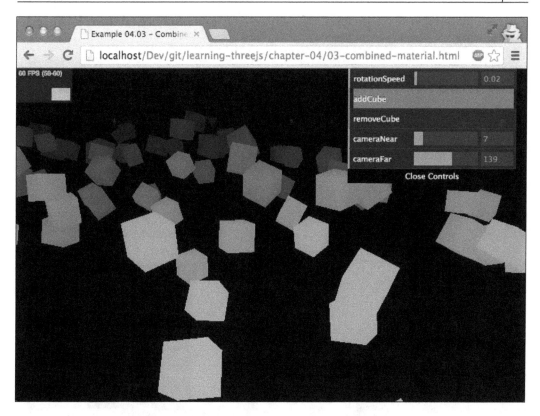

Let's look at the steps that you need to take to get this specific result. First, we need to create our two materials. For the `MeshDepthMaterial` we don't do anything special; for the `MeshBasicMaterial`, however, we will set `transparent` to `true`, and define a `blending` mode. If we don't set the `transparent` property to `true`, we'll just have solid green objects, since the Three.js library won't apply any blending. With `transparent` set to `true`, Three.js will check the `blending` property to see how the green `MeshBasicMaterial` should interact with the background. The background in this case is the `cube` rendered with the `MeshDepthMaterial`. In *Chapter 9, Animations and Moving the Camera*, we'll discuss the various blend modes that are available in more detail. For this example, though, we have used the `THREE.MultiplyBlending` object. This blend mode multiplies the foreground color with the background color, and gives you the desired effect. The last line in this code fragment is also an important one. What will happen when we create a mesh with the `createMultiMaterialObject()` function is that the geometry gets copied, and two exactly the same meshes are returned in a group. If we render these without the last line, you'll see some flickering effect, because they are rendered directly on top of each other. By scaling down the mesh created with the `MeshDepthMaterial`, we can avoid this.

The next material is also a material that won't have any influence on the colors used in rendering.

The MeshNormalMaterial for normal-based colors

The easiest way to understand what this material does is by first looking at an example. Open up example `03-mesh-normal-material.html` from the `chapter-04` folder. If you select the `sphere` as the mesh, you'll see something like the following screenshot:

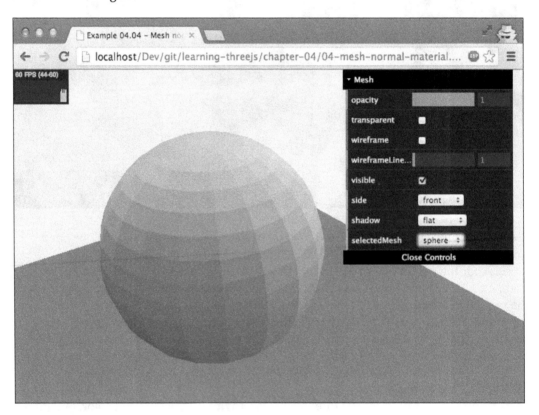

As you can see, each face of the mesh is rendered in a slightly different color, and even though the sphere rotates, the colors pretty much stay at the same place. This happens because the color of each face is based on the normal pointing out from the face. This normal is the vector that is perpendicular to the face. The normal vector is used in many different parts of the Three.js library. It is used to determine the light reflections, helps in mapping textures to 3D models, and gives information on how to light, shade, and color the pixels on a surface. Luckily, though, the Three.js library handles the computation of these vectors and uses them internally. The following screenshot shows an example of this normal:

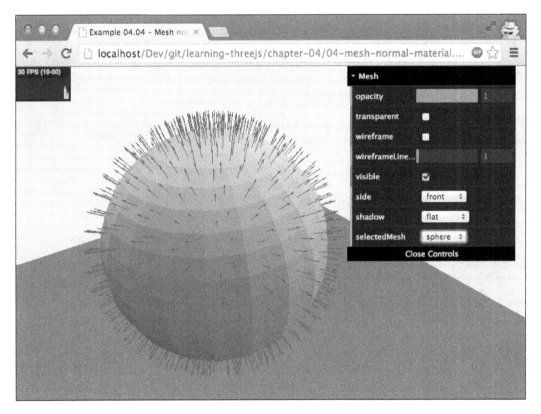

The direction that this normal points to determines the color that a face gets with the MeshNormalMaterial. Since all the normals for the faces of a sphere point in a different direction, we get the colorful sphere that you can see in the examples.

To add these normal arrows you can use the THREE.ArrowHelper object, as in the following code snippet:

```
for (var f = 0, fl = sphere.geometry.faces.length; f <
fl; f++) {
    var face = sphere.geometry.faces[ f ];
    var arrow = new THREE.ArrowHelper(
            face.normal,
            face.centroid,
            2,
            0x3333FF);
    sphere.add(arrow);
}
```

The given piece of code adds an arrow that shows the normal vector on each face of the sphere with a length of 2 and the color 0x333ff.

There are a couple of other properties that you can set on the MeshNormalMaterial object, as shown in the following table:

Name	Description
wireframe	This property defines whether to show the wireframe
wireframeLinewidth	This defines the width of the wireframe
shading	This is used to configure shading: flat shading with the THREE.FlatShading or smooth shading with the THREE.SmoothShading object

We've already seen the wireframe and wireframeLinewidth properties, but skipped over the shading property in our example on the MeshBasicMaterial. With the shading property, we can tell the Three.js library how to render our objects. If you use the THREE.FlatShading object, each face will be rendered as it is (as you can see in the previous couple of screenshots), or you can use the THREE.SmoothShading object, which smoothens out the faces of our object. For instance, if we render the sphere by using the THREE.SmoothShading object, the result will look like the screenshot that follows:

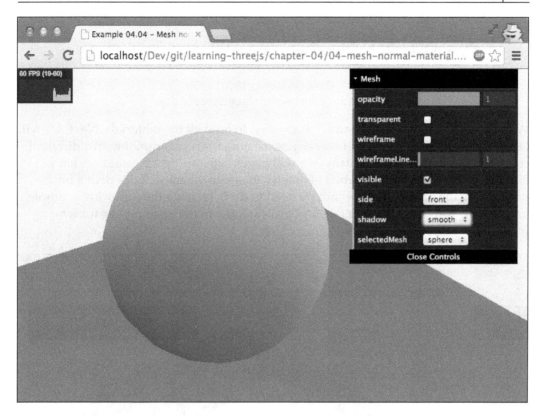

We're almost done with the simple materials. The last one is the MeshFaceMaterial.

The MeshFaceMaterial for assigning a material to each face

The last of the basic materials isn't really a material, but more of a container of the other materials. The MeshFaceMaterial allows you to assign a different material to each face of your geometry. For instance, if you have a cube, which has six faces, you can use this material to assign a different material (for example, with a different color) to each side of the cube. Using this material is really simple, as you can see from the following piece of code:

```
var matArray = [];
matArray.push(new THREE.MeshBasicMaterial( { color: 0x009e60 }));
matArray.push(new THREE.MeshBasicMaterial( { color: 0x0051ba }));
matArray.push(new THREE.MeshBasicMaterial( { color: 0xffd500 }));
matArray.push(new THREE.MeshBasicMaterial( { color: 0xff5800 }));
matArray.push(new THREE.MeshBasicMaterial( { color: 0xC41E3A }));
```

```
matArray.push(new THREE.MeshBasicMaterial( { color: 0xffffff }));

var faceMaterial = new THREE.MeshFaceMaterial(materialArray);

var cubeGeom = new THREE.CubeGeometry(3,3,3);
var cube = new THREE.Mesh(cubeGeom, faceMaterial);
```

We will first create an array, named `matArray`, to hold all the materials. Next, we will create a new material (`THREE.MeshBasicMaterial` in this example) with a different color for each face. With this array, we will instantiate the `THREE.MeshFaceMaterial` and use it together with the cube's geometry to create the mesh. Let's dive a bit deeper into the code and see what you need to do to recreate the following example: a simple 3D Rubik's cube. You can find this example in the `chapter-04` folder (`04-mesh-face-material.html`).

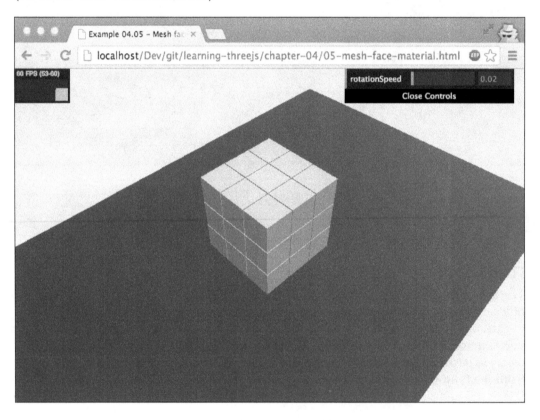

This Rubik's cube consists of a number of smaller cubes: three cubes along the x axis, three along the y axis, and three along the z axis, as shown in the following code snippet:

```
var group = new THREE.Mesh();
// add all the rubik cube elements
var mats = [];
mats.push(new THREE.MeshBasicMaterial({ color: 0x009e60 }));
mats.push(new THREE.MeshBasicMaterial({ color: 0x0051ba }));
mats.push(new THREE.MeshBasicMaterial({ color: 0xffd500 }));
mats.push(new THREE.MeshBasicMaterial({ color: 0xff5800 }));
mats.push(new THREE.MeshBasicMaterial({ color: 0xC41E3A }));
mats.push(new THREE.MeshBasicMaterial({ color: 0xffffff }));
var faceMaterial = new THREE.MeshFaceMaterial(mats);

for (var x = 0; x < 3; x++) {
    for (var y = 0; y < 3; y++) {
        for (var z = 0; z < 3; z++) {
            var cubeGeom = new THREE.CubeGeometry(2.9, 2.9, 2.9);
            var cube = new THREE.Mesh(cubeGeom, faceMaterial);
            cube.position =
                new THREE.Vector3(x * 3 - 3, y * 3, z * 3 - 3);
            group.add(cube);
        }
    }
}
```

In this piece of code we will first create the `MeshFaceMaterial`. Next, we will create three loops to make sure that we create the right number of cubes. In this loop, we will create each of the individual cubes, assign the material, position them, and add them to the group. What you should remember is that the position of the cubes is relative to the position of this group. If we move or rotate the group, all the cubes will move and rotate with it. For more information on how to work with groups, look at *Chapter 8, Creating and Loading Advanced Meshes and Geometries*.

If you open the example in your browser, you can see that the complete Rubik's cube rotates, and not the individual cubes. This happens because we use the following in our `render` loop:

```
group.rotation.y=step+=0.01;
```

This causes the complete group to rotate about its center: (0,0,0). When we positioned the individual cubes, we made sure that they were positioned around this center point. That's why you can see the -3 offset in the cube.position = new THREE.Vector3(x * 3 - 3, y * 3, z * 3 - 3); code.

The MeshFaceMaterial was the last of our basic materials. In the next section, we'll look at some of the more advanced materials available in the Three.js library.

Learning about the advanced materials

In this section we'll look at the more advanced materials that the Three.js library has to offer. We'll first look at the MeshPhongMaterial and then the MeshLambertMaterial. These two materials, react to light sources and can be used to create shiny and dull-looking materials respectively. In this section we'll also look at one of the most versatile but most difficult-to-use materials: ShaderMaterial. With the ShaderMaterial, you can create your own shader programs that will define how the material and object should be shown. For the last subject in this section on advanced materials, we'll look at how you can create a mesh that has multiple materials assigned to it instead of just one.

The MeshLambertMaterial for dull, non-shiny surfaces

This material can be used to create dull-looking, non-shiny surfaces. This is a very easy-to-use material, one that responds to the lighting sources available in the scene. It can be configured with a number of properties that we've already seen before: color, opacity, shading, blending, depthTest, depthWrite, wireframe, wireframeLinewidth, wireframeLinecap, wireframeLinejoin, vertexColors, and fog. We won't go into detail on these properties, but focus on the ones that are specific to this material. That just leaves us with the following two properties:

Name	Description
ambient	This is the ambient color of the material. It works together with the AmbientLight source that we saw in the previous chapter. This color is multiplied with the color provided by the AmbientLight source. Defaults to white.
emissive	This is the color that the material emits. It doesn't really act as a light source, but it is a solid color that is unaffected by the other lighting. Defaults to black.

This material is created just like all the other ones, as shown:

```
var meshMaterial = new THREE.MeshLambertMaterial({color:
0x7777ff});
```

For an example of this material, look at `05-mesh-lambert-material.html`; you'll see something like the following screenshot:

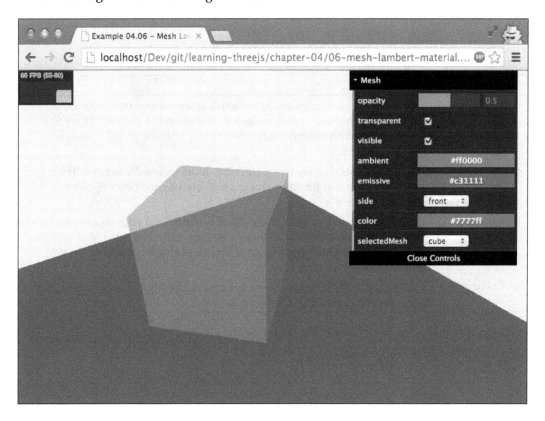

As you can see in this screenshot, the material looks rather dull. There is another material that we can use to create shiny surfaces.

The MeshPhongMaterial for shiny objects

With a `MeshPhongMaterial`, we can create a material that is shiny. The properties that you can use for it are pretty much the same as that for a non-shiny `MeshLambertMaterial`. We'll once again skip the basic properties and those already discussed: `color`, `opacity`, `shading`, `blending`, `depthTest`, `depthWrite`, `wireframe`, `wireframeLinewidth`, `wireframeLinecap`, `wireframeLinejoin`, and `vertexColors`.

The interesting properties for this material are shown in the following table:

Name	Description
ambient	This is the ambient color of the material. It works together with the `AmbientLight` source that we saw in the previous chapter. This color is multiplied with the color provided by the `AmbientLight` source. Defaults to white.
emissive	This is the color that the material emits. It doesn't really act as a light source, but it is a solid color that is unaffected by the other lighting. Defaults to black.
specular	This property defines how shiny the material is and with what color it shines. If this is set to the same color as the `color` property, you will get a more metallic-looking material. If this is set to grey, the material will become more plastic-looking.
shininess	This property defines how shiny the `specular` highlight is. The default value for the `shininess` property is `30`.

Initializing a `MeshPhongMaterial` object is done in the same way that we've already seen for all the other materials:

```
var meshMaterial = new THREE.MeshPhongMaterial({color: 0x7777ff});
```

To give you the best comparison, we've created the same example for this material as we did for the `MeshLambertMaterial`. You can use the control GUI to play around with this material. For instance, the following settings will create a plastic-looking material. You can open `06-mesh-phong-material.html` to find this example.

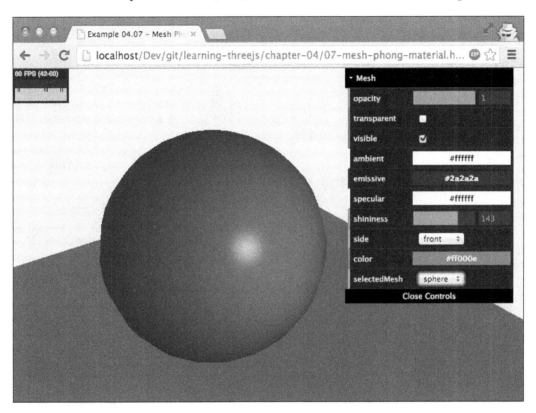

The last one of the advanced materials is also the most complex: the `ShaderMaterial`.

Creating your own shaders with the ShaderMaterial

The THREE.ShaderMaterial is one of the most versatile and complex materials available in the Three.js library. With it, you can pass in your own custom shaders that are directly run in the WebGL context. A shader is what converts the Three.js JavaScript objects into pixels on the screen. With these custom shaders, you can define exactly how your object should be rendered and overridden, or alter the defaults from the Three.js library. In this section we won't go into the details of how to write custom shaders yet; for more information on that, see *Chapter 11, Custom Shaders and Render Post Processing*. For now we'll just look at a very basic example that shows how you can configure this material.

The ShaderMaterial has a number of properties that you can set; the ones that we've already seen are as follows:

Name	Description
wireframe	This property renders the material as a wireframe. It is great for debugging purposes.
wireframeLinewidth	If you enable the wireframe property, this property defines the width of the wires from the wireframe.
shading	This defines how shading is applied. The possible values are THREE.SmoothShading and THREE.FlatShading. This property isn't enabled in the example for this material. For an example, look at the section on the MeshNormalMaterial.
vertexColors	You can define individual colors to be applied to each vertex with this property. This property doesn't work on the CanvasRenderer, but it works on the WebGLRenderer. For an example, look at the LineBasicMaterial example, where we will use this property to color the various parts of a line.
fog	This defines whether the material is affected by the global fog settings. It is not shown in action, but if set to false the global fog property that we saw in *Chapter 2, Working with the Basic Components That Make Up a Three.js Scene*, doesn't affect how this object is rendered.

Besides these properties that we've already discussed in previous sections, the ShaderMaterial has a number of specific properties that you can use to pass in and configure your custom shader. They may seem a bit obscure at the moment; for more details, see *Chapter 9*, *Animations and Moving the Camera*.

Name	Description
fragmentShader	This shader defines the color of each pixel that is passed in.
vertexShader	This shader allows you to change the position of each vertex that is passed in.
uniforms	This allows you to send information to your shader. The same information is sent to each vertex and fragment.
defines	The value of this property is converted to #define code in the vertexShader and fragmentShader. This property can be used to set some global variables in the shader programs.
attributes	This can change between each vertex and fragment. Usually used to pass positional and normal-related data. If you want to use this, you need to provide information for all the vertices of the geometry.
lights	This defines whether light data should be passed into the shaders. Defaults to false.

Before we look at an example, here's a quick explanation about the most important parts of the ShaderMaterial: to work with this material, we have to pass in two different shaders:

- vertexShader: The vertexShader is run on each vertex of the geometry. You can use this shader to transform the geometry by moving the position of the vertices around.

- fragmentShader: The fragmentShader is run on each pixel of the geometry. In the vertexShader, we will return the color that should be shown for this specific pixel.

For all the materials that we've discussed so far in this chapter, the Three.js library provides its own fragmentShader and vertexShader, so you don't have to worry about it.

For this section we'll look at a simple example that uses a very simple vertexShader that changes the x, y, and z coordinates of the vertices of a cube, and a fragmentShader that uses the shaders from glsl.heroku.com to create an animating material.

Up next you can see the complete code for the vertexShader that we'll use.

 Writing shaders isn't done in JavaScript. You have to write shaders in a C-like language called GLSL.

```
<script id="vertex-shader" type="x-shader/x-vertex">
    uniform float time;

    void main()
    {
    vec3 posChanged = position;
    posChanged.x = posChanged.x*(abs(sin(time*1.0)));
    posChanged.y = posChanged.y*(abs(cos(time*1.0)));
    posChanged.z = posChanged.z*(abs(sin(time*1.0)));

    gl_Position = projectionMatrix
                * modelViewMatrix
                * vec4(posChanged,1.0);

    }
</script>
```

We won't go into too much detail here, and just focus on the most important parts of this code snippet. To communicate with the shaders from JavaScript, we will use something called uniforms. In this example we will use the uniform float time; statement to pass in an external value. Based on this value, we will change the x, y, and z coordinates of the passed in vertex (which is passed in as the position variable):

```
vec3 posChanged = position;
posChanged.x = posChanged.x*(abs(sin(time*1.0)));
posChanged.y = posChanged.y*(abs(cos(time*1.0)));
posChanged.z = posChanged.z*(abs(sin(time*1.0)));
```

The posChanged vector now contains the new coordinates for this vertex, based on the passed in time variable. The last step that we need to do is pass this new position back to the Three.js library, which is always done as shown:

```
gl_Position = projectionMatrix * modelViewMatrix
                * vec4(posChanged,1.0);
```

The gl_Position is a special variable that is used to return the final position.

Next we need to create a `shaderMaterial` and pass in the `vertexShader`. For this we've created a simple helper function:

```
function createMaterial(vertexShader, fragmentShader) {
    var vertShader =
            document.getElementById(vertexShader).innerHTML;
    var fragShader =
            document.getElementById(fragmentShader).innerHTML;

    var attributes = {};
    var uniforms = {
        time: {type: 'f', value: 0.2},
        scale: {type: 'f', value: 0.2},
        alpha: {type: 'f', value: 0.6},
        resolution: { type: "v2", value: new THREE.Vector2() }
    };

    uniforms.resolution.value.x = window.innerWidth;
    uniforms.resolution.value.y = window.innerHeight;

    var meshMaterial = new THREE.ShaderMaterial({
        uniforms: uniforms,
        attributes: attributes,
        vertexShader: vertShader,
        fragmentShader: fragShader,
        transparent: true

    });
    return meshMaterial;
}
```

The function that we have created is used as shown: `var meshMaterial1 = createMaterial("vertex-shader","fragment-shader-1");`. The arguments point to the ID of the script element in the HTML page. Here you can also see that we have set up a `uniforms` variable. This variable is used to pass information from our `renderer` into our shader. The complete `render` loop for this example is shown as follows:

```
function render() {
    stats.update();

    cube.rotation.y = step += 0.01;
    cube.rotation.x = step;
```

```
cube.rotation.z = step;

cube.material.materials.forEach(function (e) {
    e.uniforms.time.value += 0.01;
});

// render using requestAnimationFrame
requestAnimationFrame(render);
renderer.render(scene, camera);
}
```

You can see that we have increased the `time` variable by `0.01` each time the `render` loop is run. This information is passed to our `vertexShader` and is used to calculate the new position of the vertices of our `cube`. Now open the `07-shader-material.html` example and you'll see that the cube shrinks and grows around its axis, as shown in the following screenshot:

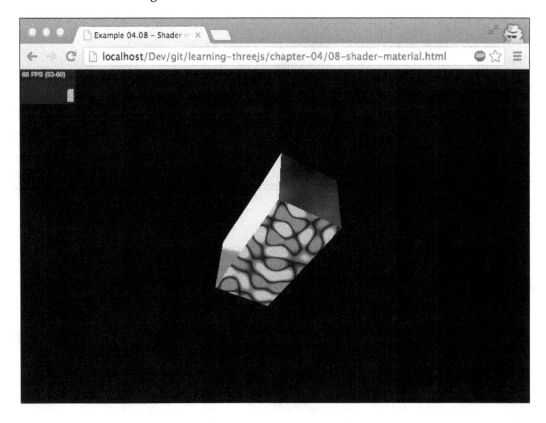

In this example you can see that each `cube` face has an animating pattern. The `fragmentShader` that is assigned to each face of the `cube` creates these patterns. As you might have guessed, we've used the `MeshFaceMaterial` for this, as shown in the following code snippet:

```
var cubeGeometry = new THREE.CubeGeometry(20, 20, 20);

var meshMaterial1 = createMaterial("vertex-shader", "fragment-
shader-1");
var meshMaterial2 = createMaterial("vertex-shader",
                                   "fragment-shader-2");
var meshMaterial3 = createMaterial("vertex-shader",
                                   "fragment-shader-3");
var meshMaterial4 = createMaterial("vertex-shader",
                                   "fragment-shader-4");
var meshMaterial5 = createMaterial("vertex-shader",
                                   "fragment-shader-5");
var meshMaterial6 = createMaterial("vertex-shader",
                                   "fragment-shader-6");

var material = new THREE.MeshFaceMaterial([meshMaterial1,
                 meshMaterial2, meshMaterial3, meshMaterial4,
                 meshMaterial5, meshMaterial6]);

var cube = new THREE.Mesh(cubeGeometry, material);
```

The only part that we haven't explained yet is the `fragmentShader`. For this example, all the fragment shaders were copied from `http://glsl.heroku.com`. This site provides an experimental playground where you can write and share fragment shaders. I won't go into detail here, but the `fragment-shader-6` used in this example looks like the code snippet that follows:

```
<script id="fragment-shader-6" type="x-shader/x-fragment">
    #ifdef GL_ES
    precision mediump float;
    #endif

    uniform float time;
    uniform vec2 resolution;


    void main( void )
```

```
    {

        vec2 uPos = ( gl_FragCoord.xy / resolution.xy );

        uPos.x -= 1.0;
        uPos.y -= 0.5;

        vec3 color = vec3(0.0);
        float vertColor = 2.0;
        for( float i = 0.0; i < 15.0; ++i ) {
        float t = time * (0.9);

        uPos.y += sin( uPos.x*i + t+i/2.0 ) * 0.1;
        float fTemp = abs(1.0 / uPos.y / 100.0);
        vertColor += fTemp;
        color += vec3( fTemp*(10.0-i)/10.0
                     ,fTemp*i/10.0, pow(fTemp,1.5)*1.5 );
        }

        vec4 color_final = vec4(color, 1.0);
        gl_FragColor = color_final;
        }
    </script>
```

The color that finally gets passed back to the Three.js library is the one set to `gl_FragColor = color_final;`. A good way to get a bit more feeling for fragment shaders is by exploring what's available at `http://glsl.heroku.com` and to use the code for your own objects. Before we move on to the next material, the following is one more example of what is possible with a custom vertex shader (`https://www.shadertoy.com/view/4dXGR4`):

Much more on the subject of fragment and vertex shaders can be found in *Chapter 11, Custom Shaders and Render Post Processing*.

Using the materials for a line geometry

The last couple of materials that we're going to look at can only be used on one specific geometry: the THREE.Line. As the name implies this is a single line that only consists of vertices and doesn't contain any faces. The Three.js library provides two different materials that you can use on a line, as follows:

- LineBasicMaterial: The basic material for a line that allows you to set the colors, line width, line cap, and line join properties
- LineDashedMaterial: Has the same properties as the LineBasicMaterial, but allows you to create a dashed effect by specifying the dash and spacing sizes

We'll start with the basic variant, and after that we'll look at the dashed variant.

The LineBasicMaterial

The materials available for the THREE.Line geometry are very simple. The following table shows the properties available to this material:

Name	Description
color	This defines the color of the line. If you specify vertexColors, this property is ignored.
linewidth	This property defines the width of the line.
LineCap	This defines how the end of a line between the two vertices looks in the wireframe mode. Possible values are butt, round, and square. The default is round. In practice, the results from changing this property are very difficult to see. This property isn't supported on the WebGLRenderer.
LineJoin	This defines how the line joins are visualized. Possible values are round, bevel, and miter. The default is round. If you look very closely, you can see this in the example by using a low opacity and a very large linewidth. This property isn't supported on the WebGLRenderer.
vertexColors	You can supply a specific color for each vertex by setting this property to the THREE.VertexColors value.
fog	This defines whether the object is affected by the global fog property.

Before we look at an example of the LineBasicMaterial, let's first have a quick look at how we can create a THREE.Line mesh from a set of vertices, and combine it with a LineBasicMaterial to create the mesh, as shown in the following code snippet;

```
var points = gosper(4, 60);
var lines = new THREE.Geometry();
var colors = [];
var i = 0;
points.forEach(function (e) {
    lines.vertices.push(new THREE.Vector3(e.x, e.z, e.y));
    colors[ i ] = new THREE.Color(0xffffff);
    colors[ i ].setHSL(e.x / 100 + 0.5, ( e.y * 20 ) / 300, 0.8);
    i++;
});

lines.colors = colors;
var material = new THREE.LineBasicMaterial({
    opacity: 1.0,
    linewidth: 1,
    vertexColors: THREE.VertexColors });

var line = new THREE.Line(lines, material);
```

The first part of this code fragment, that is, `var points = gosper(4, 60);`, is used as an example to get a set of x and y coordinates. This function returns a Gosper curve (for more information, go to the following URL: `http://en.wikipedia.org/wiki/Gosper_curve`), which is a simple algorithm that fills a 2D space. What we will do next is create a `THREE.Geometry` instance, and for each coordinate we will create a new vertex, which we push into the line properties of this instance. For each coordinate, we will also calculate a color value that is used to set the `colors` property.

> In this example we've set the color by using the `setHSL()` method. Instead of providing the values for red, green, and blue, with HSL we will provide the hue, saturation, and lightness. Using HSL is much more intuitive than RGB and it is much easier to create sets of matching colors. A very good explanation of HSL can be found in the CSS3 specification at `http://www.w3.org/TR/2003/CR-css3-color-20030514/#hsl-color`

Now that we have our geometry, we can create a `LineBasicMaterial` and use this together with the geometry to create a `THREE.Line` mesh. You can see the result in example `09-line-material.html`, as shown in the following screenshot:

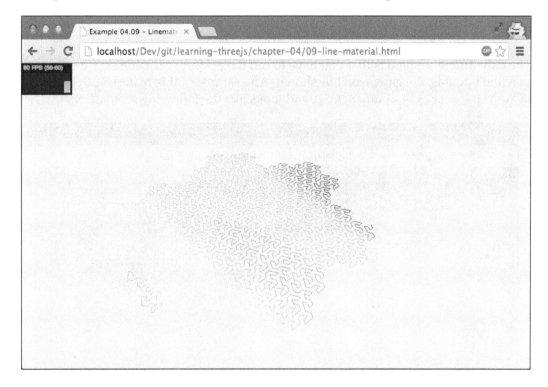

The next and last material that we will discuss in this chapter is only slightly different from the LineBasicMaterial. With the LineDashedMaterial, we can color lines, and also add a dash effect.

The LineDashedMaterial

This material has the same properties as the LineBasicMaterial, and two additional ones that you can use to define the dash width and the width of the gaps between the dashes are as follows:

Name	Description
scale	This scales the dashSize and gapSize. If the scale is smaller than 1, the dashSize and gapSize will increase; if the scale is larger than 1, the dashSize and gapSize will decrease.
dashSize	This defines the size of the dash.
gapSize	This indicates the size of the gap.

This material works in almost the same way as the LineBasicMaterial, as shown:

```
lines.computeLineDistances();
var material = new THREE.LineDashedMaterial({ vertexColors: true,
        color: 0xffffff, dashSize: 10, gapSize: 1, scale: 0.1 });
```

The only difference here is that you have to call the computeDistances() method. If you don't do this, the gaps won't be shown. An example of this material can be found in 10-line-material-dashed.html and looks like the following screenshot:

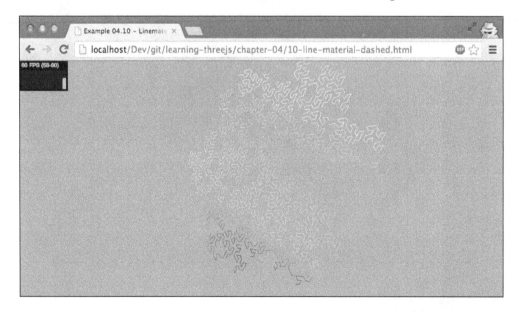

Summary

The Three.js library gives you a lot of materials that you can use to skin your geometries. The materials range from the very simple MeshBasicMaterial to the complex ShaderMaterial, where you can provide your own vertex and fragment shaders. The most important subjects that were discussed in the chapter are as follows:

- The materials share a lot of basic properties. If you know how to use a single material, you'll probably also know how to use the other materials.

- Not all materials respond to the lights in your scene. If you want a material that takes lighting into effect, use the MeshPhongMaterial or MeshLambertMaterial.

- When you want to create a transparent material, it isn't enough to just set the opacity property, you also have to set the transparent property to true.

- Most of the properties of a material can be modified at runtime. Some, though, for example, side, can't be modified at runtime. If you change such a value, you need to set the needsUpdate property to true. For a complete overview of what can and cannot be changed at runtime, see the following page: https://github.com/mrdoob/three.js/wiki/Updates

- You can assign multiple materials to a single geometry. Remember, though, that this will create copies of the same geometry and result in multiple meshes.

- The THREE.Line geometry can't be skinned with normal materials. For this, you have to use either the THREE.LineBasicMaterial or the THREE. LineDashedMaterial.

- If you want a shiny object, use the MeshPhongMaterial; if you want a non-shiny object, use the MeshLambertMaterial.

- Use a dat.GUI approach to experiment with the properties of a material. It's very hard to guess the correct values of the material during development.

In this and the previous chapters, we've already talked about geometries. We've used them in our examples and already explored a couple. In the next chapter, you'll learn everything about geometries and how you can work with them.

5
Learning to Work with Geometries

In the previous chapters we've already learned a lot about how to work with Three. js. You know how to create a basic scene, add lighting, and configure the material for your meshes. In *Chapter 2, Working with the Basic Components That Make Up a Three.js Scene*, we touched upon the available geometries that Three.js provides, which you can use to create your 3D objects, but didn't really go into details. In this and the next chapter we'll walk you through all the geometries that Three.js provides out of the box. In this chapter we'll look at the following geometries:

- `PlaneGeometry`
- `CircleGeometry`
- `ShapeGeometry`
- `CubeGeometry`
- `SphereGeometry`
- `CylinderGeometry`
- `TorusGeometry`
- `TorusKnotGeometry`
- `PolyhedronGeometry`
- `IcosahedronGeometry`
- `OctahedronGeometry`
- `TetraHedronGeometry`

And in the next chapter we'll have a look at the following complex geometries:

- `ConvexGeometry`
- `LatheGeometry`
- `ExtrudeGeometry`
- `TubeGeometry`
- `ParametricGeometry`
- `TextGeometry`

So let's look at all the basic geometries that Three.js has to offer.

The basic geometries provided by Three.js

In Three.js we've got a couple of geometries that result in a two-dimensional mesh, and a larger number that create a three-dimensional mesh. In this section we'll first look at the 2D geometries: `CircleGeometry`, `PlaneGeometry`, and `ShapeGeometry`. After that we'll explore all the basic 3D geometries that are available.

Two-dimensional geometries

The two-dimensional objects look like flat objects and, as the name implies, only have two dimensions. The first two-dimensional geometry on the list is `PlaneGeometry`.

PlaneGeometry

A `PlaneGeometry` object can be used to create a very simple two-dimensional rectangle. For an example of this geometry, look at the `01-basic-2d-geometries-plane.html` example in the sources for this chapter.

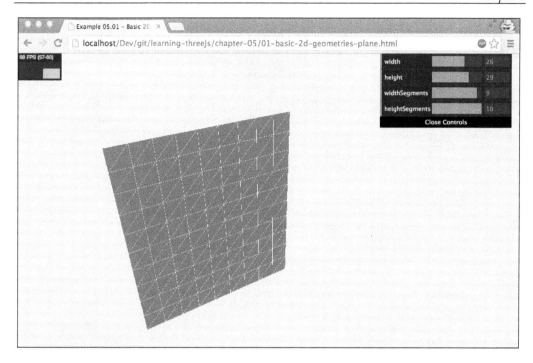

Creating this geometry is very simple as shown:

```
new THREE.PlaneGeometry(width, height, widthSegments,
    heightSegments);
```

In this example of PlaneGeometry, you can change these properties and directly see the effect it has on the resulting 3D object. An explanation of these properties is shown in the following table:

Property	Mandatory	Description
width	Yes	This property specifies the width of the rectangle.
height	Yes	This property specifies the height of the rectangle.
widthSegments	No	This property specifies the number of segments that the width should be divided in. Defaults to 1.
heightSegments	No	This property specifies the number of segments that the height should be divided in. Defaults to 1.

As you can see this is not a very complex geometry. You just specify the size and you're done. If you want to create more faces (for example, for when you want to create a checkered pattern), you can use the `widthSegments` and `heightSegments` properties to divide the geometry in smaller faces.

Before we move on to the next geometry, a quick note on the material used for this example and that we also use for most of the other examples in this chapter. We use the following method to create a mesh based on the geometry:

```
function createMesh(geometry) {

  // assign two materials
  var meshMaterial = new THREE.MeshNormalMaterial();
  meshMaterial.side = THREE.DoubleSide;
  var wireFrameMaterial = new THREE.MeshBasicMaterial();
  wireFrameMaterial.wireframe = true;

  // create a multimaterial
  var mesh = THREE.SceneUtils.createMultiMaterialObject(
    geometry, [meshMaterial,wireFrameMaterial]);
  return mesh;
}
```

In this function we create a multi-material mesh based on the provided mesh. The first material used is the `MeshNormalMaterial`. As you have learned in the previous chapter, the `MeshNormalMaterial` creates colored faces based on its normal vector (its orientation). We also set this material to be double-sided (`THREE.DoubleSide`). If we don't do this, we won't see this object when its back is turned towards the camera. We also add a `MeshBasicMaterial`, on which we enable the wireframe property. In this way, we can nicely see the 3D shape of the object and exactly see the faces that a specific geometry creates.

CircleGeometry

You can probably already guess what the `CircleGeometry` object creates. With this geometry you can create a very simple 2D circle (or a partial circle). Let's first look at the example for this geometry: `02-basic-2d-geometries-circle.html`. In the following screenshot you can find an example where we've created a simple `CircleGeometry` with a `thetaLength` property that is smaller than 2*Pi.

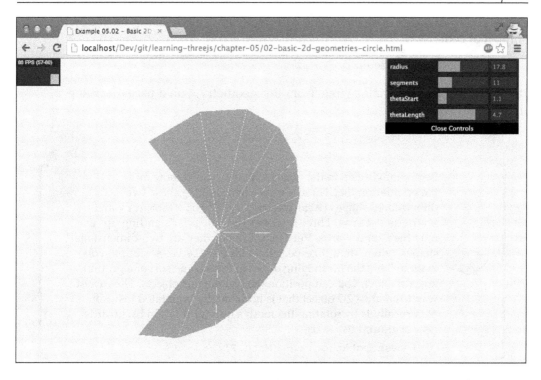

In this example you can see and control a mesh created from `CircleGeometry`. When you create a `CircleGeometry` object you can specify a couple of properties that define what the circle looks like:

Property	Mandatory	Description
radius	Yes	This property specifies the radius of a circle, which defines its size. The radius is the distance from the center of the circle to its side.
segments	No	This property defines the number of faces that are used to create the circle. The minimum is 3, and if not specified, it defaults to 8. The higher this value, the smoother the circle will look.
thetaStart	No	This property defines the position from where to start drawing the circle. This value can range from 0 to 2*Pi.
thetaLength	No	This property defines upto what extent the circle is completed. This defaults to 2*Pi (a full circle) when not specified. For instance, if you specify 0.5*Pi for this value, you'll get a quarter circle. Use this property together with the thetaStart property to define the shape of the circle.

When you look at this from code, you can create a full circle using the following snippet of code:

```
new THREE.CircleGeometry(3, 12);
```

If you wanted to create half a circle from this geometry, you'd use something like this:

```
new THREE.CircleGeometry(3, 12, 0, Math.PI);
```

Before moving on to the next geometry, a quick note on the orientation that Three.js uses when creating these two-dimensional shapes (PlaneGeometry, CircleGeometry and ShapeGeometry). Three.js creates these objects "standing up" using only the x- and y-axes. Very logical, since they are two-dimensional shapes. Often, though, especially with the PlaneGeometry, you want to have the mesh lying down to form some sort of a ground area on which you can position the rest of your objects. The easiest way to create a 2D object that is horizontally orientated instead of vertically is by rotating the mesh a quarter rotation backwards (-pi/2) around its x-axis.

```
mesh.rotation.x = -Math.PI/2;
```

That's all for the CircleGeometry; on to the last of the two-dimensional shapes: ShapeGeometry.

ShapeGeometry

The PlaneGeometry and CircleGeometry geometries have limited ways of customizing their appearance. If you want to create custom 2D shapes you can use the ShapeGeometry. With a ShapeGeometry you've got a couple of functions you can call to create your own shapes. You can compare this functionality with the path functionality that is also available for the HTML canvas element and for SVG. Let's start with an example, and after that we'll show you how you can use the various functions to draw your own shapes. The example can be found in the sources for this chapter, 03-basic-2d-geometries-shape.html:

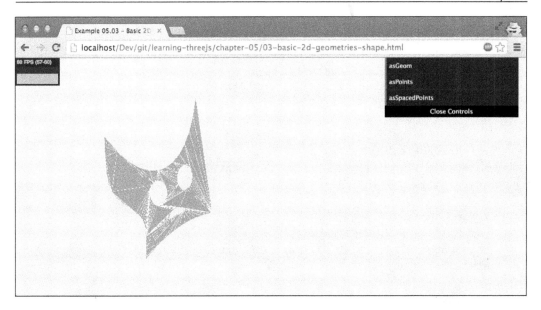

In this example you can see a custom created two-dimensional shape. Without going into a description of the properties first, let's have a look at the code that is used to create this shape:

```
function drawShape() {

  // create a basic shape
  var shape = new THREE.Shape();

  // startpoint
  shape.moveTo(10, 10);

  // straight line upwards
  shape.lineTo(10, 40);

  // the top of the figure, curve to the right
  shape.bezierCurveTo(15, 25, 25, 25, 30, 40);

  // spline back down
  shape.splineThru(
    [new THREE.Vector2(32, 30),
    new THREE.Vector2(28, 20),
    new THREE.Vector2(30, 10),
  ])

  // curve at the bottom
```

```
shape.quadraticCurveTo(20, 15, 10, 10);

// add 'eye' hole one
var hole1 = new THREE.Path();
hole1.absellipse(16, 24, 2, 3, 0, Math.PI * 2, true);
shape.holes.push(hole1);

// add 'eye hole 2'
var hole2 = new THREE.Path();
hole2.absellipse(23, 24, 2, 3, 0, Math.PI * 2, true);
shape.holes.push(hole2);

// add 'mouth'
var hole3 = new THREE.Path();
hole3.absarc(20, 16, 2, 0, Math.PI, true);
shape.holes.push(hole3);

// return the shape
return shape;
}
```

In this piece of code, you can see that we've created the outline of this shape using lines, curves, and splines. After that we've punched a number of holes in this shape by using the `holes` property of the `THREE.Shape` class. In this section, though, we're talking about a `THREE.ShapeGeometry` object and not a `THREE.Shape` object. To create a geometry from the `Shape` we need to do the following:

```
new THREE.ShapeGeometry(drawShape());
```

The result from this function is a geometry that can be used to create a mesh. The `ShapeGeometry` class has no other options you can use to configure this shape. So let's look at the list of drawing functions that you can use to create a `Shape` instead:

Name	Description
moveTo(x, y)	This function moves the drawing position to the specified x and y coordinates.
lineTo(x, y)	This function draws a line from the current position (for example, the position set by the moveTo function) to the provided x and y coordinates.

Name	Description
quadraticCurveTo(aCPx, aCPy, x, y)	You can use two different ways of specifying curves. You can use the quadraticCurveTo function or you can use the bezierCurveTo function (see the next table row). The difference between these two functions is how you specify the curvature of the curve. The following diagram explains the differences between these two options: 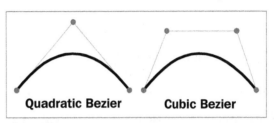 **Quadratic Bezier** **Cubic Bezier** For a quadratic curve we need to specify one additional point (using the aCPx and aCPy arguments) and the curve is based solely on that point and of course the specified end point (from the x and y arguments). For a cubic curve (used by the bezierCurveTo function), you specify two additional points to define the curve. The start point is the current position of the path.
bezierCurveTo(aCPx1, aCPy1, aCPx2, aCPy2, x, y)	Draws a curve based on the supplied arguments. For an explanation see the preceding row. The curve is drawn based on the two coordinates that define the curve (aCPx1, aCPy1, aCPx2, and aCPy2) and the end coordinates (x and y). The start point is the current position of the path.
splineThru(pts)	This function draws a fluid line through the provided set of coordinates (points). This argument should be an array of THREE.Vector2 objects. The start point is the current position of the path.
arc(aX, aY, aRadius, aStartAngle, aEndAngle, AClockwise)	Draw a circle (or part of a circle). The circle starts from the current position of the path. aX and aY are used as offset from the current position. The aRadius sets the size of the circle and aStartAngle and aEndAngle define how large a part of the circle is drawn. The Boolean property aClockwise determines whether the circle is drawn clockwise or counter-clockwise.
absArc(aX, aY, aRadius, aStartAngle, aEndAngle, AClockwise)	See description of arc. The position is absolute instead of relative to the current position.

Name	Description
ellipse(aX, aY, xRadius, yRadius, aStartAngle, aEndAngle, aClockwise)	See description of arc. As an addition, with the ellipse function we can separately set the x-radius and the y-radius.
absEllipse(aX, aY, xRadius, yRadius, aStartAngle, aEndAngle, aClockwise)	See description of ellipse. The position is absolute instead of relative to the current position.

A final property of the Shape object we need to address is the holes property. By adding THREE.Shape objects to this property (see code example at the beginning of this section) you can create holes in the shape (for instance, the eye object in this example).

In this example we've discussed about creating a ShapeGeometry from this Shape object by using the new THREE.ShapeGeometry(drawShape())) function. The Shape object itself also has a couple of helper functions you can use to create geometries.

Name	Description
makeGeometry	This function Returns a ShapeGeometry object from this Shape object.
createPointsGeometry(divisions)	This function converts the shape into a set of points. The divisions property defines how many points are returned. The higher this value, the more points are returned, and the smoother the resulting line is. The divisions apply to each part of the path separately.
createSpacedPointsGeometry (divisions)	This function also converts the shape into a set of points, but this time, applies the division to the complete path at once.

When you create a set of points using the createPointsGeometry function of the createSpacedPointsGeometry function, you can use these points to create a line:

```
new THREE.Line( shape.createPointsGeometry(10), new
    THREE.LineBasicMaterial( { color: 0xff3333, linewidth: 2 } ) );
```

When you click on the **asPoints** or **asSpacedPoints** buttons in the example you'll see something as shown in the following screenshot:

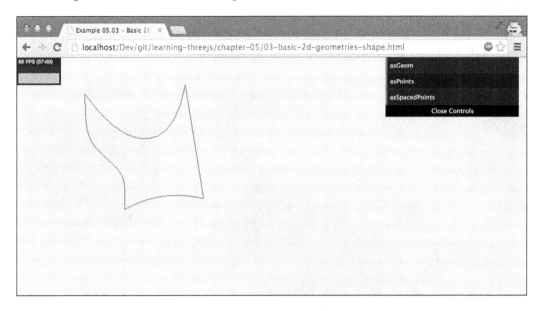

That's it for the two-dimensional shapes. The next part will show and explain the basic three-dimensional shapes.

Three-dimensional geometries

In this section on the basic three-dimension geometries we'll start with the geometry we've already seen a couple of times: the CubeGeometry.

CubeGeometry

sCubeGeometry is a very simple 3D geometry that allows you to create a cube by specifying its width, height, and depth. We've added an example where you can play around with these properties: `04-basic-3d-geometries-cube.html`. Refer to the following screenshot:

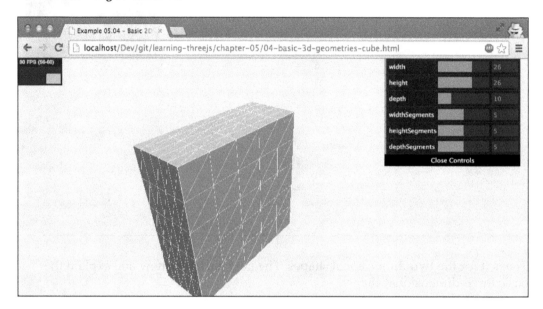

As you can see in this example, by changing the **width**, **height**, and **depth** of the CubeGeometry object you can control the size of the resulting mesh. These three properties are also mandatory when you create a new cube as shown:

```
new THREE.CubeGeometry(10,10,10);
```

In the example you can also see a couple of other properties that you can define on the cube. The following table explains all the properties:

Property	Mandatory	Description
width	Yes	This property specifies the width of the cube. This is the length of the vertices of the cube along the x-axis.
height	Yes	This property specifies the height of the cube. This is the length of the vertices of the cube along the y-axis.
depth	Yes	This property specifies the depth of the cube. This is the length of the vertices of the cube along the z-axis.

Property	Mandatory	Description
widthSegments	No	This property specifies the number of segments to divide a face into along the cube's x-axis. The default value is 1.
heightSegments	No	This property specifies the number of segments to divide a face into along the cube's y-axis. The default value is 1.
depthSegments	No	This property specifies the number of segments to divide a face into along the cube's z-axis. The default value is 1.

By increasing the various segment properties, you divide the main six faces of the cube into smaller faces. This is useful if you want to set specific material properties on parts of the cube using the MeshFaceMaterial object. The CubeGeometry is a very simple geometry. Another simple one is the SphereGeometry.

SphereGeometry

With a SphereGeometry object you can create a three-dimensional sphere. Let's dive straight into the example: 05-basic-3d-geometries-sphere.html. Refer to the following screenshot:

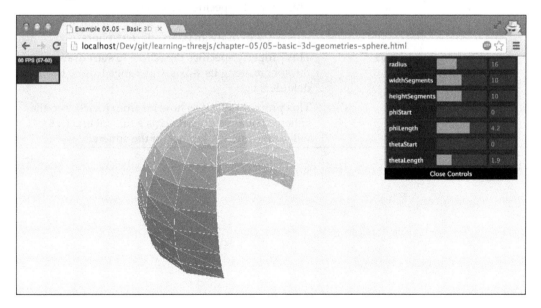

In the preceding screenshot we show you a half open sphere, which was created based on the SphereGeometry. This geometry is a very flexible one that can be used to create all kinds of sphere-related geometries. A basic SphereGeometry though can be created as easily as this: new THREE.SphereGeometry. The following properties can be used to tune what the resulting mesh looks like:

Property	Mandatory	Description
radius	No	This property sets the radius for this sphere. This defines how large the resulting mesh will be. Default is 50.
widthSegments	No	This property specifies the number of segments to use vertically. The more segments, the smoother the surface of the sphere. Default is 8, and minimum is 3.
heightSegments	No	This property specifies the number of segments to use horizontally. The more segments, the smoother the surface of the sphere. Default is 6 and minimum is 2.
phiStart	No	This property specifies the where to start drawing the sphere along its x-axis. Can range from 0 to 2*Pi; default is 0.
phiLength	No	This property specifies how far from phiStart the sphere should be drawn. 2*Pi is a full sphere; 0.5*Pi will draw an open quarter sphere.
thetaStart	No	This property specifies the where to start drawing the sphere along its x-axis. Can range from 0 to Pi; default is 0.
thetaLength	No	This property specifies how far from phiStart the sphere should be drawn. Pi is a full sphere; 0.5*Pi will draw only the top half of the sphere.

The `radius`, `widthSegments`, and `heightSegments` should be clear. We've already seen these kind of properties in other examples. The `phiStart`, `phiLength`, `thetaStart`, and `thetaLength` properties are a bit harder to understand without looking at an example. Luckily though, you can experiment with these properties from the menu in the `05-basic-3d-geometries-sphere.html` example, and create interesting geometries such as these:

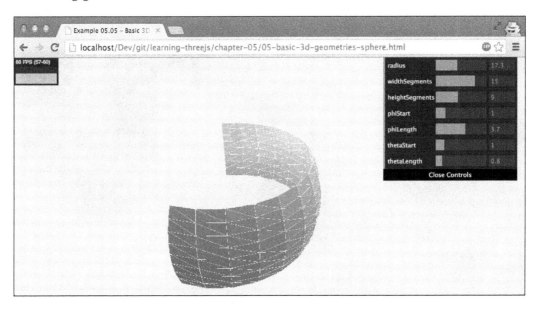

The next one on the list is the `CylinderGeometry`.

CylinderGeometry

With this geometry we can create cylinders and cylinder-like objects. As for all the other geometries we also have an example that lets you experiment with the properties of this geometry: `06-basic-3d-geometries-cylinder.html`. This is also shown in the following screenshot:

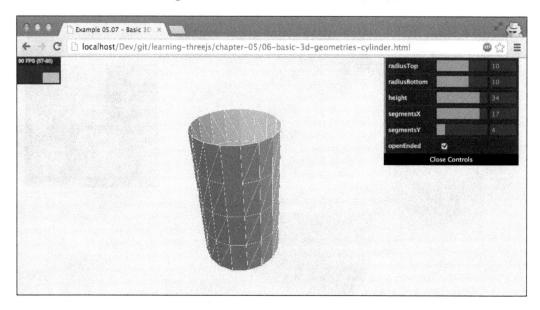

When you create a `CylinderGeometry` there aren't any mandatory arguments. So you can create a cylinder by just calling `new THREE.CylinderGeometry()`. You can pass in a number of properties, as you can see in the example, to alter the appearance of this cylinder. Some of these properties are listed as follows:

Property	Mandatory	Description
radiusTop	No	This property sets the size this cylinder will have at the top. Default value is `20`.
radiusBottom	No	This property sets the size this cylinder will have at the bottom. Default value is `20`.
height	No	This property sets the height of the cylinder. Default height is `100`.
segmentsX	No	This property sets the number of segments along the x-axis. Defaults to `8`. The higher this number, the more smooth the cylinder.

Property	Mandatory	Description
segmentsY	No	This property sets the number of segments along the y-axis. Default is 1. More segments mean more faces.
openEnded	No	This property specifies whether the mesh is closed at the top and the bottom or not. Default is false.

All these are very basic properties you can use to configure the cylinder. One interesting aspect though is using a negative radius for the top (or for the bottom). If you do this, you can use this geometry to create an hourglass-like shape as shown in the following screenshot. One thing to note here, as you can see from the colors, is that the top half in this case is turned inside out. If you use material that isn't configured with THREE.DoubleSide you won't see the top half.

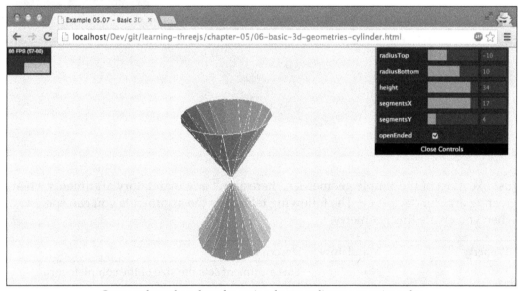

Create an hourglass shape by setting the top radius to a negative value

The next geometry is the TorusGeometry, which you can use to create donut-like shapes.

TorusGeometry

A torus is a simple shape that looks like a donut. The following screenshot, which you can get yourself by opening example 07-basic-3d-geometries-torus.html, shows the TorusGeometry in action:

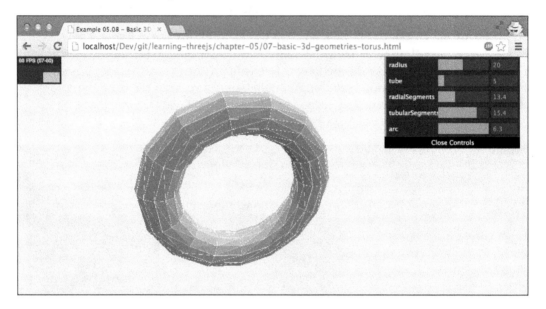

Just like most of the simple geometries, there aren't any mandatory arguments when creating a TorusGeometry. The following table lists the arguments you can specify when you create this geometry.

Property	Mandatory	Description
radius	No	This argument sets the size of the complete torus. The default is 100.
tube	No	This argument sets the radius of the tube (the actual donut). The default value for this attribute is 40.
radialSegments	No	This argument specifies the number of segments to use along the length of the torus. The default is 8. See the effect of changing this value in the demo.
tubularSegments	No	This argument specifies the number of segments to use along the width of the torus. The default is 6. See the effect of changing this value in the demo.
arc	No	With this value you can control whether the torus is drawn full circle. The default of this value is 2*Pi (a full circle).

Most of these are very basic properties that you've already seen. The `arc` property, however, is a very interesting one. With this property you define whether the donut makes a full circle, or only a partial one. By experimenting with this property you can create very interesting meshes such as the following one with an arc set to `0.5*Pi`:

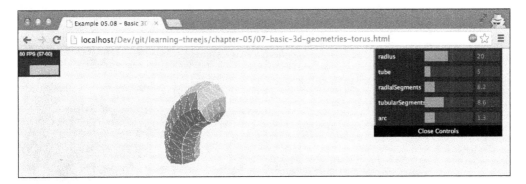

The `TorusGeometry` is a very straightforward geometry. In the next section we'll look at a geometry that almost shares its name, but is much less straightforward: the `TorusKnotGeometry`.

TorusKnotGeometry

With a `TorusKnotGeometry` you can create a torus knot. A torus knot is a special kind of knot that looks like a tube that winds around itself a couple of times. The best way to explain this is by looking at the `08-basic-3d-geometries-torus-knot.html` example:

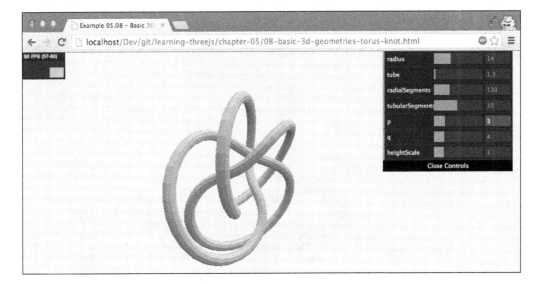

If you open this example and play around with the p and q properties you can create all kinds of beautiful geometries. The p property defines how often the knot winds around its axis, and the q property defines how much the knot winds around its interior. If this sounds a bit vague, don't worry. You don't need to understand these properties to create beautiful knots (for those interested in the details: Wikipedia has a good article on this subject at http://en.wikipedia.org/wiki/Torus_knot).

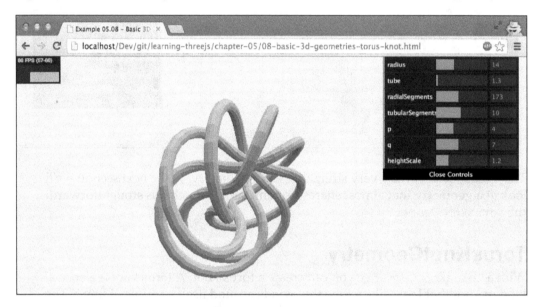

With the example for this geometry you can play around with these properties and see the effect various combinations of p and q have on this geometry as shown in the preceding screenshot.

Property	Mandatory	Description
radius	No	This property sets the size of the complete torus. The default is 100.
tube	No	This property sets the radius of the tube (the actual donut). The default value for this attribute is 40.
radialSegments	No	This property specifies the number of segments to use along the length of the torus knot. The default is 64. See the effect of changing this value in the demo.
tubularSegments	No	This property specifies the number of segments to use along the width of the torus knot. The default is 8. See the effect of changing this value in the demo.
p	No	This property defines the shape of the knot. Defaults to 2.

Property	Mandatory	Description
q	No	This property defines the shape of the knot. Defaults to 3.
heightScale	No	With this property you can stretch out the torus knot. Default value is 1.

The next geometry on the list is the last one of the basic geometries, the PolyhedronGeometry.

PolyhedronGeometry

With this geometry you can easily create polyhedrons. A polyhedron is a geometry that has only flat faces and straight edges. Most often, though, you won't use this geometry directly. Three.js provides a number of specific polyhedrons that you can use directly without having to specify the vertices and the faces of the PolyhedronGeometry directly. We'll discuss these polyhedrons further down in this section. If you do want to use the PolyhedronGeometry directly, you have to specify the vertices and the faces (just like we did for the cube in *Chapter 3, Working with the Different Light Sources Available in Three.js*). For instance, we can create a pyramid-shaped polyhedron as shown:

```
var vertices = [
    [1, 0, 1],
    [1, 0, -1],
    [-1, 0, -1],
    [-1, 0, 1],
    [0, 1, 0]
];

var faces = [
    [0, 1, 2, 3],
    [0, 1, 4],
    [1, 2, 4],
    [2, 3, 4],
    [3, 0, 4]
];

polyhedron = createMesh(new THREE.PolyhedronGeometry(vertices,
    faces, controls.radius, controls.detail));
```

To construct the `PolyhedronGeometry` object we pass in the `vertices`, the `faces`, the `radius`, and the `detail` arguments (more on these later). The resulting `PolyhedronGeometry` is shown in example `09-basic-3d-geometries-polyhedron.html` (select **type: Custom**):

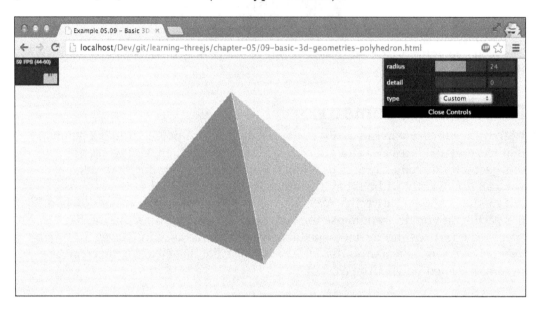

When you create a polyhedron you can pass in the following four properties:

Property	Mandatory	Description
vertices	Yes	This property specifies the points that make up the polyhedron.
faces	Yes	This property specifies the faces created from the vertices.
radius	No	This property specifies the size of the polyhedron. Default is 1.
detail	No	With this property you can add additional detail to the polyhedron. If you set this to 1, each triangle in the polyhedron will be split into 4 smaller triangles. If set to 2, those 4 smaller triangles will each be again split into 4 smaller triangles, and so on.

In the beginning of this section we mentioned that Three.js comes with a couple of polyhedrons out of the box. In the following subsections we'll quickly show you these.

All these polyhedron types can be viewed by looking at example `09-basic-3d-geometries-polyhedron.html`.

IcosahedronGeometry

The `IcosahedronGeometry` creates a polyhedron that has 20 identical triangular faces created from 12 vertices. When creating this polyhedron, all you need to specify are the `radius` and the `detail` level as shown in the following screenshot:

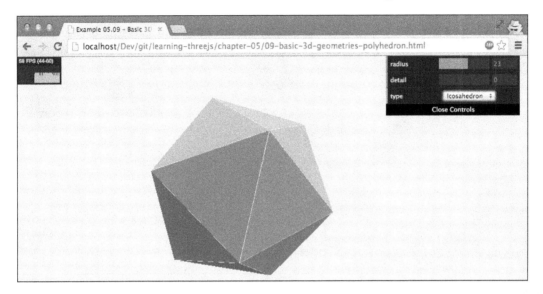

TetrahedronGeometry

A tetrahedron is one of the simplest polyhedrons. This polyhedron only contains four triangular faces created from four vertices. You create a `TetrahedronGeometry`, just like the other polyhedrons provided by Three.js, by specifying the `radius` and the `detail` level as shown in the following screenshot:

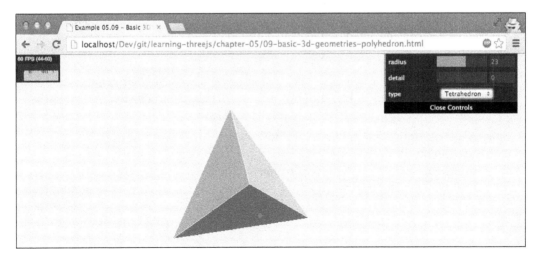

Octahedron

The last polyhedron provided by Three.js is the octahedron. As the name implies, this polyhedron has 8 faces. These faces are created from 6 vertices. The following screenshot shows this geometry:

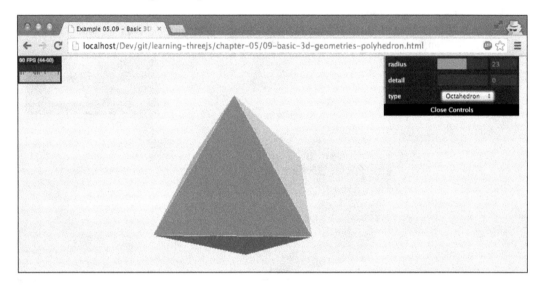

That's the end of the section on the basic two-dimensional and three-dimensional geometries provided by Three.js.

Summary

In this chapter we've discussed all of the standard geometries that Three.js has to offer. As you've seen, there are a whole lot of geometries that you can use right out of the box. The most important subjects to remember from this chapter are the following:

- Experiment with the geometries that are available. Use the examples in this chapter to get to know the properties that you can use to customize the standard set of geometries available from Three.js.

- When starting with geometries, choose an appropriate material. Don't go directly for the complex materials, but start in a simple way with a `MeshBasicMaterial` with wireframe set to `true`, or a `MeshNormalMaterial`. That way you'll get a much better picture of the true shape of the geometries.

- Remember that, when creating 2D shapes, the z-axis is ignored. If you want to have a 2D shape horizontally, you'll have to rotate the mesh around the x-axis for `-0.5*Pi`.

- If you're rotating a 2D shape, or a 3D shape that is open (for example, a cylinder or a tube), remember to set the material to `THREE.DoubleSide`. If you don't do this, the inside or back of your geometry will be invisible.

In this chapter we focused on the simple, straightforward meshes. Three.js also provides ways to create complex geometries. In the following chapter you'll learn how to create these.

6
Using Advanced Geometries and Binary Operations

In the previous chapter we showed you all the basic geometries provided by Three.js. Besides these basic geometries, Three.js also offers a set of more advanced and specialized objects. In this chapter we'll show you these advanced geometries and cover the following subjects:

- You'll learn how to use advanced geometries such as ConvexGeometry, LatheGeometry, and TubeGeometry.

- We'll show you how to create 3D shapes from 2D shapes using the ExtrudeGeometry. We'll do this based on a 2D shape drawn using Three.js provided functionality, and we'll show an example where we created a 3D shape based on an externally loaded SVG image.

- If you want to create custom shapes yourself, you can append the ones we discuss in this and in the previous section. Three.js, however, also offers a ParamtericGeometry object. With this object, you can create a geometry based on a set of equations.

- Finally, we'll look at how you can create 3D text effects using the TextGeometry.

- Additionally, we'll show you how you can create new geometries from existing ones using binary operations provided by the Three.js extension: THREEBSP.

We start with the first one from this table: ConvexGeometry

ConvexGeometry

With `ConvexGeometry` we can create a convex hull around a set of points. A convex hull is the minimal shape that encompasses all these points. The easiest way to understand this is by looking at an example. If you open up example `01-advanced-3d-geometries-convex.html`, you'll see the convex hull for a random set of points:

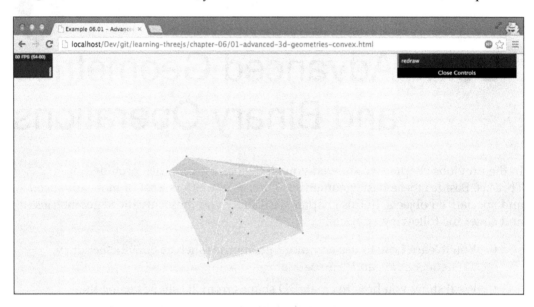

In this example we generate a random set of points and based on these points we create a `ConvexGeometry`. In the example you can click on **redraw**, which will generate 20 new points and draw the convex hull. We've also added each of these points as a small `SphereGeometry` to make it more clear how a convex hull works. The following piece of code shows how these points were created and added to the scene:

```
function generatePoints() {
  // add 10 random spheres
  var points = [];
  for (var i = 0; i < 20; i++) {
    var randomX = -15 + Math.round(Math.random() * 30);
    var randomY = -15 + Math.round(Math.random() * 30);
    var randomZ = -15 + Math.round(Math.random() * 30);
    points.push(new THREE.Vector3(randomX, randomY, randomZ));
```

```
    }

    spGroup = new THREE.Object3D();
    var material = new THREE.MeshBasicMaterial(
      {color: 0xff0000, transparent: false});
    points.forEach(function (point) {
      var spGeom = new THREE.SphereGeometry(0.2);
      var spMesh = new THREE.Mesh(spGeom, material);
      spMesh.position = point;
      spGroup.add(spMesh);
    });

    // add the points as a group to the scene
    scene.add(spGroup);
  }
```

As you can see in these couple of lines of code, we create 20 random points (THREE. Vector3), which we push into an array. Next we iterate over this array and create a SphereGeometry whose position we set to one of these points. All the points are added to a group (more on this in *Chapter 7, Particles and the Particle System*), so we can rotate them easily.

Creating a ConvexGeometry object from these points is very easy:

```
    // use the same points to create a convexgeometry
    var convexGeometry = new THREE.ConvexGeometry(points);
    convexMesh = createMesh(convexGeometry);
    scene.add(convexMesh);
```

An array containing vertices (of the type THREE.Vector3) is the only argument the ConvexGeometry constructor takes. One final note on the createMesh() function we call here. In the previous examples we've used this method to create a mesh using MeshNormalMaterial. For this example we changed this to a translucent green MeshBasicMaterial, to better show the convex hull we've created.

The next complex geometry is the LatheGeometry, which can be used to create vase-like objects.

LatheGeometry

A `LatheGeometry` allows you to create shapes from a smooth curve. This curve is defined by a number of points (also called knots) and is most often called a spline. This spline is rotated around a fixed point and results in vase- and bell-like shapes. Once again, the easiest way to understand what a `LatheGeometry` does is by looking at an example. This geometry is shown in `02-advanced-3d-geometries-lathe.html`:

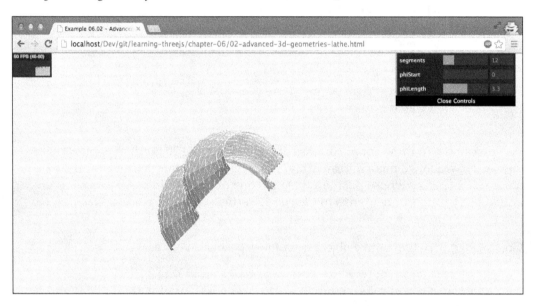

In this screenshot you can see the spline as a set of small red spheres. The positions of these spheres are passed into the `LatheGeometry` constructor, together with a couple of other arguments. In this example we rotate this spline for half a circle and based on this spline we extract the shape you can see. Before we look at all the arguments, let's look at the code used to create the spline, and how the `LatheGeometry` uses this spline:

```
function generatePoints(segments, phiStart, phiLength) {
  // add 10 random spheres
  var points = [];
  var height = 5;
  var count = 30;
  for (var i = 0; i < count; i++) {
    points.push(new THREE.Vector3((Math.sin(i * 0.2)
      + Math.cos(i * 0.3)) * height + 12,
      0, ( i - count ) + count / 2));
```

```
    }

    ...

    // use the same points to create a convexgeometry
    var latheGeometry = new THREE.LatheGeometry
        (points, segments, phiStart, phiLength);
    latheMesh = createMesh(latheGeometry);
    scene.add(latheMesh);
}
```

In this piece of JavaScript, you can see that we generate 30 points whose x coordinate is based on a combination of a `sinus` and `cosinus` function, while the z -coordinate is based on the `i` and `count` variables. This creates the spline visualized by the red dots in the screenshot we saw earlier.

Based on these points we can create the `LatheGeometry`. The `LatheGeometry` takes a couple of other arguments besides the array of vertices. The following table lists all the arguments:

Property	Mandatory	Description
points	Yes	This property specifies the points that make up the spline used to generate the bell/vase shape from.
segments	No	This property specifies the number of segments to use when creating the shape. The higher this number, the more round the resulting shape will be. The default value for this is `12`.
phiStart	No	This property specifies where to start, on a circle, when generating the shape. This can range from `0` to `2*Pi`. The default value is `0`.
phiLength	No	This property defines how fully generated the shape is. For instance a quarter shape will be `0.5*Pi`. The default is the full `360` degrees or `2*Pi`.

In the beginning of this chapter we showed you a couple of two-dimensional shapes. In the next section we'll look at how we can create three-dimensional shapes from these two-dimensional shapes by something called extruding.

Create a geometry by extruding

Three.js provides a couple of ways we can extrude a 2D shape to a 3D shape. With extruding we mean stretching out a 2D shape along its z-axis to convert it to 3D. For instance, if we extrude the THREE.CircleGeometry object, we get a shape that looks like a cylinder and if we extrude a THREE.PlaneGeometry object, we get a cube-like shape.

The most versatile way of extruding a shape is by using the THREE.ExtrudeGeometry object.

ExtrudeGeometry

With the ExtrudeGeometry you can create a 3D object from a 2D shape. Before we dive into the details of this geometry, let's first look at an example, 03-extrude-geometry.html, shown in the following screenshot:

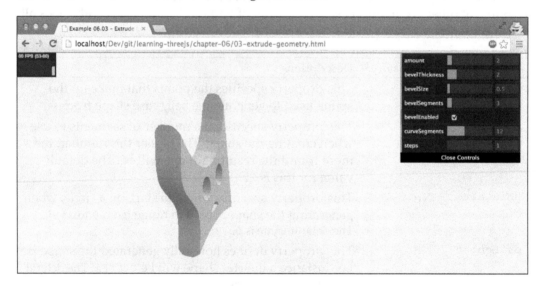

In this example we've taken the 2D shape that we created earlier in this chapter and used the ExtrudeGeometry to convert it to 3D. As you can see in this screenshot, the shape is extruded along the z-axis, which results in a 3D shape. The code to create this ExtrudeGeometry is very easy:

```
var options = {
  amount: 10,
  bevelThickness: 2,
  bevelSize: 1,
  bevelSegments: 3,
```

```
    bevelEnabled: true,
    curveSegments: 12,
    steps: 1
};

shape = createMesh(new THREE.ExtrudeGeometry(drawShape(),
    options));
```

In this code example we create the shape with the drawShape() function, just like we did earlier in the previous chapter. This shape is passed on to the THREE.ExtrudeGeometry constructor along with an options object. With the options you can define exactly how the shape should be extruded. The following table explains the options you can pass into the THREE.ExtrudeGeometry.

Property	Mandatory	Description
amount	No	This property specifies how far the shape should be extruded. Default is 100.
bevelThickness	No	This property specifies the depth of the bevel. The bevel is the rounded corner between the front and back faces and the extrusion. Default is 6.
bevelSize	No	This property specifies the height of the bevel. Default is bevelThickness-2.
bevelSegments	No	This property defines the number of segments that will be used by the bevel. The more that are used, the smoother the bevel will look. Default is 3.
bevelEnabled	No	If set to true, a bevel is added. Default is true.
curveSegments	No	This property specifies how many segments will be used when extruding the curves of shapes. The more that are used, the smoother the curves will look. Default is 12.
steps	No	This property defines into how many segments the extrusion will be divided. Default is 1.
extrudePath	No	This property specifies the path along which the shape should be extruded. If this isn't specified, the shape is extruded along the z-axis.

Property	Mandatory	Description
material	No	This property specifies the index of the material to use for the front and the back faces. Use the THREE.SceneUtils. createMultiMaterialObject function to create the mesh.
extrudeMaterial	No	This property specifies the index of the material to use for the bevel and the extrusion. Use the THREE.SceneUtils. createMultiMaterialObject function to create the mesh.

You can experiment with these options using the menu from example 12-extrude-geometry.html.

In this example we extruded the shape along its z-axis. As you could have seen in the options, you can also extrude a shape along a path. In the following geometry, the TubeGeometry, we'll do just that.

TubeGeometry

A TubeGeometry creates a tube that extrudes along a 3D spline. You specify the path using a number of vertices, and the TubeGeometry will create the tube. An example you can experiment with can be found in the sources for this chapter: 13-extrude-tube.html. Refer to the following screenshot:

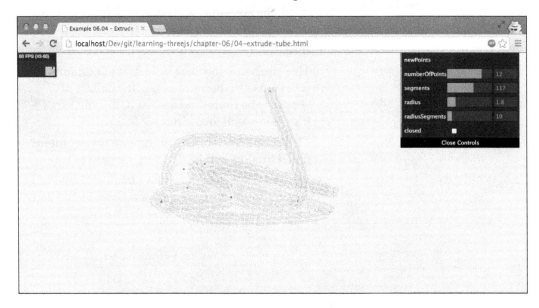

As you can see in this example, we generate a number of random points, and use those points to draw the tube. With the controls in the upper-right corner, we can define how the tube looks or generate a new tube by clicking on the **newPoints** button. The code needed to create a tube is very simple:

```
var points = [];
for (var i = 0 ; i < controls.numberOfPoints ; i++) {
  var randomX = -20 + Math.round(Math.random() * 50);
  var randomY = -15 + Math.round(Math.random() * 40);
  var randomZ = -20 + Math.round(Math.random() * 40);

  points.push(new THREE.Vector3(randomX, randomY, randomZ));
}

var tubeGeometry = new THREE.TubeGeometry(
  new THREE.SplineCurve3(points),
    segments, radius, radiusSegments, closed);

var tubeMesh = createMesh(tubeGeometry);
scene.add(tubeMesh);
```

What we need to do is, first get a set of vertices of the type THREE.Vector3. Just like we did for the THREE.ConvexGeometry class or the THREE.LatheGeometry class. Before we can use these points, however, to create the tube, we first need to convert these points to a THREE.SplineCurve3 class. In other words we need to define a smooth curve through the points we've defined. We can simply do this by passing the array of vertices to the constructor of THREE.SplineCurve3. With this spline, and the other arguments (which we'll explain in a bit), we can create the tube and add it to the scene.

Besides the THREE.SplineCurve3 object, the TubeGeometry constructor takes some other arguments. The following table lists all the arguments for the TubeGeometry:

Property	Mandatory	Description
path	Yes	This property specifies the THREE.SplineCurve3 object that describes the path this tube should follow.
segments	No	This property specifies the segments used to build up the tube. Default value is 64. The longer the path, the more segments you should specify.
radius	No	This property specifies the radius of the tube. Default is 1.

Property	Mandatory	Description
radiusSegments	No	This property specifies the number of segments to use along the length of the tube. Default is 8. The more you use, the more round the tube will look.
closed	No	If set to true, the start of the tube and the end will be connected together. Default is false.
debug	No	If set to true, extra debug information will be added to the tube.

The last extrude example we'll show in this chapter isn't really a different geometry. In the next section we'll show you how you can use the ExtrudeGeometry to create extrusions from existing SVG paths.

Extrude from SVG

When we discussed the ShapeGeometry, we mentioned that SVG and canvas follow pretty much the same approach to drawing shapes. SVG especially has a very close match with how Three.js handles shapes. In this section we'll look at how you can use a small library from https://github.com/asutherland/d3-threeD to convert SVG paths to a Three.js shape.

As an example, I've taken an SVG drawing of the Batman logo and used the ExtrudeGeometry to convert it to 3D. An example you can experiment with can be found in the sources for this chapter, 05-extrude-svg.html:

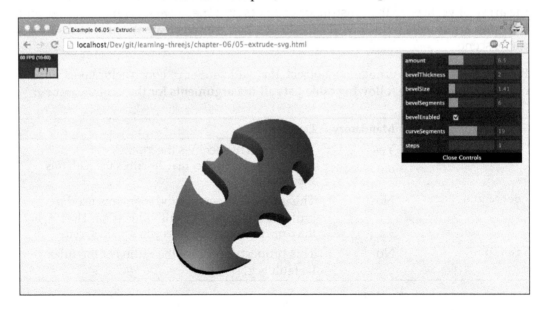

First let's look at what the original SVG looks like (you can also see this for yourself when looking at the source code for this example):

```
<svg version="1.0" xmlns="http://www.w3.org/2000/svg"
xmlns:xlink="http://www.w3.org/1999/xlink" x="0px" y="0px"
width="1152px" height="1152px" xml:space="preserve">
<g>
<path  id="batman-path" style="fill:rgb(0,0,0);" d="M 261.135
114.535 C 254.906 116.662 247.491 118.825 244.659 119.344 C
229.433 122.131 177.907 142.565 151.973 156.101 C 111.417 177.269
78.9808 203.399 49.2992 238.815 C 41.0479 248.66 26.5057 277.248
21.0148 294.418 C 14.873 313.624 15.3588 357.341 21.9304 376.806 C
29.244 398.469 39.6107 416.935 52.0865 430.524 C 58.2431 437.23
63.3085 443.321 63.3431 444.06 ... 261.135 114.535 "/>
</g>
</svg>
```

Unless you're an SVG guru, this will probably mean nothing to you. Basically though, what you see here, are a set of drawing instructions. For instance: `C 277.987 119.348 279.673 116.786 279.673 115.867` tells the browser to draw a cubic Bezier curve and the `L 489.242 111.787` tells us that we should draw a line on that specific position. Luckily, though, we won't have to write the code to interpret this ourselves. With the `d3-threeD` library, we can convert this automatically. This library was originally created for use together with the excellent `D3.js` library, but with some small adaptions we can also use this specific functionality standalone.

 SVG stands for **Scalable Vector Graphics**. This is an XML-based standard that can be used to create vector-based 2D images for the web. This is an open standard that is supported by all of the modern browsers. Directly working with SVG and manipulating it from JavaScript, however, isn't very straightforward. Luckily there are a couple of open source JavaScript libraries that make working with SVG a lot easier. `D3.js` and `Raphael.js` are two of the best.

The following code fragment shows how you can load in the SVG you saw earlier convert it to an `ExtrudeGeometry` and show it on screen:

```
function drawShape() {

  var svgString = $("#batman-path").attr("d");
  var shape = transformSVGPathExposed(svgString);
  return shape;
}

var options = {
  amount: 10,
```

```
        bevelThickness: 2,
        bevelSize: 1,
        bevelSegments: 3,
        bevelEnabled: true,
        curveSegments: 12,
        steps: 1
    };

    shape = createMesh(new THREE.ExtrudeGeometry(drawShape(),
        options));
```

In this code fragment you'll see a call to the `transformSVGPathExposed` function. This function is provided by the d3-ThreeD library and takes as argument an SVG string. We get this SVG string directly from the SVG element with the expression: `$("#batman-path").attr("d")`. In SVG the d attribute contains the path statements used to draw a shape. Add a nice-looking, shiny material, a spotlight and you've recreated this example.

The last geometry we'll discuss in this section is the `ParametricGeometry`. With this geometry, you can specify a couple of functions that are used to programmatically create geometries.

ParametricGeometry

With the `ParametricGeometry` you can create a geometry based on an equation. Before we dive into our own example, a good starting point is looking at the examples already provided by Three.js. When you download the Three.js distribution you get the following file: `examples/js/ParametricGeometries.js`. In this file you can find a couple of examples of equations you can use together with the `ParametricGeometry`. The most basic example is the function to create a plane:

```
function plane(u, v) {
    var x = u * width;
    var y = 0;
    var z = v * depth;
    return new THREE.Vector3(x, y, z);
}
```

This function is called by the `ParametricGeometry`. The u and v values will range from 0 to 1 and will be called a large number of times for all the values from 0 to 1. In this example the u value is used to determine the x coordinate of the vector and the v value is used to determine the z coordinate. When this is run, you'll have a basic plane with a width of `width` and depth of `depth`.

In our example we do something similar. But instead of creating a flat plane, we create a wave-like pattern, as you can see in example `06-parametric-geometries.html`:

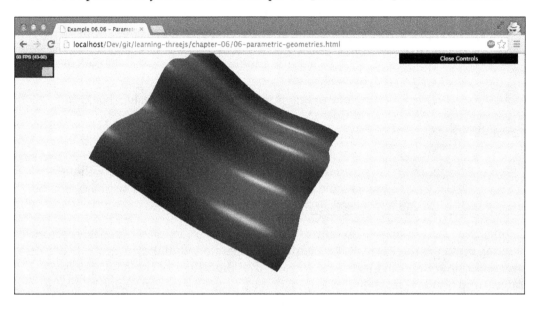

To create this shape we've passed the following function into the `ParametricGeometry`:

```
radialWave = function (u, v) {
    var r = 50;

  var x = Math.sin(u) * r;
  var z = Math.sin(v / 2) * 2 * r;
  var y = (Math.sin(u * 4 * Math.PI)
    + Math.cos(v * 2 * Math.PI)) * 2.8;

  return new THREE.Vector3(x, y, z);
}

var mesh = createMesh(new THREE.ParametricGeometry(radialWave,
  120, 120, false));
```

As you can see in this example, with a couple of lines of code, we can create really interesting geometries. In this example you can also see the arguments we can pass into the `ParametricGeometry`. These are explained in the following table:

Property	Mandatory	Description
function	Yes	The THREE.SplineCurve3 that describes the path this tube should follow.
slices	Yes	Defines into how many parts the u value should be divided.
stacks	Yes	Defines into how many parts the v value should be divided.
useTris	No	Default is false. If set to true, the geometry will be created using triangle faces. If set to false quads will be used.

I'd like to make a final note on how to use the `slices` and `stacks` property, before moving on to the final part of this chapter. We mentioned that the u and v properties are passed into the provided `function` and that the values of these two properties range from 0 to 1. With the `slices` and `stacks` property we can define how often the passed in function is called. If, for instance, we set `slices` to 5 and `stacks` to 4, the function will be called with the following values:

```
u:0/5, v:0/4
u:1/5, v:0/4
u:2/5, v:0/4
u:3/5, v:0/4
u:4/5, v:0/4
u:5/5, v:0/4
u:0/5, v:1/4
u:1/5, v:1/4
...
u:5/5, v:3/4
u:5/5, v:4/4
```

So the higher this value, the more vertices you get to specify, and the more smooth your created geometry will look.

For more examples you can look at `examples/js/ParametricGeometries.js` in the Three.js distribution. This file contains functions to create the following geometries:

- Klein bottle
- Plane
- Flat Mobius strip

- 3d Mobius strip
- Tube
- Torus knot
- Sphere

The last part of this chapter deals with creating 3D text objects.

Creating 3D text

In the last part of this chapter we'll have a quick look at how you can create 3D text effects. First, we'll look at how to render text using the fonts provided by Three.js, and after that we'll have a quick look at how you can use your own fonts for this.

Rendering text

Rendering text in Three.js is very easy. All you have to do is define the font you want to use, and the basic extrude properties we've seen when we discussed the ExtrudeGeometry. The following screenshot shows an example of how to render text in Three.js: 07-text-geometry.html

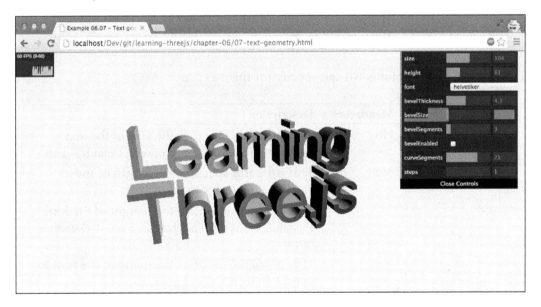

The code required to print these couple of lines is shown next:

```
var options = {
  size: 90,
  height: 90,
  weight: 'normal',
  font: 'helvetiker',
  style: 'normal',
  bevelThickness: 2,
  bevelSize: 4,
  bevelSegments: 3,
  bevelEnabled: true,
  curveSegments: 12,
  steps: 1
};


text1 = createMesh(new THREE.TextGeometry("Learning", options));
text1.position.z = -100;
text1.position.y = 100;
scene.add(text1);

text2 = createMesh(new THREE.TextGeometry("Three.js", options));
scene.add(text2);
};
```

Let's look at all the options we can specify for this TextGeometry:

Property	Mandatory	Description
size	No	This property specifies the size of the text, defaults to the height property. Default is 100.
height	No	This property specifies the length of the extrusion, defaults to 50.
weight		This property specifies the weight of the font. Possible values are normal and bold. Default is normal.
font		This property specifies the name of the font to use. Default is helvetiker.
style		This property specifies the weight of the font. Possible values are normal and italic. Default is normal.

Property	Mandatory	Description
bevelThickness	No	This property specifies the depth of the bevel. The bevel is the rounded corner between the front and back faces and the extrusion. Default is 10.
bevelSize	No	This property specifies the height of the bevel. Default is 8.
bevelSegments	No	This property defines the number of segments that will be used by the bevel. The more that are used, the smoother the bevel will look. Default is 3.
bevelEnabled	No	This property if set to true, a bevel is added. Default is false.
curveSegments	No	This property specifies the how many segments will be used when extruding the curves of shapes. The more that are used, the smoother the curves will look. Default is 4.
steps	No	This property defines how many segments the extrusion will be divided into. Default is 1.
extrudePath	No	This property specifies the path along which the shape should be extruded. If this isn't specified, the shape is extruded along the z-axis.
material	No	This property specifies the index of the material to use for the front and the back faces. Use the THREE.SceneUtils. createMultiMaterialObject function to create the mesh.
extrudeMaterial	No	This property specifies the index of the material to use for the bevel and the extrusion. Use the THREE.SceneUtils. createMultiMaterialObject function to create the mesh.

The fonts that are included in Three.js are also added to the sources for this book. You can find them in the assets/fonts folder.

If you want to render fonts in 2D, for instance, to use them as a texture for a material, you shouldn't use `TextGeometry`. A `TextGeometry` and the JavaScript fonts introduce a lot of overhead. For simple 2D font rendering, it is better to just use the HTML5 canvas. With the `context.font` property you can set the font to use and with `context.fillText` you can output text to the canvas.

It's also possible to use other fonts with this geometry, but you first need to convert them to JavaScript. How to do this is shown in the next section.

Adding custom fonts

There are a couple of fonts provided by Three.js that you can use in your scenes. These fonts are based on the fonts provided by typeface.js (`http://typeface.neocracy.org`). typeface.js is a library that can convert TrueType or OpenType fonts to JavaScript. The resulting JavaScript file can be included in your page, and the font can then be used in Three.js.

To convert an existing OpenType or TrueType font you can use the webpage at `http://typeface.neocracy.org/fonts.html`. On this page you can upload a font, and it will be converted to JavaScript for you. To include that font just add the following line to the top of your HTML page:

```
<script type="text/javascript"
  src="../assets/fonts/bitstream_vera_sans_mono_roman.typeface.js">
</script>
```

This will load the font, and make it available to Three.js. If you want to know the name of the font (to use with the `font` property), you can print out the font cache to the console using the following line of JavaScript:

```
console.log(THREE.FontUtils.faces);
```

This will print out something as shown in the following screenshot:

```
▼ Object
  ▼ bitstream vera sans mono: Object
    ▶ normal: Object
    ▶ __proto__: Object
  ▼ helvetiker: Object
    ▶ bold: Object
    ▶ normal: Object
    ▶ __proto__: Object
  ▶ __proto__: Object
```

Here you can see that we can use the `helvetiker` font with weight `bold` and `normal`. And the `bitstream vera sans mono` font with weight `normal`. An alternative way of determining the font name is by looking at the JavaScript source file for the font. At the end of the file you'll find a property with the name `familyName`. This property also contains the name of the font.

```
"familyName":"Bitstream Vera Sans Mono"
```

In the next part of this chapter we'll introduce the THREEBSP library to create very interesting looking geometries using the binary operations: intersect, subtract, and union.

Using binary operations to combine meshes

In this section we'll look at a different way of creating geometries. In this chapter so far and in the previous chapter we use the default geometries provided by Three.js to create interesting-looking geometries. With the default set of properties you can create beautiful models, but you are limited to what Three.js provides. In this section we'll show you how you can combine various of these standard geometries to create new ones. For this we use the Three.js extension `THREEBSP`, which you can find online here: `https://github.com/skalnik/ThreeBSP`. This additional library provides the following three functions:

Name	Description
`intersect`	This function allows you to create a new geometry based on the intersection of two existing geometries. The area where both geometries overlap, will define the shape of this new geometry.
`union`	The `union` function can be used to combine two geometries to create a new one. You can compare this with the `mergeGeometry` function we'll look at in *Chapter 8, Creating and Loading Advanced Meshes and Geometries*.
`subtract`	The `subtract` function is the opposite of the `union` function. With the function you can create a new geometry by removing the overlapping area from the first geometry.

In the following sections we'll look at each of these functions in more detail.

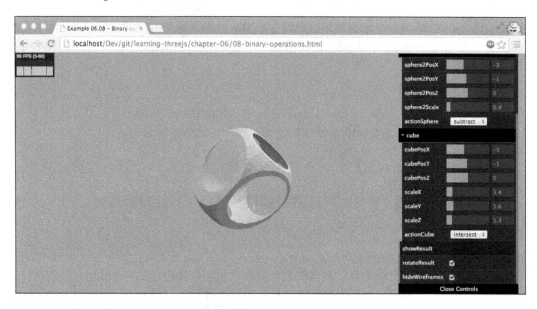

The preceding screenshot shows an example of what you can create by just using the union and subtract functionality one after the other. To use this library we need to include it in our page. This library is written in coffee-script, a more user-friendly variant of JavaScript. To get this working we have two options. We can add the coffee-script file and compile it on the fly, or we can precompile it to JavaScript and include directly. For the first approach we need to do the following:

```
<script type="text/javascript"
  src="../libs/coffee-script.js"></script>
<script type="text/coffeescript"
  src="../libs/ThreeBSP.coffee"></script>
```

The ThreeBSP.coffee file contains the functionality we need for this example, and the coffee-script.js file can interpret the coffee language used for ThreeBSP. A final step we need to take is to make sure the ThreeBSP.coffee file has been parsed completely before we start using the ThreeBSP functionality. For this we add the following to the bottom of the file:

```
<script type="text/coffeescript">
  onReady();
</script>
```

And we rename our initial anonymous jQuery function to `onReady`:

```
function onReady() {
  // Three.js code
}
```

If we precompile the coffee-script to JavaScript using the `coffee-script` command line tool, we can include the resulting JavaScript file directly. To convert it to JavaScript use the following command:

coffee --compile ThreeBSP.coffee

This command creates a `ThreeBSP.js` file that we can include in our example like we do for the other JavaScript files. In our examples we use this second approach, since it'll load quicker than compiling the coffee-script each time we load the page.

The subtract function

Before we start with the `subtract` function, there is one important step you need to keep in mind. These three functions use the absolute position of the mesh for calculations. So if you group meshes or use multiple materials before applying these functions you'll probably get strange results. For the best and most predictable result make sure you're working with ungrouped meshes.

Let's start by demonstrating the `subtract` functionality. For this we've provided an example: `08-binary-operations.html`. With this example you can experiment with the three operations. When you first open the example you'll see something like this:

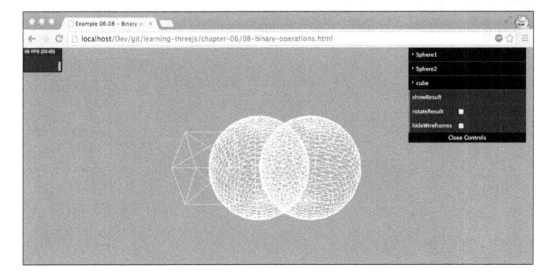

It consists of three wireframes: a cube and two spheres. **Sphere1**, the center sphere, is the object on which all operations are executed, **Sphere2** is the right sphere and "cube" is the left cube. On **Sphere2** and **Cube** you can define one of four actions: **subtract, union, intersect,** and **none.** These actions are applied from the point of view of **Sphere1**. When we set **Sphere2** to subtract and select **showResult**, (and hide the wireframes) the result will show **Sphere1** minus the area where **Sphere1** and **Sphere2** overlap. Note that some of these operations might take a couple of seconds to complete after you've pushed the **showResult** button.

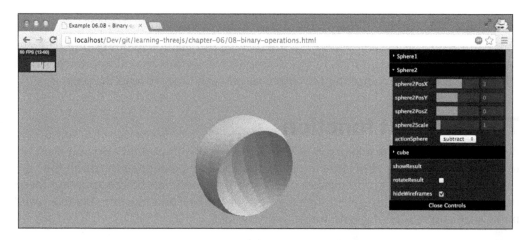

In this example, first the action defined for **Sphere2** is executed and then the action for the cube is executed. So if we subtract both **Sphere2** and the cube (which we scale a bit along the x-axis), we get the following result:

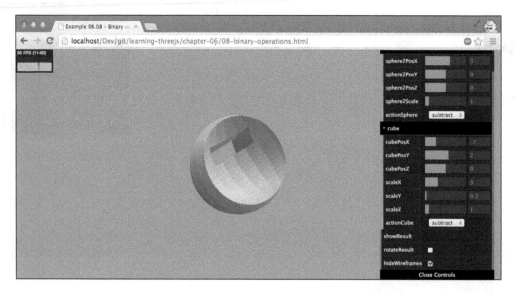

The best way to understand the subtract functionality, is to just play around with the example. The ThreeBSP code to accomplish this is very trivial and in this example it is implemented in the `redrawResult` function, which is called whenever the **showResult** button from the example is clicked.

```
function redrawResult() {
  scene.remove(result);
  var sphere1BSP = new ThreeBSP(sphere1);
  var sphere2BSP = new ThreeBSP(sphere2);
  var cube2BSP = new ThreeBSP(cube);

  var resultBSP;

  // first do the sphere
  switch (controls.actionSphere) {
    case "subtract":
      resultBSP = sphere1BSP.subtract(sphere2BSP);
      break;
    case "intersect":
      resultBSP = sphere1BSP.intersect(sphere2BSP);
      break;
    case "union":
      resultBSP = sphere1BSP.union(sphere2BSP);
      break;
    case "none": // noop;
  }

  // next do the cube
  if (!resultBSP) resultBSP = sphere1BSP;
  switch (controls.actionCube) {
    case "subtract":
      resultBSP = resultBSP.subtract(cube2BSP);
      break;
    case "intersect":
      resultBSP = resultBSP.intersect(cube2BSP);
      break;
    case "union":
      resultBSP = resultBSP.union(cube2BSP);
```

```
        break;
    case "none": // noop;
    }


    if (controls.actionCube === "none"
        && controls.actionSphere === "none") {
        // do nothing
    }
    else {
        result = resultBSP.toMesh();
        result.geometry.computeFaceNormals();
        result.geometry.computeVertexNormals();
        scene.add(result);
    }
}
```

The first thing we do in this code is wrap our meshes (the wireframes you can see) in a ThreeBSP object. This allows us to apply the substract, intersect, and union functions on these objects. Now we can just call the specific function we want on the ThreeBSP object wrapped around the center sphere (sphere1BSP), and the result from this function will contain all the information we need to create a new mesh. To create this mesh we just call the toMesh() function, make sure all the normals are computed correctly by first calling computeFaceNormals and then calling computeVertexNormals(). These compute functions need to be called since, by running one of the binary operations, the vertices and faces of the geometry are probably changed. Three.js uses the face normal and the vertex normal in shading calculations. Explicitly recalculating them will make sure your new object is shaded smoothly (when shading on the material has been set to THREE.SmoothShading) and renders correctly and we can add the result to the scene.

For intersect and union we use exactly the same approach.

The intersect function

With everything we've explained in the previous section, there isn't much left to explain for the `intersect` function. With this function only that part of the meshes that overlap is left.

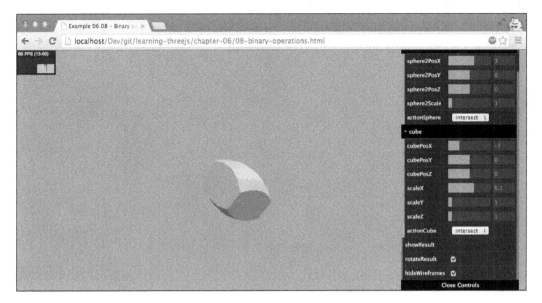

If you look at the example and play around with the settings you'll see that it's very easy to create these kinds of objects. And remember, this can be applied to every mesh you can create, even the complex ones we saw in this chapter such as: `ParametricGeometry` and `TextGeometry`.

The functions subtract and intersect work great together. The example we showed in the beginning of this chapter was created by first subtracting a smaller sphere to create a hollow sphere. After that we used a cube to intersect with this hollow sphere to get the desired result:

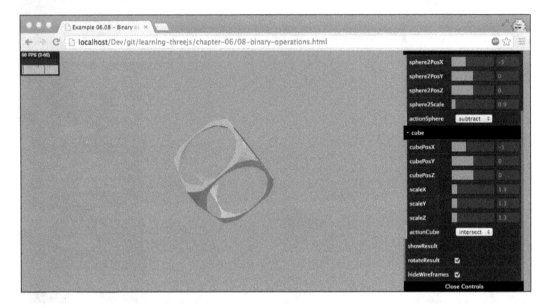

The last function provided by ThreeBSP is the union function.

The union function

The final function is the least interesting one. With this function we can combine two meshes together to create a new one. So when we apply this to the two spheres and the cube, we get a single object:

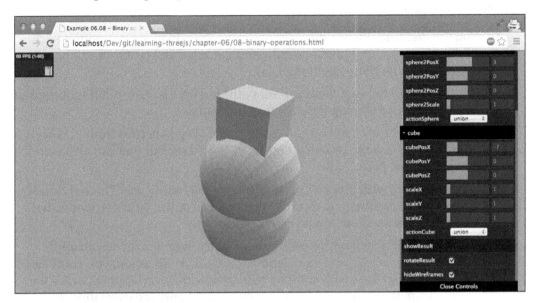

Not really that useful, since this is also functionality provided by Three.js itself (see *Chapter 8*, *Creating and Loading Advanced Meshes and Geometries*, where we explain how to use THREE.GeometryUtils.merge for this), and also offers slightly better performance. If you enable rotation, you can see that this union is applied from the perspective of the center sphere, since it is rotating around the center of that sphere. The same applies for the other two operations.

Summary

We've seen a lot in this chapter. We've introduced a couple of advanced geometries and even showed you how you can create interesting looking geometries using a couple of simple binary operations. The most important things to remember from this chapter are these:

- You can create really beautiful shapes using the advanced geometries such as ConvexGeometry, TubeGeometry, and LatheGeometry. Once again, experiment with these geometries.

- It is possible to convert existing SVG paths to Three.js. You still might need to fine-tune the paths using tools such as **Inkscape**.

- With ExtrudeGeometry you can easily create 3D geometries from 2D shapes. Normally this is done by extruding along the z-axis, but you can also extrude along a custom path.

- When working with text you need to specify the font to use. Three.js comes with a couple of fonts you can use. You can also create your own fonts, but more complex fonts often won't convert correctly.

- With ThreeBSP you have access to three binary operations you can apply to your Mesh: union, subtract, and intersect. With union, you combine two meshes together, with subtract you remove the overlapping part of the meshes from the source mesh, and with intersect only the overlapping part is kept.

So far we've looked at solid (or wireframe) geometries, where vertices are connected to each other to form faces. In the following chapter we'll look at an alternative way of visualizing geometries using something called particles. With particles we don't render complete geometries, we just render the vertices as points in space. This allows you to create great-looking, good-performing 3D effects.

7
Particles and the Particle System

In the previous chapters we've discussed the most important concepts, objects, and APIs that Three.js has to offer. In this chapter, we'll look into the only concept we've skipped so far: **particles**. With particles it is very easy to create many small objects that you can use to simulate rain and snow. You can also use particles as a way to create interesting 3D effects. For instance, you can render individual geometries as a set of particles and control these particles separately. In this chapter we'll explore the various particle features provided by Three.js. To be more specific we'll look at the following subjects in this chapter:

- Creating and styling particles using the ParticleBasicMaterial.
- Using a particle system to create a grouped set of particles.
- Creating a particle system from existing geometries
- Animating particles and the particle system
- Using a texture to style the particles
- Using the canvas to style a particle with the ParticleCanvasMaterial

Let's start by exploring what a particle is, and how you can create one.

Understanding particles

Like we do with most new concepts we'll start with an example. In the sources for this chapter, you'll find an example with the name `01-particles.html`. Open this example and you'll see a couple of very uninteresting looking white cubes as shown in the following screenshot:

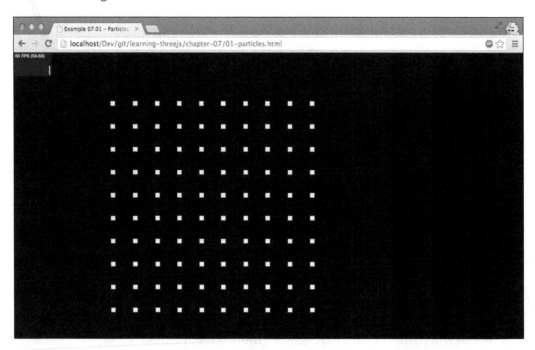

What you see in this screenshot are 100 particles. If you create a particle without any properties, they are rendered as small, white, two-dimensional squares. These particles were created with the following lines of code:

```
function createParticles() {
    var material = new THREE.ParticleBasicMaterial();
    for (var x = -5; x < 5; x++) {
        for (var y = -5; y < 5; y++) {
            var particle = new THREE.Particle(material);
            particle.position.set(x * 10, y * 10, 0);
            scene.add(particle);
        }
    }
}
```

In this example, we create the particles manually with the `THREE.Particle(material)` constructor. The only item we pass in is a material. This has to be either a `ParticleBasicMaterial` or a `ParticleProgramMaterial`. We'll look at both of these materials in more depth in the rest of this chapter.

Before we move on to more interesting particles, let's look a bit closer at the `THREE.Particle`. A `THREE.Particle` extends from the `THREE.Object3D` object, just like a `THREE.Mesh` does. This means that most of the properties and functions you know from a `THREE.Mesh` can be used on a `THREE.Particle`. You can set its position using the `position` attribute, scale it using the `scale` property and move it relatively using the relevant `translate` properties.

We'd just like to add a last note on creating particles this way. If you look at the complete source code for this example, you might notice that we used the `CanvasRenderer` class for this, instead of the `WebGLRenderer` we used for most examples. The reason is that creating particles and adding them to the scene directly, only works for the `CanvasRenderer`. For the `WebGLRenderer` class we first have to create a `THREE.ParticleSystem` object and add create particles from there. To get the same result as the screenshot we saw earlier, for the `WebGLRenderer` we have to use the following code:

```
function createParticles() {


  var geom = new THREE.Geometry();
  var material = new THREE.ParticleBasicMaterial({size: 4,
    vertexColors: true, color: 0xffffff});

  for (var x = -5; x < 5; x++) {
    for (var y = -5; y < 5; y++) {
      var particle = new THREE.Vector3(x * 10, y * 10, 0);
      geom.vertices.push(particle);
      geom.colors.push(
        new THREE.Color(Math.random() * 0x00ffff));
    }
  }

  var system = new THREE.ParticleSystem(geom, material);
  scene.add(system);
}
```

As you can see, for each particle, we need to create a vertex (represented by Vector3), add it to a geometry, create a ParticleSystem object, and add the ParticleSystem object to the scene. An example of the WebGLRenderer in action (with colored squares) can be found in example 02-particles-webgl.html, also shown in the following screenshot:

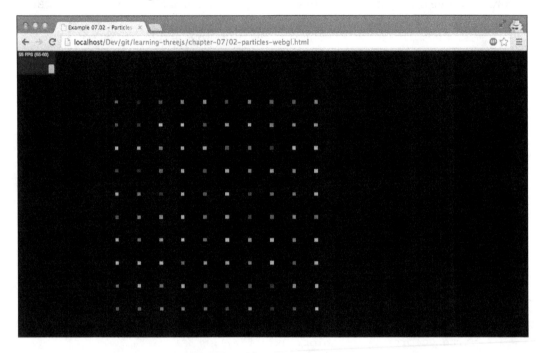

In the following sections we'll explore this ParticleSystem class further.

Particles, the particle system, and the BasicParticleMaterial

At the end of the previous section we quickly introduced the ParticleSystem class. Unless you're using the CanvasRenderer class, you'll need a ParticleSystem class to show particles. The constructor of the ParticleSystem class takes two properties: a geometry and a material. The material is used to color and texturize the particles (as we'll see later on), and the geometry defines where the particles are positioned. Each vertex, each point used to define the geometry of the supplied geometry is shown as a particle. When we create a ParticleSystem object based on a CubeGeometry object, we get eight particles, one for each corner of the cube.

Normally, though, you won't create a `ParticleSystem` from one of the standard Three.js geometries, but add the vertices manually to a geometry created from scratch, just like we did at the end of the previous section. In this section we'll dive a bit deeper into this approach and look at how you can use the `BasicParticleMaterial` to style the particles. We'll explore this using example `03-basic-particle-system.html` that looks as shown in the following screenshot:

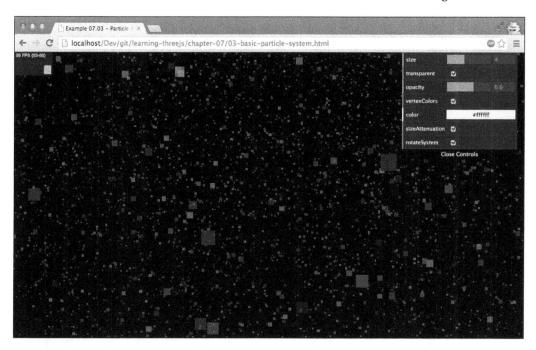

In this example we create a `ParticleSystem` which we fill with 15,000 particles. All the particles are styled with a `BasicParticleMaterial`. To create this `ParticleSystem` we used the following code:

```
function createParticles(size, transparent, opacity,
    vertexColors, sizeAttenuation, color) {


    var geom = new THREE.Geometry();
    var material = new THREE.ParticleBasicMaterial({
        size: size,
        transparent: transparent,
        opacity: opacity,
        vertexColors: vertexColors,
        sizeAttenuation: sizeAttenuation,
        color: color
```

```
  });

  var range = 500;
  for (var i = 0; i < 15000; i++) {
    var particle = new THREE.Vector3(
      Math.random() * range - range / 2,
      Math.random() * range - range / 2,
      Math.random() * range - range / 2
    );
    geom.vertices.push(particle);
    var color = new THREE.Color(0x00ff00);
    color.setHSL(color.getHSL().h,
    color.getHSL().s,
    Math.random() * color.getHSL().l);
    geom.colors.push(color);
  }

  system = new THREE.ParticleSystem(geom, material);
  scene.add(system);
}
```

In this listing we first create a THREE.Geometry object. We'll add the particles, represented as a THREE.Vector3 object, to this geometry. For this we've created a simple loop that creates a THREE.Vector3 at a random position and add it. In this same loop we also specify the array of colors: geom.colors that are used when we set the vertexColors property of the ParticleBasicMaterial object to true. The last thing to do is create a ParticleBasicMaterial object, using the supplied properties, create the ParticleSystem and add it to the scene. The following table explains all the properties you can set on the ParticleBasicMaterial object:

Name	Description
color	The color of all the particles in the ParticleSystem object. Setting the vertexColors property to true and specifying the colors using the colors property of the geometry overrides this property. The default value is 0xFFFFFF
map	With this property you can apply a texture to the particles. You can, for instance, make them look like snowflakes. This property isn't shown in this example, but is explained further down in this chapter.
size	This property specifies the size of the particle. Default is 1.

Name	Description
sizeAnnutation	If set to `false` all the particles will have the same size, regardless of how far from the camera they are located. If this is set to `true`, the size is based on the distance from the camera. Default is `true`.
vertexColors	Normally all the particles in the `ParticleSystem` have the same color. If this property is set to `true`, and the `colors` array in the geometry has been filled, the colors from that array will be used instead. Default value is `false`.
opacity	Along with the `transparent` property sets the opacity of the particle. Default is `1` (no opacity).
transparent	If set to `true`, the particle will be rendered with the opacity set by the `opacity` property. Default is `false`.
blending	The blend mode to use when rendering the particle. See *Chapter 9, Animations and Moving the Camera,* for more information on blend modes.
fog	Whether the particles are affected by fog added to the scene. Defaults to `true`.

The previous example provides a simple control menu that you can use to experiment with the `ParticleBasicMaterial` specific properties.

So far we've only rendered the particles as small cubes which is the default behavior. There are, however, two different ways you can follow to style the particles. We can apply the `ParticleCanvasMaterial` to use the results from an HTML canvas element as a texture, or load an external image file using the map property of the `ParticleBasicMaterial`. In the next section we look into how you can do this.

Styling particles with the HTML5 canvas

Three.js offers two different ways in which you can use an HTML5 canvas to style your particles. If you use the `CanvasRenderer` class you can directly reference an HTML5 canvas from the `ParticleCanvasMaterial` object. When you use the `WebGLRenderer` class you need to take a couple of extra steps to use an HTML5 canvas as a style for your particle. In the following two sections we'll show you both of these approaches.

Using HTML5 canvas with the CanvasRenderer class

With the `ParticleCanvasMaterial` you can use the output from the HTML5 Canvas as a texture for your particles. This material is specifically created for the `CanvasRenderer` and only works when you use this specific renderer. Before we look at how to use this material, let's first look at the attributes you can set on this material:

Name	Description
color	The color of the particle. Depending on the specified `blending` mode this affects the color of the canvas image.
program	A function that takes a canvas context as parameter. This function is called when the particle is rendered. The output from the calls to this 2D drawing context are shown as the particle.
opacity	The opacity of the particle. Default is 1, no opacity.
transparent	Whether the particle is transparent or not. Works together with the `opacity` property.
Blending	The blend mode to use. See *Chapter 9, Animations and Moving the Camera*, for more details.

To see the `ParticleCanvasMaterial` in action, you can open example `04-program-based-particle-system.html`:

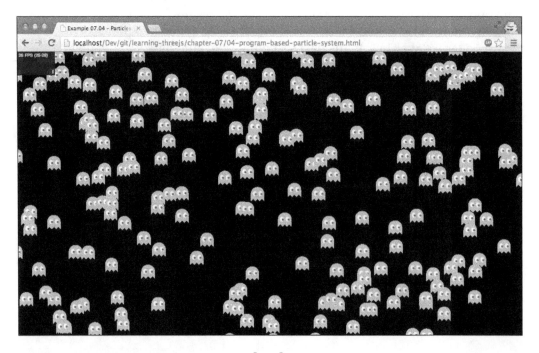

In this example the particles are created in the `createParticles` function:

```
function createParticles() {

    var material = new THREE.ParticleCanvasMaterial({
        program: draw,
        color: 0xffffff});
    var range = 500;
    for (var i = 0; i < 1000; i++) {
        var particle = new THREE.Particle(material);
        particle.position = new THREE.Vector3(
            Math.random() * range - range / 2,
            Math.random() * range - range / 2,
            Math.random() * range - range / 2);
        particle.scale = 0.1;
        particle.rotation.z = Math.PI;
        scene.add(particle);
    }
}
```

This code looks a lot like the code we saw in the previous section. The main change is that, because we're working with the `CanvasRenderer`, we create `THREE.Particle` objects directly, instead of using a `ParticleSystem`. In this code we also define a `ParticleCanvasMaterial` with a `program` attribute that points to the `draw` function. This `draw` function defines what a particle will look like (a ghost from Pac-Man):

```
var draw = function(ctx) {
    ctx.fillStyle = "orange";
    ...
    // lots of other ctx drawing calls
    ...
    ctx.beginPath();
    ctx.fill();
}
```

We won't dive into the actual canvas code required to draw our shape. What's important here is that we define a function that accepts a 2D canvas context as its parameter. Everything that is drawn onto that context is used as the shape for the `THREE.Particle`.

Using HTML5 canvas with the WebGLRenderer class

If we want to do the same thing with the WebGLRenderer class, we have to take a slightly different approach. The ParticleCanvasMaterial class won't work so we have to use the ParticleBasicMaterial for this purpose. In the attributes for the ParticleBasicMaterial we already mentioned the map property. With the map property we can load a texture for the particle. With Three.js, this texture can also be the output from an HTML5 canvas. An example showing this concept can be found here: 05-program-based-particle-system-webgl.html. The output is also shown in the following screenshot:

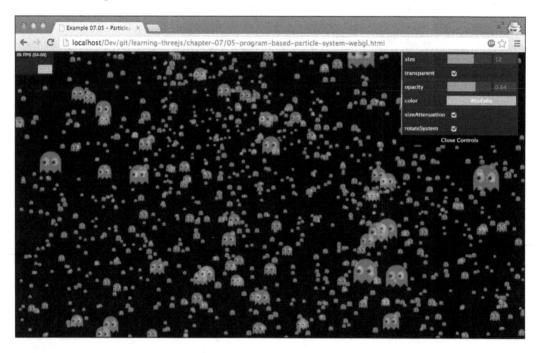

Let's look at the code we wrote to get this effect. Most of the code is the same as our previous WebGL example, so we won't go too much into detail. The important code changes that were made to get this example are shown in the following code snippet:

```
var getTexture = function() {
  var canvas = document.createElement('canvas');
  canvas.width = 32;
```

```
  canvas.height = 32;

  var ctx = canvas.getContext('2d');
  ...
  // draw the ghost
  ...
  ctx.fill();
  var texture = new THREE.Texture(canvas);
  texture.needsUpdate = true;
  return texture;
}

function createParticles(size, transparent, opacity,
  sizeAttenuation, color) {

    var geom = new THREE.Geometry();


    var material = new THREE.ParticleBasicMaterial({
      size: size,
      transparent: transparent,
      opacity: opacity,
      map: getTexture(),
      sizeAttenuation: sizeAttenuation,
      color: color});


    var range = 500;
    for (var i = 0; i < 5000; i++) {
      var particle = new THREE.Vector3(
        Math.random() * range - range / 2,
        Math.random() * range - range / 2,
        Math.random() * range - range / 2);
        geom.vertices.push(particle);
    }

    system = new THREE.ParticleSystem(geom, material);
    system.sortParticles = true;
    system.name = "particles";
    scene.add(system);
}
```

In the first of these two JavaScript functions, getTexture, we create a THREE.
Texture object based on an HTML5 canvas element. In the second function,
createParticles, we assign this texture to the map property. In this function you
can also see that we set sortParticles property of the ParticleSystem object to
true. This property ensures that before the particles are rendered, they are sorted
according to their z-position on screen. If you see partly overlapping particles or
incorrect transparency, setting this property to true will in most of the cases fix
that. While we're talking about ParticleSystem properties, there is one additional
property you can set on the ParticleSystem: FrustrumCulled. If this property is
set to true, it means that if particles fall outside the visible camera range, they aren't
rendered. This can be used to improve performance and framerate if needed.

The result of this is that everything we draw to the canvas in the getTexture()
method is used for our particles. In the following section, we'll look a bit deeper
into how this works with the textures that we load from external files. Note that
in this example, we only see a very small part of what is possible with textures.
In *Chapter 10, Loading and Working with Textures*, we'll dive into the details of
what can be done with textures.

Using textures to style particles

In the previous example we saw how you could style a particle system using an
HTML5 canvas. Since you can draw anything you want, even load external images,
you can use this approach to add all kinds of styles to the particle system. There is,
however, also a more direct way to use an image to style your particles. Three.js allows
you to load external images with the THREE.ImageUtils.loadTexture() function.

In this section we'll show you two examples, and explain how to create them. Both
these examples use an image as a texture for your particles. In the first example
we create an example that simulates rain 06-rainy-scene.html as shown in the
following screenshot:

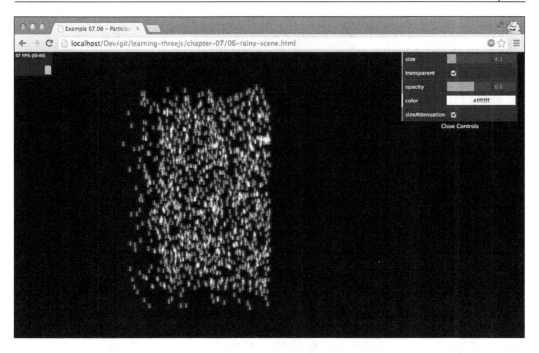

The first thing we need to do is get a texture that will represent our raindrop. You can find a couple of examples in the `assets/textures/particles` folder. In *Chapter 9, Animations and Moving the Camera*, we'll explain all the details and requirements for textures. For now, all you need to know is that the texture should be a square and a power of 2 (for example, 64x64, 128x128, 256x256). For this example we'll use this texture:

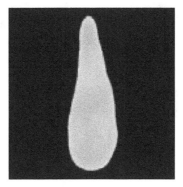

This image uses a black background (needed for correct blending) and shows the shape and color of a raindrop. Before we can use this texture in our ParticleBasicMaterial, we first need to load it. This can be done with the following line of code:

```
var texture = THREE.ImageUtils.loadTexture(
    "../assets/textures/particles/raindrop-2.png");
```

With this line of code Three.js will load the texture, and we can use it in our material. For this example we defined the material as shown in the following code snippet:

```
var material = new THREE.ParticleBasicMaterial({
    size: 3,
    transparent: true,
    opacity: true,
    map: texture,
    blending: THREE.AdditiveBlending,
    sizeAttenuation: true,
    color: 0xffffff}
);
```

In this chapter we've already discussed all of these properties. The main thing to understand here is that the map property points to the texture we loaded with the THREE.ImageUtils.loadTexture() function and we specify THREE.AdditiveBlending as blending mode. This blending mode means that when a new pixel is drawn, the color of the background pixel, is added to the color of this new pixel. For our raindrop texture, this means that the black background won't be shown. An alternative would be to define the black color from our texture as transparent, but that's a combination that doesn't work with particles and WebGL.

That takes care of styling the particle system. What you'll also see when you open up this example is that the particles themselves are moving. In the previous examples we moved the entire particle system, this time we position the individual particles within the particle system. Doing this is actually very simple. Each particle is represented as a vertex that makes up the geometry that was used to create the ParticleSystem object. Let's look at how we add the particles for this ParticleSystem:

```
var range = 40;
for (var i = 0; i < 1500; i++) {
    var particle = new THREE.Vector3(
        Math.random() * range - range / 2,
        Math.random() * range * 1.5,
```

```
        Math.random() * range - range / 2);
    particle.velocityY = 0.1 + Math.random() / 5;
    particle.velocityX = (Math.random() - 0.5) / 3;
    geom2.vertices.push(particle);
}
```

This isn't that different from the previous examples we saw. The only thing we added here is that to each particle (a THREE.Vector3 object) two additional properties are added: velocityX and velocityY. The first one defines how a particle (a raindrop) moves horizontally, and the second one defines how fast the raindrop falls down. The horizontal velocity ranges from -0.16 to +0.16 and the vertical speed ranges from 0.1 to 0.3. Now that each raindrop has its own speed, we can move the individual particles inside the render loop as shown in the following code snippet:

```
var vertices = system2.geometry.vertices;
vertices.forEach(function (v) {
    v.y = v.y - (v.velocityY);
    v.x = v.x - (v.velocityX);

    if (v.y <= 0) v.y = 60;
    if (v.x <= -20 || v.x >= 20) v.velocityX = v.velocityX * -1;
});
```

In this piece of code we get all the vertices (particles) from the geometry that was used to create the ParticleSystem object. For each of the particles we take velocityX and velocityY and use them to change the current position of the particle. The last two lines make sure the particles stay within the range we've defined. If the y position drops below zero, we add the raindrop back to the top and if the x position reaches any of the edges, we make it bounce back by inverting the horizontal velocity.

Let's look at another example. This time we won't make rain, but we'll make snow. Additionally we won't be using a single texture, but we'll use five separate images (taken from the Three.js examples). Let's start by looking at the result again (see 07-snowy-scene.html):

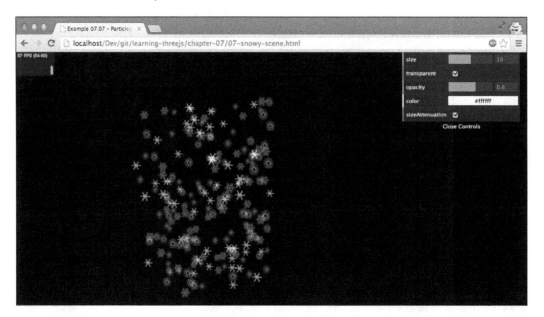

In this image you can see that instead of using a single image as texture, we've used multiple. You might wonder how we did this. As you probably remember, we can only have a single material for a ParticleSystem. If we want to have multiple materials, we just have to make multiple particle systems:

```
function createParticles(size, transparent, opacity,
  sizeAttenuation, color) {

  var texture1 = THREE.ImageUtils.loadTexture(
    "../assets/textures/particles/snowflake1.png");
  var texture2 = THREE.ImageUtils.loadTexture(
    "../assets/textures/particles/snowflake2.png");
  var texture3 = THREE.ImageUtils.loadTexture(
    "../assets/textures/particles/snowflake3.png");
  var texture4 = THREE.ImageUtils.loadTexture(
    "../assets/textures/particles/snowflake5.png");

  scene.add(createSystem("system1", texture1, size, transparent,
    opacity, sizeAttenuation, color));
  scene.add(createSystem("system2", texture2, size, transparent,
    opacity, sizeAttenuation, color));
```

```
  scene.add(createSystem("system3", texture3, size, transparent,
    opacity, sizeAttenuation, color));
  scene.add(createSystem("system4", texture4, size, transparent,
    opacity, sizeAttenuation, color));
}
```

Here you can see that we load the textures separately, and pass all the information on how to create the `ParticleSystem` for the `createSystem` function. This function looks as shown in the following code snippet:

```
function createSystem(name, texture, size, transparent, opacity,
  sizeAttenuation, color) {
    var geom = new THREE.Geometry();

    var color = new THREE.Color(color);
    color.setHSL(color.getHSL().h,
      color.getHSL().s,
      (Math.random()) * color.getHSL().l);

    var material = new THREE.ParticleBasicMaterial({
      size: size,
      transparent: transparent,
      opacity: opacity,
      map: texture,
      blending: THREE.AdditiveBlending,
      depthWrite: false,
      sizeAttenuation: sizeAttenuation,
      color: color});

    var range = 40;
    for (var i = 0; i < 50; i++) {
      var particle = new THREE.Vector3(
        Math.random() * range - range / 2,
        Math.random() * range * 1.5,
        Math.random() * range - range / 2);
      particle.velocityY = 0.1 + Math.random() / 5;
      particle.velocityX = (Math.random() - 0.5) / 3;
      particle.velocityZ = (Math.random() - 0.5) / 3;
      geom.vertices.push(particle);
    }

    var system = new THREE.ParticleSystem(geom, material);
    system.name = name;
    system.sortParticles = true;
    return system;
}
```

The first thing we do in this function is define the color the particles for this specific texture should be rendered in. This is done by randomly changing the 'lightness' of the color that is passed in. Next the material is created in the same manner as we did before. The only change here is that the depthWrite property is set to false. This property defines whether this object affects the WebGL depth buffer. By setting this to false we make sure that the various particle systems don't interfere with each other. If this property isn't disabled, you'll see that the black background from the texture is sometimes shown when a particle is in front of a particle from another particle system. The last step taken in this piece of code is randomly placing the particles and adding a random speed to each particle. In the render loop we can now update each particle from each particle system as shown in the following code snippet:

```
scene.children.forEach(function (child) {
  if (child instanceof THREE.ParticleSystem) {
    var vertices = child.geometry.vertices;
    vertices.forEach(function (v) {
      v.y = v.y - (v.velocityY);
      v.x = v.x - (v.velocityX);
      v.z = v.z - (v.velocityZ);

      if (v.y <= 0) v.y = 60;
      if (v.x <= -20 || v.x >= 20)
        v.velocityX = v.velocityX * -1;
      if (v.z <= -20 || v.z >= 20)
        v.velocityZ = v.velocityZ * -1;
    });
  }
});
```

With this approach we can have particles that have different textures. This approach, however, is a bit limited. The more different textures we want, the more particle systems we'll have to create and manage. It would be easier if we could use a single particle, like we showed in the beginning of this chapter for the CanvasRenderer, and style that instead. With the CanvasRenderer class we'll quickly run into performance issues, though. Using single THREE.Particle class objects doesn't work with the WebGLRenderer. There is, however, an alternative I haven't mentioned yet —the THREE.Sprite.

Working with sprites

The `THREE.Sprite` object can be used for two different goals:

- Create an object that is moved, positioned, and scaled based on screen coordinates. You can use this to create a **Head-Up display** (**HUD**) like a layer for your 3D content.

- Create a particle like object that can be moved in the 3D space just like the `THREE.Particle` allows for the `CanvasRenderer`. Using sprites in a 3D environment is also sometimes called billboarding. Billboarding means that the sprite always faces the camera, just like a billboard along the highway faces the driver.

We'll look at both of these cases, starting with the first one. For an example we're going to create a simple `THREE.Sprite` that moves from left to right over the screen. In the background we'll render a 3D scene with a moving camera to illustrate that the `THREE.Sprite` moves independently. The following screenshot shows what we'll be creating for the first example (`08-sprites.html`):

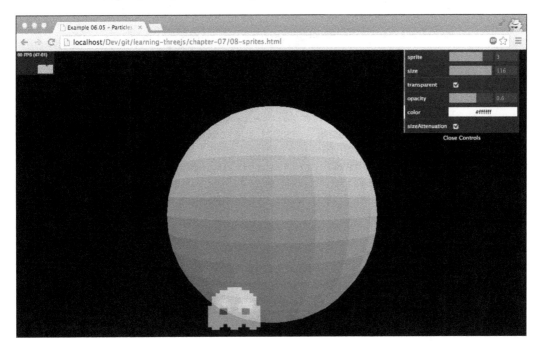

If you open this example in your browser you'll see a Pac-Man ghost like sprite moving around the screen and changing color and form whenever it hits the right edge. So a good place to start with the explanation is the construction of the THREE.Sprite and how the various shapes the sprite can take are loaded:

```
function getTexture() {
  var texture = new THREE.ImageUtils.loadTexture(
    "../assets/textures/particles/sprite-sheet.png");
  return texture;
}

function createSprite(size, transparent, opacity, color,
    spriteNumber) {
  var spriteMaterial = new THREE.SpriteMaterial({
    opacity: opacity,
    color: color,
    transparent: transparent,
    useScreenCoordinates: true,
    map: getTexture()}
  );

  // we have 1 row, with five sprites
  spriteMaterial.uvOffset.set(1 / 5 * spriteNumber, 0);
  spriteMaterial.uvScale.set(1 / 5, 1);
  spriteMaterial.alignment = THREE.SpriteAlignment.bottomCenter;
  spriteMaterial.scaleByViewport = true;
  spriteMaterial.blending = THREE.AdditiveBlending;

  var sprite = new THREE.Sprite(spriteMaterial);
  sprite.scale.set(size, size, size);
  sprite.position.set(200, window.innerHeight - 2, 0);
  sprite.velocityX = 5;

  scene.add(sprite);
}
```

In the `getTexture()` function we load a texture. But instead of loading five different images for each `ghost`, we load a single texture that contains all the sprites and looks as shown in the following screenshot:

With the `uvOffset` and the `uvScale` properties we select the correct sprite to show on screen. With the `uvOffset` property, we determine the offset for the x-axis (u) and the y-axis (v) for the texture we loaded. The scale for these properties runs from 0 to 1. In our example, if we want to select the third ghost, we set the u-offset (x-axis) to `0.4`, since we've only got one row we don't need to change the v-offset (y-axis). If we only set this property the texture shows ghost 3, 4, and 5, compressed together, on screen. To only show one ghost we need to zoom in. We do this by setting the `uvScale` property for the u-value to `1/5`. This means that we zoom in (only for the x-axis) to only show 20% of the texture, which is exactly one ghost.

One other property we'd like to explain is the `useScreenCoordinates` property. If this property is set to `true` you position the sprite using only its x and y coordinate, relative to the top-left corner of the window. The camera from the screen is completely ignored with this property set to `true`. For the other properties see the following table:

Name	Description
Color	The color of the sprite.
Map	The texture to use for this sprite. This can be a sprite sheet as shown in the example in this section.
sizeAnnutation	If set to `false` the size of the sprite won't be affected by the distance its removed from the camera. Default is `true`.
opacity	Sets the transparency of the sprite. Default is `1` (no opacity).
blending	The blend mode to use when rendering the sprite. See *Chapter 9, Animations and Moving the Camera*, for more information on blend modes.
fog	Whether the sprite is affected by fog added to the scene. Defaults to `true`.
useScreenCoordinates	If set to `true`, the position of the sprite is absolute. Based on the upper left corner of the screen.

Name	Description
scaleByViewport	Size of the sprite is based on the size of the viewport. If set to true, size = imageWidth / viewportHeight. If set to false, size = imageWidth / 1.0.
alignment	When the sprite is scaled (using the scale property) this property defines from where the sprite is scaled. For instance, if set to THREE.SpriteAlignment.topLeft, the sprite's top-left corner stays at the same position when increasing or decreasing the scale of the sprite.
uvOffset	Use along with with the uvOffset property to select a part of the texture to use for the sprite. For an explanation see the code example in this section.
uvScale	Use along with the uvScale property to select a part of the texture to use for the sprite. For an explanation see the code example in this section.

You can also set depthTest and depthWrite properties on this material. For more information on these properties see *Chapter 4, Working with Three.js materials*.

Before moving on to the last section on particles, let's look at the second use of the THREE.Sprite: using it as a single particle that can be positioned in 3D space. For this we've also created an example: 09-sprites-3D.html, the output of which is shown in the following screenshot:

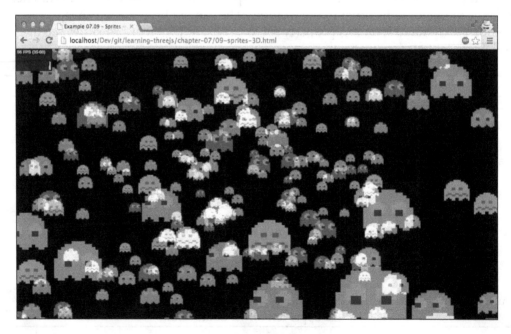

If you've looked closely at the properties in the previous table, you can pretty much guess the code required to get this effect:

```
function createSprite(size, transparent, opacity, color,
    spriteNumber, range) {

    var spriteMaterial = new THREE.SpriteMaterial({
        opacity: opacity,
        color: color,
        transparent: transparent,
        useScreenCoordinates: false,
        sizeAttenuation: true,
        map: getTexture()}
    );

    // we have one row, with five sprites
    spriteMaterial.uvOffset.set(1 / 5 * spriteNumber, 0);
    spriteMaterial.uvScale.set(1 / 5, 1);
    spriteMaterial.alignment = THREE.SpriteAlignment.bottomCenter;
    spriteMaterial.blending = THREE.AdditiveBlending;

    var sprite = new THREE.Sprite(spriteMaterial);
    sprite.scale.set(size, size, size);
    sprite.position = new THREE.Vector3(
        Math.random() * range - range / 2,
        Math.random() * range - range / 2,
        Math.random() * range - range / 2);
    sprite.velocityX = 5;
    return sprite;
}
```

In this code we create 400 sprites based on the sprite sheet we showed earlier. You'll probably know and understand most of the properties and concepts shown here. The main thing to remember when you want to use a sprite in the 3D space is to set the useScreenCoordinates property to false. With that property set to false, the sprites will behave like the particles we discussed in the rest of the chapter. Rotating all the separate sprites is very easy since we've added them to a group and can be done as shown in the following line of code:

```
group.rotation.x+=0.1;
```

In this chapter, so far we've mainly looked at creating particles, sprites, and particle systems from scratch. An interesting option, though, is to create a particle system from an existing geometry.

Creating a particle system from an advanced geometry

As you remember, a particle system renders each particle based on the vertices from the supplied geometry. This means that if we provide a complex geometry; for example, a torus knot or a tube, we can create a particle system based on the vertices from that specific geometry. For the last section of this chapter we'll create a torus knot, like the one we saw in the previous chapter, and render it as a particle system.

We've already explained the torus knot in the previous chapter so we won't go into much detail here. We're using the exact code from the previous chapter, and we've added a single menu option that you can use to transform the rendered mesh to a particle system. You can find the example in the sources for this `10-create-particle-system-from-model.html`, the output of which is shown in the following screenshot:

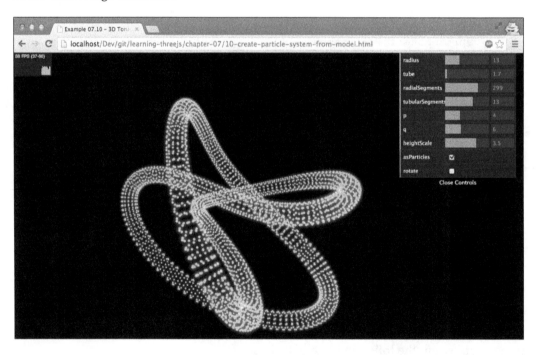

As you can see in this image, every vertex used to generate the torus knot is used as a particle. In this example, we've added a nice looking material, based on an HTML canvas, to create this glowing effect. We'll only look at the code to the create the material and the particle system, since we've already discussed the other properties in this chapter.

```
function generateSprite() {

  var canvas = document.createElement('canvas');
  canvas.width = 16;
  canvas.height = 16;

  var context = canvas.getContext('2d');
  var gradient = context.createRadialGradient(
    canvas.width / 2, canvas.height / 2,
    0,
    canvas.width / 2, canvas.height / 2,
    canvas.width / 2);

  gradient.addColorStop(0,  'rgba(255,255,255,1)');
  gradient.addColorStop(0.2, 'rgba(0,255,255,1)');
  gradient.addColorStop(0.4, 'rgba(0,0,64,1)');
  gradient.addColorStop(1,  'rgba(0,0,0,1)');

  context.fillStyle = gradient;
  context.fillRect(0, 0, canvas.width, canvas.height);

  var texture = new THREE.Texture(canvas);
  texture.needsUpdate = true;
  return texture;
}

function createParticleSystem(geom) {
  var material = new THREE.ParticleBasicMaterial({
    color: 0xffffff,
    size: 3,
    transparent: true,
    blending: THREE.AdditiveBlending,
    map: generateSprite()
  });

  var system = new THREE.ParticleSystem(geom, material);
  system.sortParticles = true;
  return system;
```

```
}

// use it like this
var geom = new THREE.TorusKnotGeometry(...);
var knot = createParticleSystem(geom);
```

In this code fragment you can see two functions: createParticleSystem()
and generateSprite(). In the first function we create a simple ParticleSystem
directly from the provided geometry (in this example a torus knot) and set the
texture (the map property) to a glowing dot (generated on an HTML5 Canvas
element) with the generateSprite() function.

Summary

That's a wrap for this chapter. We've explained what a particle, a sprite, and a
particle system are and how you can style these objects with the available materials.
The important parts to remember are listed here:

- You can use a THREE.Particle object directly when you use the
  CanvasRenderer class.

- When you use the WebGLRenderer class, you can't use a THREE.Particle
  object, but you can create singular particles using the THREE.Sprite object.

- If you want to create a large number of particles that share a material you
  should use the THREE.ParticleSystem class. With this object each vertex is
  rendered as a particle using the supplied material.

- You can easily animate particles by changing their position. This works the
  same for a THREE.Particle, a THREE.Sprite, and the vertices from the
  geometry used to create the THREE.ParticleSystem.

- With the map property you can use images or the output from an HTML5
  Canvas element to style your particles.

- You can also use the THREE.Sprite class to create objects that function as an
  overlay to the 3D scene. These objects are positioned at absolute positions on
  the screen by setting the property useScreenCoordinates to true.

In the chapters so far we've created meshes based on geometries provided by Three.
js. This works great for simple models such as spheres and cubes, but isn't the best
approach when you want to create complex 3D models. For those models you'd
usually use a 3D modeling application such as Blender or 3D Studio max. In the
next chapter, you'll learn how you can load and display models created by such 3D
modeling applications.

8

Creating and Loading Advanced Meshes and Geometries

In this chapter, we'll look at a couple of different ways you can create advanced and complex geometries and meshes. In *Chapter 5, Learn to work with geometries*, we already showed you how to create some advanced geometries using the built-in objects from Three.js. In this chapter we'll use the following two approaches to create advanced geometries and meshes:

- **Grouping and merging**: The first approach we explain uses built-in functionality from Three.js to group and merge existing geometries. This creates new meshes and geometries from existing objects.

- **Load from external**: In this section we'll explain how you can load meshes and geometries from external sources. For instance, we'll show you how you can use Blender to export meshes in a format Three.js supports.

We start with the "group and merge" approach. With this approach we use the standard Three.js grouping and the `GeometryUtils.merge()` function to create new objects.

Geometry grouping and merging

In this section we'll look at two basic features of Three.js: grouping objects together and merging multiple meshes into a single mesh. We'll start with grouping objects.

Grouping objects together

In some of the previous chapters, you've already seen this when working with multiple materials. When you create a mesh from a geometry using multiple materials, Three.js creates a group. To this group, multiple copies of your geometry are added, each with their own specific material. This group is returned, so it looks like a mesh that uses multiple materials. In truth, however, it is a group that contains a number of meshes.

Creating groups is very easy. Every mesh you create can contain child elements that can be added using the add function. The effect of adding a child object to a group is that you can move, scale, rotate, and translate the parent object, and all the child objects will also be affected. Let's look at an example, 01-grouping.html, as shown in the following screenshot:

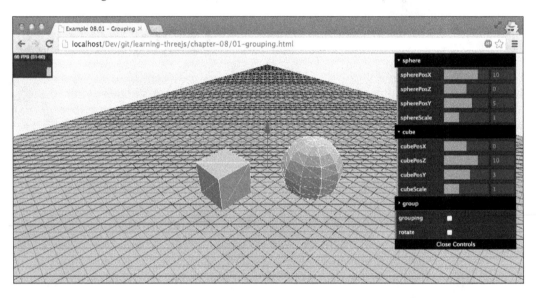

In this example you can use the menu to move the sphere and the cube around. If you check the **rotate** option, you'll see these two meshes rotating around their center. This isn't anything new and is not very exciting. However, these two objects haven't been added to the scene directly, but have been added as a group:

```
sphere = createMesh(new THREE.SphereGeometry(5, 10, 10));
cube = createMesh(new THREE.CubeGeometry(6, 6, 6));

group = new THREE.Object3D();
group.add(sphere);
group.add(cube);

scene.add(group);
```

In this code fragment you can see that we create a `THREE.Object3D` object. This is the base class of a `THREE.Mesh` object and a `THREE.Scene` object, but in itself doesn't contain anything or cause anything to be rendered. In this example, we use the `add` function to add `sphere` and `cube` to this object and we add it to the `scene` instance. If you look at the example you can still move the cube and sphere around, and scale and rotate these two objects. You can also do these things in the group they are in. If you look at the group menu, you'll see the `position` and `scale` options. You can use these to scale and move the entire group around. The scale and position of the objects inside this group are relative to the scale and position of the group itself.

Scale and position are very straightforward. One thing to keep in mind though, is when you rotate a group, it doesn't rotate the objects inside it separately, it rotates the entire group around its center. In this example I placed an arrow at the center of the group:

```
var arrow = new THREE.ArrowHelper(
   new THREE.Vector3(0, 1, 0), group.position, 10, 0x0000ff);
scene.add(arrow);
```

If you check both the **grouping** and **rotate** checkboxes, the group will rotate. And you'll see the sphere and cube rotating around the center of the group (indicated by the arrow) as shown in the following screenshot:

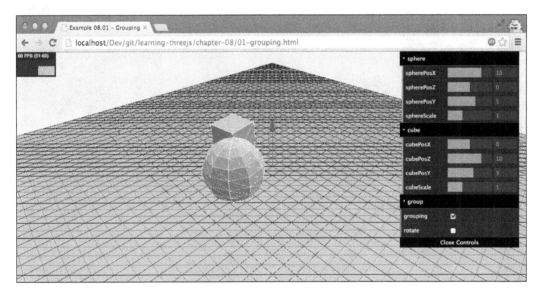

When using a group you can still reference and modify the individual geometries. In the next section, we'll look at merging, where you'll end up with a single new geometry.

Merging multiple meshes into a single mesh

In most cases using groups allows to easily manipulate and manage a large number of meshes. When you're dealing with a very large number of objects, however, performance will become an issue. With groups you're still working with individual objects that each need to be handled and rendered separately. With `THREE.GeometryUtils.merge` you can merge geometries together and create a combined one. In the following example, you can see how this works and the effect it has on performance. If you open example `02-merging.html`, you see a scene with a randomly distributed set of semi-transparent cubes. With the slider in the menu you can set the number of cubes you want in the scene, and redraw the scene by clicking on the **redraw** button. Depending on the hardware you're running on, you'll see a performance degradation at a certain number of cubes. In my case, as you can see in the following screenshot, this happens at around 4000 objects, where the refresh rate drops to around 40 fps instead of the normal 60 fps:

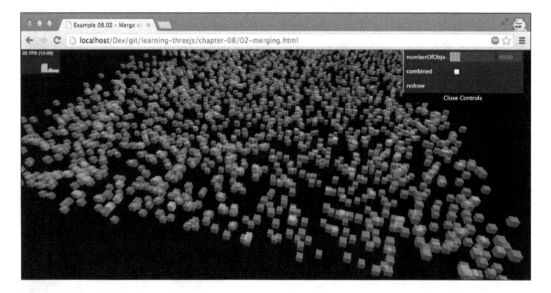

As you can see there is a certain limit to the number of meshes you can add to the scene. Normally, though, you probably wouldn't need that many meshes, but when creating specific games (for example, Minecraft) or advanced visualizations you might run into these kind of performance issues. With `THREE.GeometryUtils.merge` you can solve this problem. Before we look at the code, let's run this same example, but this time, with the **combined** checkbox selected as shown in the following screenshot:

As you can see we can easily render 20,000 cubes, without any drop in performance. To do this we use the following couple of lines of code:

```
var geometry = new THREE.Geometry();
for (var i = 0; i < controls.numberOfObjects; i++) {
  THREE.GeometryUtils.merge(geometry, addCube());
}
scene.add(new THREE.Mesh(geometry, cubeMaterial));
```

In this code fragment the `addCube()` function returns a `THREE.CubeGeometry` object. With the `THREE.GeometryUtils.merge(geometry, addCube());` statement we merge the cube geometry in the initially empty, `THREE.Geometry`. We do this 20,000 times and are left with a single geometry that we add to the scene. If you look at the code you can probably see a couple of drawbacks from this approach. Since you're left with a single geometry, you can't apply a material to each individual cube. This, however, can be somewhat solved, by using a `THREE.MeshFaceMaterial` object. The biggest drawback, however, is that you lose control over the individual cubes. If you want to move, rotate, or scale a single cube, you can't (unless you search for the correct faces and vertices and position them individually).

With the grouping and merging approach you can create large and complex geometries using the basic geometries provided by Three.js. If you want to create more advanced geometries, using the programmatic approach provided by Three.js isn't always the best and easiest option. Three.js, luckily, offers a couple of other options to create geometries. In the next section, we'll look at how you can load geometries and meshes from external resources.

Loading geometries from external resources

Three.js can read a number of 3D file formats and import geometries and meshes defined in those files. The following table shows the file formats supported by Three.js and the ones we'll look at in this section.

Format	Description
JSON	Three.js has its own JSON format that you can use to declaratively define a geometry or a scene. Even though this isn't an official format, it's very easy to use, and comes in as very helpful when you want to reuse complex geometries or scenes.
OBJ en MTL	OBJ is a simple 3D format first developed by Wavefront Technologies. It's one of the most widely adopted 3D file formats and is used to define the geometry of an object. MTL is a companion format to OBJ. In an MTL file the material of the objects in an OBJ file is specified.
	Three.js also has a custom OBJ exporter, called `OBJExporter.js`, should you want to export your models to OBJ from Three.js.
Collada	Collada is a format for defining digital assets in an XML based format. This is also a widely used format that is supported by pretty much all 3D applications and rendering engines.
STL	STL stands for STereoLithography and is widely used for rapid prototyping. For instance, models for 3D printers are often defined as an STL file.
	Three.js also has a custom STL exporter, named `STLExporter.js`, should you want to export your models to STL from Three.js.
CTM	CTM is a file format created by **openCTM**. It's used as a format for storing 3D triangle-based meshes in a compact format.

Format	Description
VTK	VTK is the file format defined by the Visualization Toolkit, and is used to specify vertices and faces. There are two formats available and Three.js supports the old, ASCII format.
PDB	This is a very specialized format, created by the Protein Databank, that is used to specify what proteins look like. Three.js can load and visualize proteins specified in this format.
PLY	This format is called the polygon file format. This is most often used to store information from 3D scanners.

In the next chapter we'll revisit some of these formats (and look at one additional one MD2), when we look at animation. For now we start with the first one on the list, Three.js own internal format.

Saving and loading in Three.js JSON format

You can use Three.js' JSON format for two different scenarios in Three.js. You can use it to save and load a single geometry, or you can use it to save and load a complete scene.

Saving and loading a geometry

To demonstrate saving and loading we created a simple example based on a `THREE.TorusKnotGeometry` class. With this example you can create a torus knot, just like we did in *Chapter 5, Learn to work with geometries*, and using the **save** button from the **Save & Load** menu you can save the current geometry. For this example, we save using the HTML5 local storage API. This API allows us to easily store persistent information in the client's browser and retrieve it at a later time (even after the browser is shut down and restarted).

The example can be found at `03-load-save-json-object.html` as shown in the following screenshot:

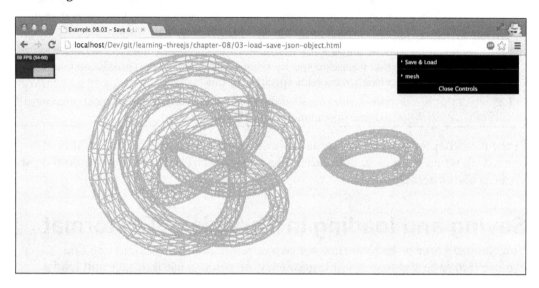

To get this to work, you first have to include the `GeometryExporter.js` file from the Three.js distribution, you can find this file in the `examples/js/exporters` directory, into your page:

```
<script type="text/javascript"
  src="../libs/GeometryExporter.js"></script>
```

Now you can use the following JavaScript to save a geometry to your browser's local storage:

```
var exporter = new THREE.GeometryExporter();
var result = exporter.parse(knot.geometry);
localStorage.setItem("json", JSON.stringify(result));
```

Before saving it, we first convert the result from the `GeometryExporter` object, a JavaScript object, to a string using the `JSON.stringify` function. This results in a JSON string that looks like the following code listing (most of the vertices and faces are left out):

```
{
  "metadata": {
    "version": 4,
    "type": "geometry",
    "generator": "GeometryExporter"
  },
```

```
    "vertices": [14.000030624610355, -0.006999878543058498, ...],
    "uvs": [
       []
    ],
    "faces": [49, 0, 8, ...]
}
```

As you can see Three.js saves the raw geometry. It saves all the faces and vertices, but you don't know whether it was a torus, a cube, or something else. To save this information using the HTML5 local storage API all we have to do is call the `localStorage.setItem` function. The first argument is the key value (`json`) that we can later use to retrieve the information we pass in as the second argument.

Loading this geometry back into Three.js also requires just a couple of lines of code.

```
var json = localStorage.getItem("json");

if (json) {
  var loadedGeometry = JSON.parse(json);

  var loader = new THREE.JSONLoader();
  var geom = loader.parse(loadedGeometry);
  loadedMesh = createMesh(geom.geometry);
  loadedMesh.position.x = -35;
  loadedMesh.position.z = -5;
  scene.add(loadedMesh);
}
```

Here we first get the geometry from local storage, using the name we saved it with (`json` in this case). For this we use the `localStorage.getItem` function provided by the HTML5 localStorage API. Next we convert the string back to a JavaScript object (`JSON.parse`) and use the `THREE.JSONLoader` class to convert the JSON object back to a geometry. We can create a mesh from this geometry and add it to the scene. In this example I've use the `parse` method on the loader to directly parse a JSON string, the loader also provides a `load` function where you can pass in the URL to a file containing the JSON definition.

As you can see here, we only save the geometry. We lose everything else. If you want to save the complete scene, including materials, lights, positions and so on, you can use the `SceneExporter` object.

Saving and loading a scene

If you want to save a complete scene, you use the same approach as we saw in the previous section for the geometry. A working example showing this can be found at `04-load-save-json-scene.html` as shown in the following screenshot:

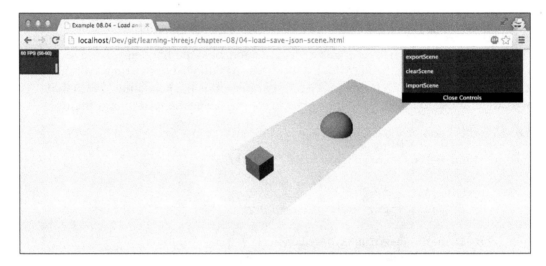

In this example you've got three options: **exportScene**, **clearScene**, and **importScene**. With **exportScene** the current state of the scene will be saved in the browser's local storage. To test the import functionality, you can remove the scene by clicking on the **clearScene** button, and load it from local storage with the **importScene** button. The code to do all this is very simple, but before you can use it, you have to again import the required exporter from the Three.js distribution (look in the `examples/js/exporters` directory).

```
<script type="text/javascript"
  src="../libs/SceneExporter.js"></script>
```

With these loaders included in the page you can export a scene with the following JavaScript:

```
var exporter = new THREE.SceneExporter();
var sceneJson = JSON.stringify(exporter.parse(scene));
localStorage.setItem('scene', sceneJson);
```

This approach is exactly the same as we did for the `GeometryExporter` class from the previous section, only this time we use the `THREE.SceneExporter()` method. The resulting JSON looks a bit different though:

```
{
  "metadata": {
```

```
    "formatVersion": 3.2,
    "type": "scene",
    "generatedBy": "SceneExporter",
    "objects": 5,
    "geometries": 3,
    "materials": 3,
    "textures": 0
},
"urlBaseType": "relativeToScene",
"objects": {
    "Object_78B22F27-C5D8-46BF-A539-A42207DDDCA8": {
        "geometry": "Geometry_5",
        "material": "Material_1",
        "position": [15, 0, 0],
        "rotation": [-1.5707963267948966, 0, 0],
        "scale": [1, 1, 1],
        "visible": true
        }
    ... // removed all the other objects for legibility
},
"geometries": {
    "Geometry_8235FC68-64F0-45E9-917F-5981B082D5BC": {
        "type": "cube",
        "width": 4,
        "height": 4,
        "depth": 4,
        "widthSegments": 1,
        "heightSegments": 1,
        "depthSegments": 1
    }
    ... // removed all the other objects for legibility
}
    ... other scene information like textures
```

The main difference is that instead of exporting the raw information from an object, this exporter creates a JSON file that very specifically declares the objects, lights, materials, and other data used in a scene. When you load this again, Three.js just recreates the objects exactly as they were exported. Loading a scene is done as shown in the following code snippet:

```
var json = (localStorage.getItem('scene'));
var sceneLoader = new THREE.SceneLoader();
sceneLoader.parse(JSON.parse(json), function(e) {
    scene = e.scene;
}, '.');
```

The last argument passed into the loader (' . ') defines the relative URL. For instance, if you've got materials that use textures (for example, external images), those will be retrieved using this relative URL. In this example, where we don't use textures, we just pass in the path of current directory. Just like with GeometryLoader, you can also load a JSON file directly by using the load function.

There are many different 3D programs that you can use to create complex meshes. A popular open source one is Blender (www.blender.org). Three.js has an exporter for Blender (and for Maya and 3D Studio Max) that directly exports to Three.js' own JSON format. In the next section we'll walk you through getting Blender configured to use this exporter and show you how you can export a complex model in Blender and show it in Three.js.

Working with Blender

Before we get started with the configuration, we'll show the result that we'll be aiming for. In the following screenshot, you can see a simple Blender model that we exported with the Three.js plugin and imported in Three.js with the JSONLoader class.

Installing the Three.js exporter in Blender

To get Blender to export Three.js models, we first need to add the Three.js exporter to Blender. The following steps are for Mac OS X, but are pretty much the same on Windows and Linux. You can download Blender from `www.blender.org` and follow the specific installation instructions for your platform. After installation you can add the Three.js plugin. First, locate the `addons` directory from your Blender installation using a terminal window as shown in the following screenshot:

On my Mac it's located here: `./blender.app/Contents/MacOS/2.68/scripts/addons`. For Windows this folder can be found at the following location:

```
C:\Users\USERNAME\AppData\Roaming\Blender
Foundation\Blender\2.6X\scripts\addons
```

And for Linux you can find this directory here:

```
/home/USERNAME/.config/blender/2.6X/scripts/addons
```

Next you need to get the Three.js distribution and unpack it locally. In this distribution you can find the following directory: `utils/exporters/blender/2.66/scripts/addons/`. In this directory there is a single subdirectory with the name: `io_mesh_threejs`. Copy this directory to the `addons` folder of your Blender installation.

Now all we need to do is start Blender and enable the exporter. In Blender open the **Blender User Preferences** (**File | User Preferences**). In the window that opens, navigate to the **Addons** tab and in the search box type **three**. This will show the following screen:

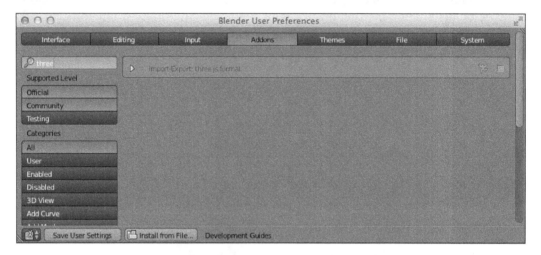

At this point, the Three.js plugin is found, but it is still disabled. Select the small checkbox at the right, and the Three.js exporter will be enabled. As a final check to see whether everything is working correctly, open the **File | Export** menu option, and you'll see Three.js listed as an **Export** option.

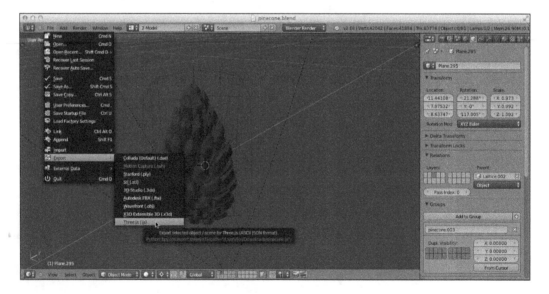

With the plugin installed we can load our first model.

Loading and exporting a model from Blender

As an example, we've added a simple Blender model named `misc_chair01.blend` in the `assets/models` folder, which you can find in the sources for this book. In this section, we'll load this model, and show the minimal steps it takes to export this model to Three.js.

First, we need to load this model in Blender. Use **File** | **Open** and browse to the folder containing the `misc_chair01.blend` file. Select this file and click on **Open**. This will show you a screen looking somewhat like this:

Exporting this model to the Three.js JSON format is pretty straightforward. From the **File** menu navigate to **Export** | **Three.js**, type in the name of the export file, and select **Export Three.js**. This will create a JSON file in a format Three.js understands. A part of the contents of this file are shown next:

```
{

  "metadata" :
  {
    "formatVersion" : 3.1,
    "generatedBy"   : "Blender 2.66 Exporter",
    "vertices"      : 208,
    "faces"         : 124,
    "normals"       : 115,
    "colors"        : 0,
    "uvs"           : [270,151],
```

```
         "materials"       : 1,
         "morphTargets"    : 0,
         "bones"           : 0
      },
   . . .
```

As you can see, this is very similar to the format we saw earlier. If you look closely you might notice a different `formatVersion`. In the previous example, this property was set to `3.2` and in this example it is set to `3.1`. The reason is that version `3.2` was only recently introduced. The Blender exporter hasn't been updated to this latest version yet. We aren't completely done however. In the previous screenshot, you can see that the chair contains a wooden texture. If you look through the JSON export you can see that the export for the chair also specifies a material:

```
"materials": [{
   "DbgColor": 15658734,
   "DbgIndex": 0,
   "DbgName": "misc_chair01",
   "blending": "NormalBlending",
   "colorAmbient": [0.53132, 0.25074, 0.147919],
   "colorDiffuse": [0.53132, 0.25074, 0.147919],
   "colorSpecular": [0.0, 0.0, 0.0],
   "depthTest": true,
   "depthWrite": true,
   "mapDiffuse": "misc_chair01_col.jpg",
   "mapDiffuseWrap": ["repeat", "repeat"],
   "shading": "Lambert",
   "specularCoef": 50,
   "transparency": 1.0,
   "transparent": false,
   "vertexColors": false
}],
```

This material specifies a texture for the `mapDiffuse` property: `misc_chair01_col.jpg`. So besides exporting the model, we also need to make sure the texture file is also available to Three.js. Luckily, we can save this texture directly from Blender.

In Blender open the **UV/Image Editor** view. You can select this view from the dropdown menu, which is at the left of the **File** menu option. This will replace the top menu with the menu as shown in the following screenshot:

Make sure the texture, **misc_chair_01_col.jpg** in our case, you want to export is selected (you can select a different one using the small image icon). Next click on the **Image** menu and use the **Save as Image** menu option to save the image. Save it in the same folder where you saved the model, using the name specified in the JSON export file. At this point we're ready to load the model into Three.js.

The code to load this into Three.js at this point looks like the following code snippet:

```
var loader = new THREE.JSONLoader();
loader.load('../assets/models/misc_chair01.js', function
  (geometry, mat) {
    mesh = new THREE.Mesh(geometry, mat[0]);

    mesh.scale.x = 15;
    mesh.scale.y = 15;
    mesh.scale.z = 15;

    scene.add(mesh);

}, '../assets/models');
```

We've already seen the JSONLoader class before, but this time we use the load function instead of the parse function. In this function, we specify the URL we want to load (points to the exported JSON file), we specify a callback that is called when the object is loaded, and we specify the location, ../assets/models, where the texture can be found (relative to the page). This callback takes two parameters: geometry and mat. The geometry parameter contains the model and the mat parameter contains an array of material objects. We know that there is only one material, so when we create the THREE.Mesh instance, we directly reference that material. If you open example 05-blender-from-json.html, you can see the chair we just exported from Blender.

Using the Three.js exporter isn't the only way of loading models from Blender into Three.js. Three.js understands a number of 3D file formats, and Blender can already export in a couple of those formats. Using the Three.js format, however, is very easy, and if things go wrong, they are often found quickly.

In the following section, we'll look at a couple of formats Three.js supports, and also show a Blender based example for the OBJ and MTL file format.

Importing from 3D file formats

In the beginning of this chapter we listed a number of formats that are supported by Three.js. In this section we'll quickly walk through a couple of examples for those formats. Note that for all these formats an additional JavaScript file needs to be included. You can find all these files in the Three.js distribution in the `examples/js/loaders` directory.

OBJ and MTL format

OBJ and MTL are companion formats and often used together. The OBJ file defines the format of the geometry, and the MTL file defines the materials that are used. Both OBJ and MTL are text based formats. A part of the OBJ file looks like the following code snippet :

```
v -0.032442 0.010796 0.025935
v -0.028519 0.013697 0.026201
v -0.029086 0.014533 0.021409
usemtl Material
s 1
f 2731 2735 2736 2732
f 2732 2736 3043 3044
```

And the MTL file defines materials like the following code snippet:

```
newmtl Material
Ns 56.862745
Ka 0.000000 0.000000 0.000000
Kd 0.360725 0.227524 0.127497
Ks 0.010000 0.010000 0.010000
Ni 1.000000
d 1.000000
illum 2
```

OBJ and MTL are well understood formats by Three.js and are also supported from Blender. So as an alternative, you could choose to export models from Blender in OBJ/MTL format instead of the Three.js JSON format. Three.JS has two different loaders you can use. If you only want to load the geometry you can use the OBJLoader. We used this loader for the following example `06-load-obj.html`, the output of which is as shown in the following screenshot:

To import this in Three.js you have to add the `ObjLoader.js` file:

```
<script type="text/javascript"
  src="../libs/OBJLoader.js"></script>
```

And import the model as shown in the following code snippet:

```
var loader = new THREE.OBJLoader();
loader.load('../assets/models/pinecone.obj', function(geometry) {
  var material = new THREE.MeshLambertMaterial({
    color: 0x5C3A21
  });

  // geometry is a group of children.
  // If a child has one additional child it's probably a mesh
  geometry.children.forEach(function(child) {
    if (child.children.length == 1) {
      if (child.children[0] instanceof THREE.Mesh) {
        child.children[0].material = material;
      }
    }
  });

  geometry.scale.set(100, 100, 100);
  geometry.rotation.x = -0.3;
  scene.add(geometry);
});
```

In this code we use the `OBJLoader` class to load the model from an URL. Once the model is loaded the callback we provide is called, and we add the model to the scene. Usually a good first step is to print out the response from the callback to console to understand how the geometry is built up. Often with these loaders the geometry is returned as a hierarchy of groups and geometries. Understanding this makes it much easier to place and apply the correct material. Also look at the position of a couple of vertices to determine whether you need to scale the model up or down and where to position the camera.

The next example (`07-load-obj-mtl.html`) uses the `OBJMTLLoader` class to load a model and directly assign material.

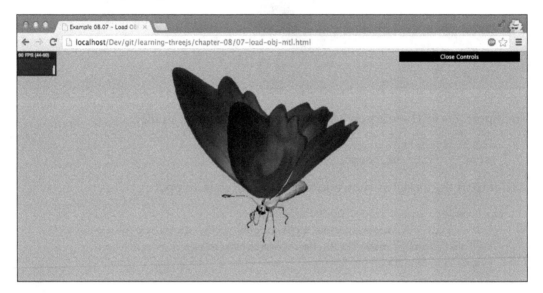

First we need to add the correct loaders to the page:

```html
<script type="text/javascript"
  src="../libs/OBJLoader.js"></script>
<script type="text/javascript"
  src="../libs/MTLLoader.js"></script>
<script type="text/javascript"
  src="../libs/OBJMTLLoader.js"></script>
```

And we can load the model from the OBJ and MTL file like this:

```
var loader = new THREE.OBJMTLLoader();
loader.addEventListener( 'load', function ( event ) {

  var object = event.content;
  var wing2 = object.children[5].children[0];
  var wing1 = object.children[4].children[0];

  wing1.material.alphaTest = 0.5;
  wing1.material.opacity = 0.6;
  wing1.material.transparent = true;

  wing2.material.alphaTest = 0.5;
  wing2.material.opacity = 0.6;
  wing2.material.transparent = true;

  object.scale.set(140, 140, 140);
  object.rotation.x = 0.2;
  object.rotation.y = -1.3;

  scene.add(object);
});


loader.load('../assets/models/butterfly.obj',
  '../assets/models/butterfly.mtl');
```

The first thing to mention, before we look at the code, is that if you receive an OBJ and MTL file and the required texture files, you'll have to check how the MTL file references the textures. These should be referenced relatively to the MTL file, not as an absolute path. The code itself isn't that special. For this loader, it is required to specify an event listener for the `load` event. When the model, material, and textures are loaded, this listener is called. In this specific case, we change some properties from the materials of the wings of the butterfly. The opacity in the source files was set incorrectly, which caused the wings to be invisible. This is something that you'll encounter with complex models that reference materials and textures. Sometimes you'll have to look at how the material is defined and determine what you need to change to get it working.

But, as you can see, you can easily load complex models directly into Three.js and render them in real time in your browser.

Loading a collada model

Collada models (extension is .dae) are another very common format for defining scenes and models (and animations as we'll see in the following chapter). In the collada model not just the geometry is defined, but also the materials. It's even possible to define light sources.

To load Collada models you have to take pretty much the same steps as for the OBJ and MTL models. You start by including the correct loader:

```
<script type="text/javascript"
  src="../libs/ColladaLoader.js"></script>
```

For this example we'll load the following model:

Loading a collada model is once again pretty trivial:

```
var mesh;
loader.load("../assets/models/dae/Truck_dae.dae",
  function (result) {
    mesh = result.scene.children[0].children[0].clone();
    mesh.scale.set(4, 4, 4);
    scene.add(mesh);
});
```

The main difference here is the `result` object that is returned to the callback. The `result` object has the following structure:

```
var result = {

    scene: scene,
    morphs: morphs,
    skins: skins,
    animations: animData,
    dae: {
        ...
    }
};
```

In this chapter we're interested in the objects that are in the scene parameter. I first printed out the scene (which was `result.scene.children[0].children[0]`) to the console to lock where the mesh that I was interested in was,. All that was left to do, was scale it to a reasonable size and add it to the scene. A final note on this specific example, when I loaded this model for the first time, the materials didn't render correctly. The reason was, that the textures used the TGA format, which isn't supported in WebGL. To fix this, I had to convert the TGA files to PNG, and edit the XML of the `.dae` model to point to these PNGs.

As you can see, for most of the complex models, including materials, you often have to take some additional steps to get the desired results. By looking closely at how the materials are configured (using `console.log()`) or replacing them with test materials, problems are often easy to spot.

Loading STL, CTM, and VTK models

We're going to quickly skip over the next couple of file formats, since they all follow the same principle:

1. Include the `[NameOfFormat]Loader.js` file in your webpage.

2. Use the `[NameOfFormat]Loader.load()` function to load an URL.

3. Check what the response format for the callback looks like and render the result.

We did include an example for all these formats:

Name	Example	Screenshot
STL	09-load-STL.html	
CTM	10-load-CTM.html	
VTK	11-load-vtk.html	

We've showed almost all the supported file formats. In the next two sections we'll take a different approach. First we'll look at how to render proteins from the protein databank (PDB format), and finally we'll use a model defined in the PLY format to create a particle system.

Showing proteins from the protein databank

The protein databank (www.rcsb.org) contains detailed information about a lot of different molecules and proteins. Besides the explanation of these proteins, they also provide a way to download the structure of these molecules in the PDB format. Three.js provides a loader for files specified in the PDB format. In this section we'll give an example on how you can parse PDB files and visualize them with Three.js.

The first thing we always need to do to load in a new file format is include the correct loader in Three.js:

```
<script type="text/javascript"
    src="../libs/PDBLoader.js"></script>
```

With this loader included, we're going to create the following 3D model of the provided molecule description:

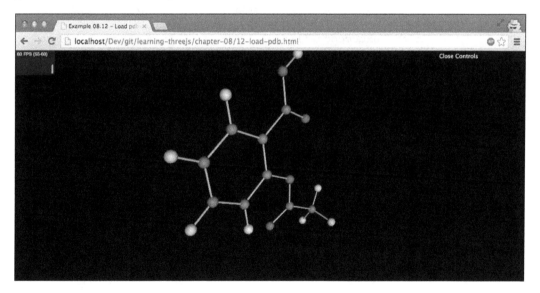

Loading a PDB file is done in the same manner we already saw for the previous formats:

```
var loader = new THREE.PDBLoader();
var group = new THREE.Object3D();
loader.load("../assets/models/diamond.pdb", function (geometry,
  geometryBonds) {
    var i = 0;

    geometry.vertices.forEach(function (position) {
      var sphere = new THREE.SphereGeometry(0.2);
      var material = new THREE.MeshPhongMaterial(
        {  color: geometry.colors[i++]  });
      var mesh = new THREE.Mesh(sphere, material);
      mesh.position = position;
      group.add(mesh);
    });

    for (var j = 0; j < geometryBonds.vertices.length; j += 2) {
      var path = new THREE.SplineCurve3(
        [geometryBonds.vertices[j],
         geometryBonds.vertices[j + 1]]);
      var tube = new THREE.TubeGeometry(path, 1, 0.04)
      var material = new THREE.MeshPhongMaterial(
        {  color: 0xcccccc  });
      var mesh = new THREE.Mesh(tube, material);
      group.add(mesh);
    }
    console.log(geometry);
    console.log(geometryBonds);

    scene.add(group);
});
```

As you can see from this example, we instantiate a `PDBLoader` object, pass in the model file we want to load, and provide a callback that is called when the model is loaded. For this specific loader, the `callback` function is called with two arguments: `geometry` and `geometryBonds`. The vertices from the supplied `geometry` contain the positions of the individual atoms, and the `geometryBonds` instance is used for the connections between the atoms.

For each vertex we create a sphere with the color that is also supplied by the model:

```
var sphere = new THREE.SphereGeometry(0.2);
var material = new THREE.MeshPhongMaterial({color:
  geometry.colors[i++]});
var mesh = new THREE.Mesh(sphere, material);
mesh.position = position;
group.add(mesh)
```

And each connection is defined like this:

```
var path = new THREE.SplineCurve3(
  [geometryBonds.vertices[j], geometryBonds.vertices[j + 1]]);
var tube = new THREE.TubeGeometry(path, 1, 0.04)
var material = new THREE.MeshPhongMaterial({color: 0xcccccc});
var mesh = new THREE.Mesh(tube, material);
group.add(mesh);
```

For the connection we first create a 3D path using the `THREE.SplineCurve3` object. This path is used as input for a `THREE.Tube` object and used to create the connection between the atoms. All the connections and atoms are added to a group, and this group is added to the scene. There are many models you can download from the `protein` databank. The following screenshot shows the structure of a diamond:

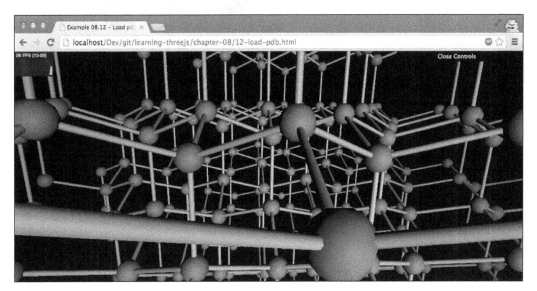

Creating a particle system from a PLY model

Working with the PLY format isn't that much different from the other formats. You include the loader, provide a callback, and visualize the model. For this last example, however, we're going to do something different. Instead of rendering the model as a mesh, we'll use the information from this model to create a particle system.

The JavaScript code to render the preceding screenshot is actually very simple:

```
var loader = new THREE.PLYLoader();
var group = new THREE.Object3D();
loader.load("../assets/models/test.ply", function (geometry) {
  var material = new THREE.ParticleBasicMaterial({
    color: 0xffffff,
    size: 0.4,
    opacity: 0.6,
    transparent: true,
    blending: THREE.AdditiveBlending,
    map: generateSprite()
  });

  group = new THREE.ParticleSystem(geometry, material);
  group.sortParticles = true;

  console.log(group);
  scene.add(group);
});
```

As you can see, we use the `PLYLoader` object to load the model. The callback returns the `geometry`, and we use this geometry as input for the `ParticleSystem` object. The material we use is the same one we used for the last example in the previous chapter. As you can see, with Three.js, it is very easy to combine models from various sources, and render them in different ways, all with a couple of lines of code.

Summary

Using models from external sources isn't that hard to do in Three.js. Especially for the simple models, you only have to take a couple of simple steps. When working with external models or creating them using grouping and merging, it is good to keep the following in mind:

- When you group objects, they remain available as individual objects. Transformations applied to the parent also affect the children.

- When you merge geometries together, you lose the individual geometries and get a single new geometry. This is especially useful, when you're dealing with thousands of geometries you need to render and you're running into performance issues.

- Remember that the Three.js `GeometryExporter` class is still a work in progress. The same goes for the `SceneExporter` class and the `SceneLoader` class.

- When using the format loaders provided by Three.js look through the source code, and print out the information received in the callback. This will help you understand the steps you need to take to get the correct mesh, and set it to the correct position and scale.

- Often when the model doesn't show correctly, the materials cause this. It could be that incompatible texture formats are used, opacity is incorrectly defined, or the format contains incorrect links to the texture images. Use a test material to determine the problem, and print the material to the JavaScript console, to check for strange values.

- When using Blender, you have different options for exporting the models. You can use the Three.js plugin, but OBJ in combination with MTL is also a well supported and understood format.

The models you've worked with in this chapter, and in the previous chapters, are mostly static models. They aren't animated, don't move around, and don't change shape. In the next chapter you'll learn how you can animate your models to make them come to life. Besides animations, the following chapter will also explain the various camera controls provided by Three.js. With a camera control, you can move, pan, and rotate the camera around your scene.

9
Animations and Moving the Camera

In the chapters so far we've already seen some simple animations, but nothing too complex. In the first chapter we've introduced the basic rendering loop, and in the following chapter we've used that to rotate some simple objects and show a couple of other basic animation concepts. In this chapter we're going to look in more details on how animation is supported by Three.js. We will look in detail at the following four subjects:

- **Basic animations**: The basic of all animations in Three.js deals with changing any of the following three properties of an object: its position, its rotation, and its scale. In the first part we'll quickly look back at how you can do this from the rendering loop we introduced in *Chapter 1, Creating Your First 3D Scene with Three.js*, in the *Introducing the requestAnimationFrame() method* section.

- **Moving the camera**: An important part in animations is the ability to move the camera around the scene. In this section we'll walk you through the various camera controls that are supported by Three.js.

- **Morphing and skinning**: When you look at the ways of animating complex meshes, there are two main options. Using morphs to define the transition between one geometry and another, and using bones and skinning for these transitions. In this chapter we'll explore both these options.

- **Loading external animations**: In the previous chapter we've seen how Three. js supports a number of external formats. In this chapter we'll extend on that and show you how you can load animations from external formats.

We start with the basic concepts behind animations.

Basic animations

Before we look at the examples, let's do a quick recap of what we've shown in *Chapter 1, Creating Your First 3D Scene with Three.js*, about the `render` loop. To support animations we need to tell Three.js to render the scene every so often. For this we use the standard HTML5 `requestAnimationFrame` functionality:

```
render();

function render() {

  // render the scene
  renderer.render(scene, camera);

  // schedule the next rendering using requestAnimationFrame
  requestAnimationFrame(render);
}
```

With this code fragment we only need to call the `render()` function once, when we've done initializing the scene. In the `render()` function itself, we use `requestAnimationFrame` to schedule the next rendering. This way the browser will make sure the `render()` function is called at the correct interval (usually around 60 times a second). Before `requestAnimationFrame` was added to the browsers, usually `setInterval(function, interval)` or `setTimeout(function, interval)` was used. This would call the specified function once every set interval. The problem with this approach is that it doesn't take into account what else is going on. Even if your animation isn't shown or is in a hidden tab, it is still called and it uses resources. Another issue is that these functions update the screen whenever they are called, not when it is the best time for the browser. This once again means higher CPU usage. With `requestAnimationFrame` we don't tell the browser when it needs to update the screen, we ask the browser to run the supplied function when it's most opportune. Usually this results in a frame rate of about 60 fps. With `requestAnimationFrame` your animations will run more smoothly and will be more CPU and GPU resource friendly and you don't have to worry about timing issues yourself.

Simple animations

With this approach we can very easily animate objects by changing their rotation, scale, position, material, vertices, faces, and anything you can imagine. In the next `render` loop Three.js will render the changed properties. A very simple example, based on the one we already saw in *Chapter 1, Creating Your First 3D Scene with Three.js*, is available as: `01-basic-animation.html` as shown in the following screenshot:

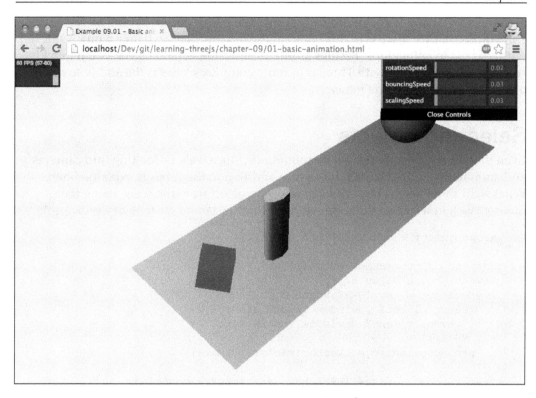

The `render` loop for this is very simple. You just need to change the properties of the involved meshes and Three.js handles the rest:

```
function render() {
  cube.rotation.x += controls.rotationSpeed;
  cube.rotation.y += controls.rotationSpeed;
  cube.rotation.z += controls.rotationSpeed;

  step += controls.bouncingSpeed;
  sphere.position.x = 20 + ( 10 * (Math.cos(step)));
  sphere.position.y = 2 + ( 10 * Math.abs(Math.sin(step)));

  scalingStep += controls.scalingSpeed;
  var scaleX = Math.abs(Math.sin(scalingStep / 4));
  var scaleY = Math.abs(Math.cos(scalingStep / 5));
  var scaleZ = Math.abs(Math.sin(scalingStep / 7));
  cylinder.scale.set(scaleX, scaleY, scaleZ);

  renderer.render(scene, camera);
  requestAnimationFrame(render);
}
```

Nothing spectacular here, but it nicely shows the basic concept behind all the animations that we discuss in this book. In the next section we'll take a quick sidestep with regards to animations. Besides animations, an important aspect, you'll quickly run into when working with Three.js in more complex scenes is the ability to select objects on screen using the mouse.

Selecting objects

Even though not directly related to animations, since we'll be looking into cameras and animations in this chapter, it is a nice addition to the subjects explained here. What we'll show here is how you can select an object from the scene using the mouse. We'll first look at the code required for this, before we look at the example.

```
var projector = new THREE.Projector();

function onDocumentMouseDown(event) {
  event.preventDefault();
  var vector = new THREE.Vector3(
    (event.clientX / window.innerWidth ) * 2 - 1,
    -( event.clientY / window.innerHeight ) * 2 + 1,
      0.5);
  projector.unprojectVector(vector, camera);

  var raycaster = new THREE.Raycaster(camera.position,
    vector.sub(camera.position).normalize());

  var intersects = raycaster.intersectObjects(
    [sphere, cylinder, cube]);

  if (intersects.length > 0) {
    intersects[ 0 ].object.material.transparent = true;
    intersects[ 0 ].object.material.opacity = 0.1;
  }
}
```

In this code we use the THREE.Projector class together with the THREE.Raycaster class to determine whether we've clicked on a specific object. What happens when we click on the screen is:

1. First, a vector is created based on the position that we've clicked on, on the screen.

2. Next, with the unprojectVector function we convert the clicked position on the screen, to coordinates in our Three.js scene.

3. Next, we use a THREE.Raycaster object (returned from the projector.pickingRay function) to send out a ray into the world from the position we've clicked on, on the screen.

4. Finally we use the `raycaster.intersectObjects` function to determine whether any of the supplied objects are hit by this ray.

The result from this final step contains information on any object that is hit by this ray. The following information is provided:

```
distance: 49.9047088522448
face: THREE.Face4
faceIndex: 4
object: THREE.Mesh
point: THREE.Vector3
```

The `object` property is the mesh that was clicked on, `face` and `faceIndex` point to the face of the mesh that was selected. The `distance` property is measured from the camera to the clicked object and the `point` is the exact position on the mesh where the object was clicked. In the example `02-selecting-objects.html` you can test this out. Any object you'll select will become transparent and the details of the selection will be printed to the console. If you want to see the path of the ray that is cast you can enable the **showRay** property from the menu as shown in the following screenshot:

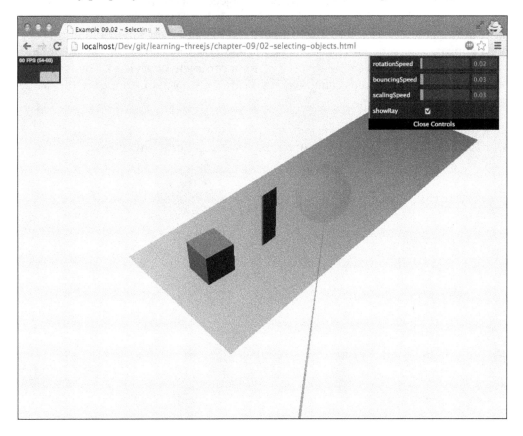

So far we've changed the properties in our render loop ourselves. In the next section we'll look at a small library that makes defining animations a lot easier.

Animating with Tween.js

Tween.js is a small JavaScript library that you can download from `https://github.com/sole/tween.js/`, and use to easily define the transition of a property between two values. All the intermediate points between the start and end value are calculated for you. This process is called **tweening**. For instance, you can use this library to change the x position of a mesh from 10 to 3 within 10 seconds:

```
var tween = new TWEEN.Tween({x: 10})
  .to({x: 3}, 10000)
  .easing(TWEEN.Easing.Elastic.InOut)
  .onUpdate( function () {
    // update the mesh
  })
```

In this example we've created a `TWEEN.Tween` object. This tween will make sure that the x property is changed from 10 to 3 over a period of 10000 milliseconds. Tween.js also allows you to define how this property is changed over time. Should this be done in linear, quadratic, or any of the other possibilities (see `http://sole.github.io/tween.js/examples/03_graphs.html` for a complete overview). The way the value is changed over time is called **easing**. With Tween.js, you configure this using the `easing()` function.

Using this library from Three.js is very simple. If you open example `03-animation-tween.html`, you can see the Tween.js library in action as shown in the following screenshot:

In this example, we've taken a particle system, from *Chapter 7, Particles and the Particle System*, where all the particles drop down to the ground. The position of these particles is based on a tween created with the Tween.js library:

```
// first create the tweens
var posSrc = {pos: 1}
var tween = new TWEEN.Tween(posSrc).to({pos: 0}, 5000);
tween.easing(TWEEN.Easing.Sinusoidal.InOut);

var tweenBack = new TWEEN.Tween(posSrc).to({pos: 1}, 5000);
tweenBack.easing(TWEEN.Easing.Sinusoidal.InOut);

tween.chain(tweenBack);
```

```
tweenBack.chain(tween);

var onUpdate = function () {
  var count = 0;
  var pos = this.pos;

  loadedGeometry.vertices.forEach(function (e) {
    var newY = ((e.y + 3.22544) * pos) - 3.22544;
    particleSystem.geometry.vertices[count++].set(e.x,
      newY, e.z);
  });

  particleSystem.sortParticles = true;
};

tween.onUpdate(onUpdate);
tweenBack.onUpdate(onUpdate);
```

With this piece of code we create two tweens: tween and tweenBack. The first one defines how the position property transitions from 1 to 0 and the second one does the opposite. With the chain() function we chain these two tweens to each other, so these tweens will start looping when started. The final thing we define here is the onUpdate method. In this method we walk through all the vertices of the particle system and change their position according to the position provided by the tween (this.pos).

We start the tween when the model is loaded, so at the end of the following function we call the tween.start() function:

```
var loader = new THREE.PLYLoader();
loader.load( "../assets/models/test.ply", function (geometry) {
  ...
  tween.start()
  ...
});
```

When the tween is started, we need to tell the Tween.js library when we want it to update all the tweens that it knows about. We do this by calling the TWEEN.update() function:

```
function render() {
  TWEEN.update();
  webGLRenderer.render(scene, camera);
  requestAnimationFrame(render);
}
```

With these steps in place, the tween library will take care of positioning the various particles of the particle system. As you can see, using this library is much easier than having to manage the transitions yourself.

Besides animating and changing objects, we can also animate a scene by moving the camera around. In the previous chapters we've already done this a couple of times, by manually updating the position of the camera. Three.js also provides a number of additional ways of updating the camera.

Working with the camera

Three.js has a number of camera controls that you can use to control the camera throughout a scene. These controls are located in the Three.js distribution and can be found in the examples/js/controls directory. In this section we'll look at the following controls:

Name	Description
FirstPersonControls	Controls that behave like those in first person shooters. Move around with the keyboard, and look around with the mouse.
FlyControls	Flight simulator like controls. Move and steer with the keyboard and the mouse.
RollControls	A simpler version of the FlyControls. Allows you to move around and roll around the z-axis.
TrackBallControls	Most used controls, allow you to use the mouse (or the trackball) to easily move, pan, and zoom around the scene.
OrbitControls	Simulates a satellite in orbit around a specific scene. Allows you to move around with the mouse and keyboard.
PathControls	With this control the camera's position moves around a predefined path. You can compare it with a rollercoaster ride where you can look around you, but have no influence on your position.

Besides using these camera controls, you can of course also move the camera around yourself by setting it's position and change where it is pointed to using the lookAt() function.

The first of the controls we'll look at are the TrackballControls.

TrackballControls

Before you can use the `TrackballControls` you first need to include the correct JavaScript file into your page:

```
<script type="text/javascript"
  src="../libs/TrackballControls.js"></script>
```

With this included, we can create the controls and attach them to camera:

```
var trackballControls = new THREE.TrackballControls(camera);
trackballControls.rotateSpeed = 1.0;
trackballControls.zoomSpeed = 1.0;
trackballControls.panSpeed = 1.0;
```

Updating the position of the camera is something we do in the `render` loop:

```
var clock = new THREE.Clock();
function render() {
  var delta = clock.getDelta();
  trackballControls.update(delta);
  requestAnimationFrame(render);
  webGLRenderer.render(scene, camera);
}
```

In the previous code fragment we see a new Three.js object: `THREE.Clock`. `THREE.Clock` can be used to exactly calculate the elapsed time a specific invocation or rendering loop took. You can do this by calling the `clock.getDelta()` function. This function will return the elapsed time between this call and the previous call to `getDelta()`. To update the position of the camera we call the `trackballControls.update()` function. In this function we need to provide the time that is passed since the last time this `update` function was called. For this we use the `getDelta()` function from the `THREE.Clock` object. You might wonder why we don't just pass in the frame rate (1/60 seconds) to the `update` function. The reason is that when we request an animation frame, we can expect 60 fps, but this isn't guaranteed. Depending on all kind of external factors this frame rate might change. To make sure that the camera turns and rotates smoothly we need to pass in the exact elapsed time.

A working example for this can be found here: `04-trackball-controls-camera.html`, also shown in the following screenshot:

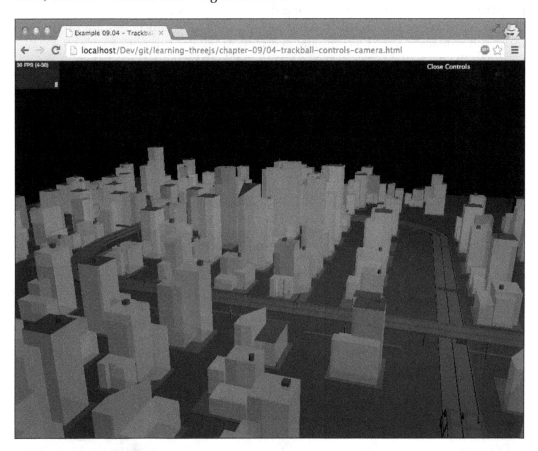

You can control the camera in the following manner:

Control	Action
Left mouse button and move	Rotate and roll the camera around the scene.
Scroll wheel	Zoom in and zoom out.
Middle mouse button and move	Zoom in and zoom out.
Right mouse button and move	Pan around the scene.

There are a couple of properties that you can use to fine tune how the camera acts. For instance, you can set how fast the camera rotates with the `rotateSpeed` property and disable zooming by setting the `noZoom` property to `true`. In this chapter we won't go into detail on what each property does since they are pretty much self-explanatory. For a complete overview of what is possible, look at the source of the `TrackballControls.js` file where these properties are listed.

FlyControls

The next one we'll look at are `FlyControls`. With `FlyControls` you can fly around a scene using controls that are also found in flight simulators. An example can be found in `05-fly-controls-camera.html` as shown in the following screenshot:

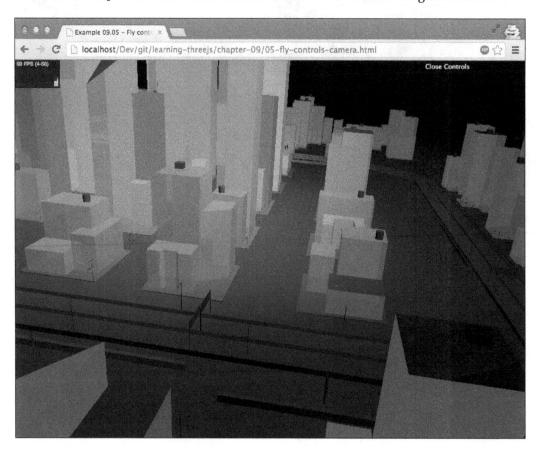

Enabling `FlyControls` works in the same manner as the `TrackballControls`. First
load the correct JavaScript file:

```
<script type="text/javascript"
  src="../libs/FlyControls.js"></script>
```

And next we can configure the control and attach it to the camera:

```
var flyControls = new THREE.FlyControls(camera);
flyControls.movementSpeed = 25;
flyControls.domElement = document.querySelector('#WebGL-output');
flyControls.rollSpeed = Math.PI / 24;
flyControls.autoForward = true;
flyControls.dragToLook = false;
```

Once again, we won't look into all the specific properties. Look at the source of the
`FlyControls.js` file for that. Let's just pick out the properties we need to configure
correctly to get this control working. The property that needs to be set correctly is the
`domElement` property. This property should point to the element in which we render
the scene. For the examples in this book we use the following element for our output:
`<div id="WebGL-output"></div>`, and we set the property by using `flyControls.`
`domElement = document.querySelector('#WebGL-output');`. If we don't set this
property correctly, moving around the mouse will result in strange behavior.

You can control the camera with this control in the following manner:

Control	Action
Left and middle mouse button	Start moving forward
Right mouse button	Move backwards
Mouse movement	Look around
W	Start moving forward
S	Move backwards
A	Move left
D	Move right
R	Move up
F	Move down
Left, right, up and down arrows	Look left, right, up, and down
G	Roll left
E	Roll right

The next control we'll look at are the `THREE.RollControls`.

RollControls

The `RollControls` behave much the same as the `FlyControls`, so we won't go into detail here. `RollControls` can be created like this:

```
var rollControls = new THREE.RollControls(camera);
rollControls.movementSpeed = 25;
rollControls.lookSpeed = 3;
```

If you want to play around with this control, look at the `06-roll-controls-camera.html` example. Note that if you see only a black screen, move the mouse to the bottom of your browser. The cityscape will pan into view. This camera can be moved around with the following controls:

Control	Action
Left mouse button	Move forward
Right mouse button	Move backwards
Left, right, up, and down arrows	Move left, right, forward, and backwards
W	Move forward
A	Move left
S	Move backwards
D	Move right
Q	Roll left
E	Roll right
R	Move up
F	Move down

The last of the basic controls we'll look at are the `FirstPersonControls`.

FirstPersonControls

As the name implies the `FirstPersonControls` allows you to control the camera just like in a first person shooter. The mouse is used to look around and the keyboard is used to walk around. You can find an example here: `07-first-person-camera.html`. Refer to the following screenshot:

Creating these controls follow the same principle as for the other controls we've seen so far. The example we've just shown used the following configuration:

```
var camControls = new THREE.FirstPersonControls(camera);
camControls.lookSpeed = 0.4;
camControls.movementSpeed = 20;
camControls.noFly = true;
camControls.lookVertical = true;
camControls.constrainVertical = true;
camControls.verticalMin = 1.0;
camControls.verticalMax = 2.0;
camControls.lon = -150;
camControls.lat = 120;
```

The only properties that you should carefully look at when using this control for yourself are the last two, the lon and the lat properties. These two properties define where the camera is pointed at when the scene is rendered for the first time.

The controls for this control are pretty straightforward:

Control	Action
Mouse movement	Look around
Left, right, up and down arrows	Move left, right, forward and backwards
W	Move forward
A	Move left
S	Move backwards
D	Move right
R	Move up
F	Move down
Q	Stop all movement

For the next controller we'll move from this first person perspective to the perspective from space.

OrbitControl

The OrbitControl controller is a great way to rotate and pan around an object in the center of the scene. We've included an example that shows how this controller works: 08-controls-orbit.html. Refer to the following screenshot:

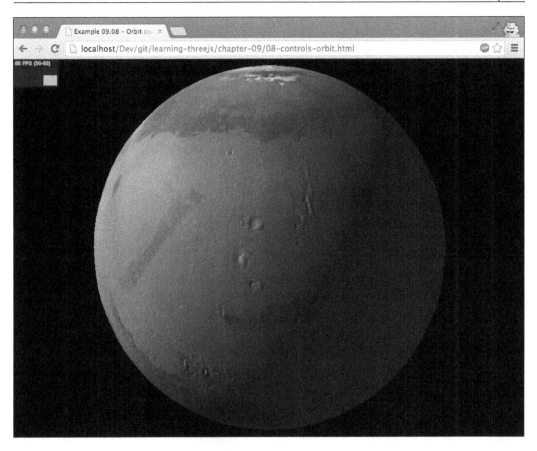

Using the `OrbitControl` controller is as simple as using the other controls. Include the correct JavaScript file, set up the control to the camera, and use a `THREE.Clock` object again to update the control:

```
<script type="text/javascript"
  src="../libs/OrbitControls.js"></script>
...
var orbitControls = new THREE.OrbitControls(camera);
orbitControls.autoRotate = true;
var clock = new THREE.Clock();
...
var delta = clock.getDelta();
orbitControls.update(delta);
```

The controls for `OrbitControl` are focused on using the mouse:

Control	Action
Left mouse click + move	Rotate the camera around the center of the scene
Scroll wheel or Middle mouse click + move	Zoom in and zoom out
Right mouse click + move	Pan around the scene
Left, right, up, and down arrows	Pan around the scene

As the last control we'll look at the `PathControl`. With this control you can move the camera around a fixed path.

PathControl

The `PathControl` is a really cool control. With this control you can set out a path that the camera should follow and the user can move the camera to look around. As an example, we load a model of the Statue of Liberty and use the `PathControl` to slowly spiral upwards. See example `09-path-controls.html`. Refer to the following screenshot:

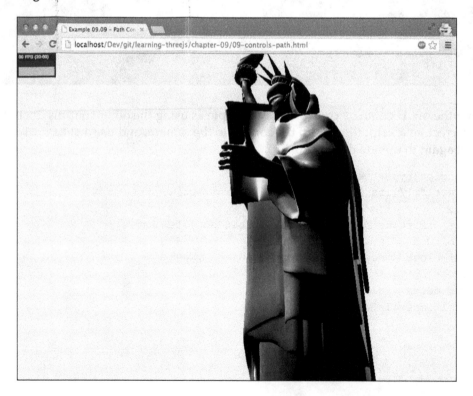

This control takes a little bit of more work to get up and running. First thing we need to do is create the path along which the camera will move:

```
function getPath() {
  var points = [];
  var r = 20;
  var cX = 0;
  var cY = 0;

  for (var i = 0; i < 1440; i += 5) {

    var x = r * Math.cos(i * (Math.PI / 180)) + cX;
    var z = r * Math.sin(i * (Math.PI / 180)) + cY;
    var y = i / 30;

    points.push(new THREE.Vector3(x, y, z));
  }
  return points;
}
```

This function returns the points that create a spiral with a radius of 20, that starts at the bottom and slowly moves up. These points make up our path, so now we can set up the PathControls. First thing, though, is that we need to load the correct JavaScript file.

```
<script type="text/javascript"
  src="../libs/PathControls.js"></script>
```

Before we can load the controller, you need to make sure that you don't manually set the camera's position or use its lookAt() function, since it can interfere with this specific control. Now we can configure the pathControls object and add it to the scene:

```
var pathControls = new THREE.PathControls(camera);

// configure the controller
pathControls.duration = 70
pathControls.useConstantSpeed = true;
pathControls.lookSpeed = 0.1;
pathControls.lookVertical = true;
pathControls.lookHorizontal = true;
pathControls.verticalAngleMap =
  {srcRange: [ 0, 2 * Math.PI ], dstRange: [ 1.1, 3.8 ]};
```

```
pathControls.horizontalAngleMap =
  {srcRange: [ 0, 2 * Math.PI ], dstRange: [ 0.3, Math.PI - 0.3 ]};
pathControls.lon = 300;
pathControls.lat = 40;

// add the path
controls.points.forEach(function(e) {
  pathControls.waypoints.push([e.x, e.y, e.z])});

// when done configuring init the control
pathControls.init();

// add the animationParent to the scene and start the animation
scene.add(pathControls.animationParent);
pathControls.animation.play(true, 0 );
```

For this controller we need to do a couple of things more than the ones for the other controllers. The first part is the same as we've already done earlier. We set some specific properties to fine tune the controller. Next we add the points we defined earlier to the waypoints property. This will be the path that the camera will follow. Now that everything is configured we can use the init() function to finalize the initialization of this controller.

The last step from this code fragment is required to run the animation and move the camera automatically. All that is left now is one final step. In our render loop, we need to add the following:

```
var delta = clock.getDelta();
THREE.AnimationHandler.update(delta);
pathControls.update(delta);
```

This will result in our camera moving automatically along the path.

That's it for the camera and moving it around. In this part we've seen a lot of controls that allow you to create interesting camera actions. In the next section we'll look at a more advanced way of animation: morphing and skinning.

Morphing and skeletal animation

When you create animations in external programs (for instance Blender) you usually have two main options for defining animations:

- **Morph targets**: With morph targets you define a deformed version, a key position, of the mesh. For this deformed target, all vertex positions are stored. All you need to do to animate the shape is, move all the vertices from one position to a key position and repeat that process. The following screenshot shows various morph targets used to express facial expressions (image provided by the Blender foundation).

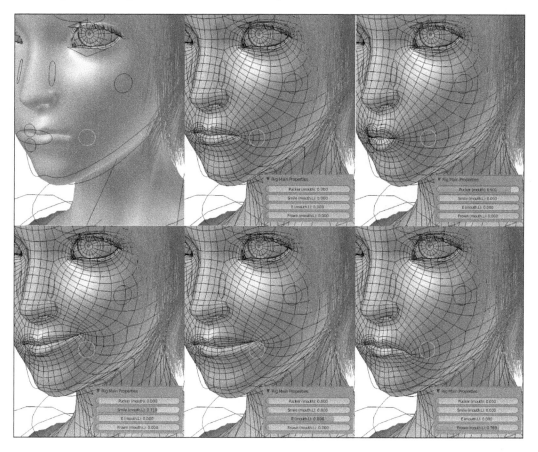

- **Skeletal animation**: An alternative is using skeletal animation. With skeletal animation you define the skeleton, the bones of the mesh, and attach vertices to the specific bones. Now when you move a bone, any connected bone is also moved appropriately, and the attached vertices are moved and deformed based on the position, movement, and scaling of the bone. The following screenshot, once again provided by the Blender foundation, shows an example of how bones can be used to move and deform an object.

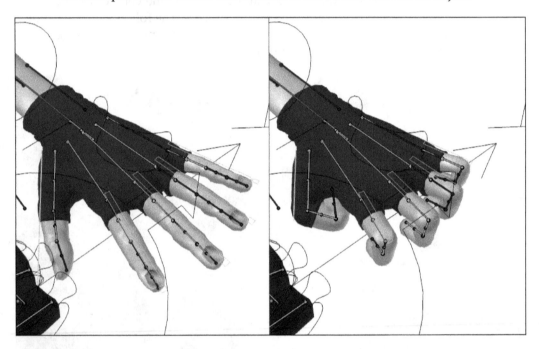

Three.js supports both modes, but generally you'll probably get better results with morph targets. The main problem with skeletal animation is getting a good export from a 3D program such as Blender that can be animated in Three.js. It's much easier to get a good working model with morph targets than it is with bones and skins.

In this section we'll look at both the options and additionally look at a couple of external formats supported by Three.js in which animations can be defined.

Animation with morph targets

Morph targets are the most straightforward way of defining an animation. You define all the vertices for each key position and tell Three.js to move the vertices from one position to the other. The disadvantage of this approach, though, is that for large meshes and large animations the model files will become very large. The reason is that for each key position all the vertices positions are repeated.

We'll show you how to work with morph targets using two examples. In the first example, we'll let Three.js handle the transition between the various key frames (or morph targets as we'll call them from now on), in the second one we'll do this manually.

Animation with MorphAnimMesh

For our first morphing example, we'll use a model that is also available from the Three.js distribution: the horse. The easiest way to understand how morph targets-based animation works is by opening up the example: `10-morph-targets.html`. Refer to the following screenshot:

In this example the horse at the right is animated and running, and the horse on the left is standing still. This second horse is rendered from the basic model, the original set of vertices. With the menu at the top right, you can browse through all the morph targets that are available and see the different positions that the left horse can take.

Three.js provides a way to move from one position to the next, but this would mean we have to manually keep track of the current position we're in, the target we want to morph into, and once we've reached the target position repeat this for the other positions. Luckily, Three.js also provides a specific mesh, the `MorphAnimMesh`, that takes care of the details for us. Before we continue, a quick note on another animation related mesh provided by Three.js called `MorphBlendMesh`. If you look through the objects provided by Three.js you might notice this object. With this specific mesh you can do pretty much the same things as you can do with `MorphAnimMesh` and when you look at the source code, you can even see that much of it is duplicated between these two objects. `MorphBlendMesh`, however, seems to be deprecated and isn't used in any of the official Three.js examples. Everything you could do with `MorhpBlendMesh` can be done with `MorphAnimMesh`, so use `MorphAnimMesh` for this kind of functionality. The following piece of code shows how to load the model and create a `MorphAnimMesh` object from it:

```
var loader = new THREE.JSONLoader();
loader.load('../assets/models/horse.js',
  function(geometry, mat) {

  var mat = new THREE.MeshLambertMaterial(
    {color: 0xffffff,
      morphNormals: false,
      morphTargets: true,
      vertexColors: THREE.FaceColors});

  morphColorsToFaceColors(geometry);
  geometry.computeMorphNormals();
  meshAnim = new THREE.MorphAnimMesh(geometry, mat );
  scene.add(meshAnim);

  },'../assets/models' );


function morphColorsToFaceColors(geometry) {

  if (geometry.morphColors && geometry.morphColors.length) {

    var colorMap = geometry.morphColors[ 0 ];
    for (var i = 0; i < colorMap.colors.length; i++) {
      geometry.faces[ i ].color = colorMap.colors[ i ];
      geometry.faces[ i ].color.offsetHSL(0, 0.3, 0);
    }
  }
}
```

The same approach as we've already seen when loading other models. Instead of creating a normal `Mesh`, we create a `MorphAnimMesh` object. There are a couple of things you need to take into account when loading animations:

- Make sure the material you use has set `morphTargets` to `true`. If not set, your mesh won't animate.

- Before creating the `MorphAnimMesh` object, make sure to call `computeMorphNormals` on the geometry so that all the normal vectors for the morph targets are calculated. This is required for correct lighting and shadow effects.

- It's possible to define colors for faces of a specific morph target. With the helper method `morphColorsToFaceColors`, we make sure the correct colors are used in the animation.

- The default setting is to play the complete animation in one go. If there are multiple animations defined for the same geometry you can use the `parseAnimations()` function together with `playAnimation(name, fps)` to play one of the defined animations. We'll use this approach in the last section of this chapter where we load animations from a MD2 model.

All that is left to do is update the animation in the `render` loop. For this, we once again use the `THREE.Clock` object to calculate the delta and use it to update the animation:

```
function render() {

  var delta = clock.getDelta();
  webGLRenderer.clear();
  if (meshAnim) {
    meshAnim.updateAnimation(delta *1000);
    meshAnim.rotation.y += 0.01;
  }

  // render using requestAnimationFrame
  requestAnimationFrame(render);
  webGLRenderer.render(scene, camera);
}
```

This approach is the easiest, and allows you to quickly set up an animation from a model that has morph targets defined. An alternative approach is to set up the animation manually.

Creating an animation by setting the morphTargetInfluence property

We'll create a very simple example where we morph a cube from one shape to another. This time, though, we manually control to which target we will be morphing. You can find the example at: `11-morph-targets-manually.html`. Refer to the following screenshot:

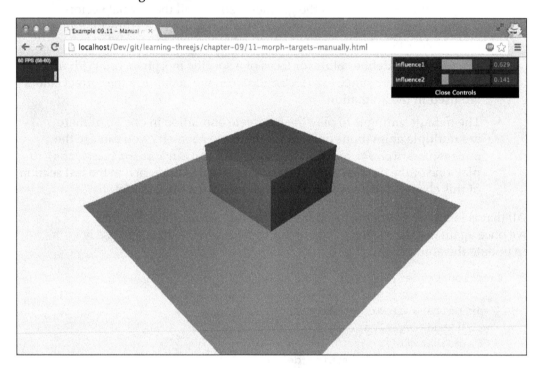

In this example we've manually created two morph targets for a simple cube:

```
// create a cube
var cubeGeometry = new THREE.CubeGeometry(4, 4, 4);
var cubeMaterial = new THREE.MeshLambertMaterial({morphTargets:
  true, color: 0xff0000});

// define morphtargets, we'll use the vertices from these
  geometries
var cubeTarget1 = new THREE.CubeGeometry(2, 10, 2);
var cubeTarget2 = new THREE.CubeGeometry(8, 2, 8);

// define morphtargets and compute the morphnormal
```

```
cubeGeometry.morphTargets[0] = {name: 't1', vertices:
  cubeTarget2.vertices};
cubeGeometry.morphTargets[1] = {name: 't2', vertices:
  cubeTarget1.vertices};
cubeGeometry.computeMorphNormals();

var cube = new THREE.Mesh(cubeGeometry, cubeMaterial);
```

As you open up this example you'll see a simple cube. With the sliders in the top-right corner you can set the `morphTargetInfluences` property. In other words, you can determine how much the initial cube should morph into the cube specified as `mt1` and how much it should morph into `mt2`. You can set the influence using the `morphTargetInfluences` property of the mesh:

```
var controls = new function () {
  this.influence1 = 0.01;
  this.influence2 = 0.01;

  this.update = function () {
    cube.morphTargetInfluences[0] = controls.influence1;
    cube.morphTargetInfluences[1] = controls.influence2;
  };
}
```

These two examples show the most important concepts behind morph target animations. In the next section we'll have a quick look at animation using bones and skinning.

Animation using bones and skinning

Morph animations are very straightforward. Three.js knows all the target vertex positions, and only needs to transition each vertex from one position to the next. For bones and skinning it becomes a bit more complex. When you use bones for animation you move the bone and Three.js has to determine how to translate the attached skin (a set of vertices) accordingly. For this example, we use a model that was exported from Blender to the Three.js format (`hand-1.js` in the models folder.). This is a model of a hand, complete with a set of bones. By moving the bones around, we can animate the complete model. Let's first look at how we loaded the model:

```
var loader = new THREE.JSONLoader();
loader.load('../assets/models/hand-1.js', function (geometry, mat) {
  var mat = new THREE.MeshLambertMaterial(
```

```
    {color: 0xF0C8C9, skinning: true});

mesh = new THREE.SkinnedMesh(geometry, mat);

// rotate the complete hand
mesh.rotation.x = 0.5 * Math.PI;
mesh.rotation.z = 0.7 * Math.PI;

// make sure to set quaternation to false for easy rotation
mesh.bones.forEach(function (e) {
  e.useQuaternion = false;
})

// add the mesh
scene.add(mesh);

// and start the animation
tween.start();

}, '../assets/models');
```

Loading a model for bone animation isn't that different from any of the other models. We just specify the model file, which contains the bone's definition, and based on the geometry we create a mesh. Three.js also provides a specific mesh for skinned geometries like this named `THREE.SkinnedMesh`. The one thing you need to specify to make sure the model is updated is set the `skinning` property of the material that you use to `true`. The last thing we do here is that we set the `useQuaternion` property of all the bones to `false`. If we don't do this, we have to specify rotations for the bones with quaternions; if we set it to `false`, we can set the rotation in the normal manner. Before we move the bones, let's look at the example: `12-bones-manually.html`. Refer to the following screenshot:

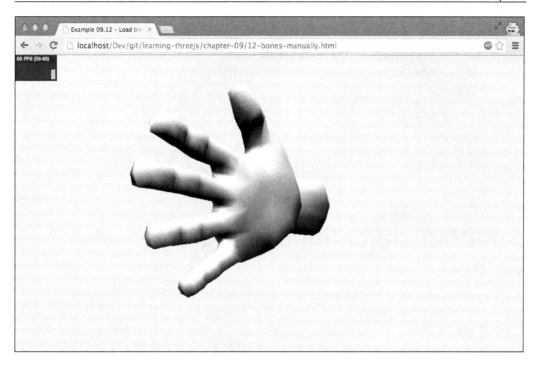

When you open this example you see the hand making a grab-like motion. We did this by setting the z-rotation property of the finger bones:

```
var onUpdate = function () {
  var pos = this.pos;

  // rotate the fingers
  mesh.bones[5].rotation.set(0, 0, pos);
  mesh.bones[6].rotation.set(0, 0, pos);
  mesh.bones[10].rotation.set(0, 0, pos);
  mesh.bones[11].rotation.set(0, 0, pos);
  mesh.bones[15].rotation.set(0, 0, pos);
  mesh.bones[16].rotation.set(0, 0, pos);
  mesh.bones[20].rotation.set(0, 0, pos);
  mesh.bones[21].rotation.set(0, 0, pos);

  // rotate the wrist
  mesh.bones[1].rotation.set(pos, 0, 0);
};
```

Any time this `update` method is called, the relevant bones are set to the `pos` position. The missing element is how to call this `update` method at a regular interval. For this we use the Tween.js library, which we've also seen in the beginning of the chapter (look in the source for more details).

As you can see working with bones takes a bit more effort, but is much more flexible than the fixed morph targets. In this example we've only moved the rotation of the bones, you can also move the position or change the scale. In the next section we look at loading animations from external models. In that section we'll revisit this example, but now we'll run a predefined animation from the model, instead of manually moving the bones around.

Creating animations using external models

In *Chapter 8, Creating and Loading Advanced Meshes and Geometries*, we've looked at a number of 3D formats that are supported by Three.js. A couple of those formats also support animations. In this chapter we'll look at the following examples:

- **Blender with the JSON exporter**: we'll start with an animation created in blender and exported to the Three.js JSON format.
- **Collada model**: the collada format has support for animations. For this example we'll load an animation from a collada file and render it with Three.js.
- **MD2 model**: the MD2 model is a simple format used in the older quake engines. Even though the format is a bit dated, it is still a very good format for storing character animations.

We'll start with the blender model.

Creating bones animation using Blender

To get started with animations from Blender you can load the example we've included in the `models` folder. You can find the `hand.blend` file there, which you can load in blender.

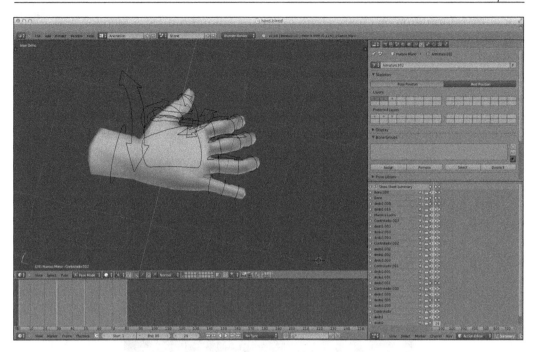

There isn't room in this book to go into much detail on how to create animations in blender, but there are a couple of things you need to keep in mind:

- Every vertex from your model must at least be assigned to a vertex group.

- The name of the vertex groups you use in blender must correspond to the name of the bone that controls it. That way Three.js can determine which vertices it needs to modify when moving the bones.

- Only the first **action** is exported. So make sure the animation you want to export is the first one.

- When creating **keyframes**, it is a good idea to select all the bones, even if they don't change.

- When exporting the model, make sure the model is in its rest post. If this is not the case, you'll see a very deformed animation.

For more information on creating and exporting animations from Blender, and the reasons for the aforementioned pointers, you can look at the following great resource: `http://devmatrix.wordpress.com/2013/02/27/creating-skeletal-animation-in-blender-and-exporting-it-to-three-js/`.

When you've created the animation in blender you can export the file using the Three. js exporter, we've also used in the previous chapter. When exporting the file using the Three.js exporter, you have to make sure the following properties are checked:

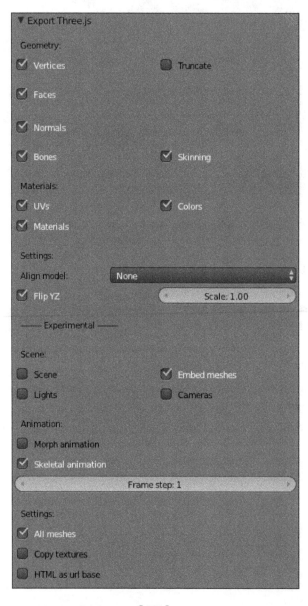

This will export the animation you've specified in Blender as a **skeletal animation** instead of a **morph animation**. With a skeletal animation, the movements of the bones is exported, which we can replay in Three.js.

Loading the model in Three.js is the same as we did for our previous example. However, when the model is loaded, we now also create an animation:

```
var loader = new THREE.JSONLoader();
loader.load('../assets/models/hand-2.js',
  function (geometry, mat) {

  // register the animation
  THREE.AnimationHandler.add(geometry.animation);

  // create a material
  var mat = new THREE.MeshLambertMaterial(
    {color: 0xF0C8C9, skinning: true});

  // create and position the mesh
  mesh = new THREE.SkinnedMesh(geometry, mat);
  mesh.rotation.x = 0.5 * Math.PI;
  mesh.rotation.z = 0.7 * Math.PI;
  scene.add(mesh);

  // create the animation
  var animation = new THREE.Animation(mesh, "wave");

  // start the animation
  animation.play();

}, '../assets/models');
```

What is different from the previous example is that we first register the animation with the central Three.js `AnimationHandler` using the `AnimationHandler.add` function. This will allow us to create the animation using the new `THREE.Animation(mesh, "wave")` statement. The name of this animation must be the same as the one you specified in Blender. Finally we set the animation to play.

As you've probably guessed, we still need to do something to actually run the animation. In our `render` loop we call the `THREE.AnimationHandler.update(clock.getDelta())` function to update the animation and Three.js will use the bones to set the model in the correct position. The result of this example is a simple waving hand: `13-animation-from-blender.html`. Refer to the following screenshot:

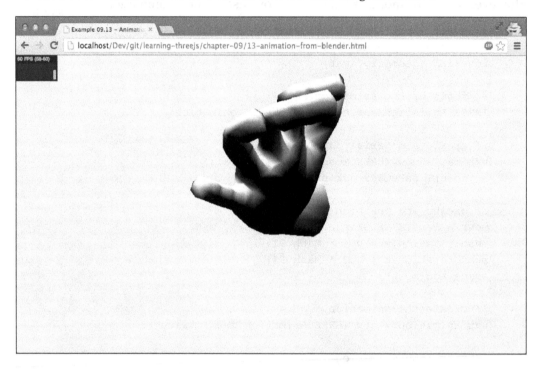

Besides Three.js's internal format, we can use a couple of other formats to define animations. The first one we'll look at is loading a collada model.

Loading an animation from a collada model

Loading a model from a collada file works in the same manner as for the other formats. First you have to include the correct loader JavaScript file:

```
<script type="text/javascript"
  src="../libs/ColladaLoader.js"></script>
```

Next we create a loader and use it to load the model file:

```
var loader = new THREE.ColladaLoader();
loader.load('../assets/models/monster.dae', function (collada) {

  var geom = collada.skins[0].geometry;
  var mat = collada.skins[0].material;

  // create a smooth skin
  geom.computeMorphNormals();
  mat.morphNormals = true;

  // create the animation
  meshAnim = new THREE.MorphAnimMesh(geom, mat);

  // position the mesh
  meshAnim.scale.set(0.15, 0.15, 0.15);
  meshAnim.rotation.x = -0.5 * Math.PI;
  meshAnim.position.x = -100;
  meshAnim.position.y = -60;

  scene.add(meshAnim);
  meshAnim.duration = 5000;
});
```

A collada file can contain much more than just a single mode, it can store complete scenes including cameras, lights, animations, and more. A good way to work with a collada model is to print out the result from the `loader.load` function to the console, and determine which components you want to use. In this case there was a single skinned mesh that used morph targets for its animation. If you look back at the section on morph targets earlier in this chapter, you'll see that in this example we use the exact same approach. We get the geometry and we get the material and create a `MorphAnimMesh` object. Even the render loop stays the same:

```
function render() {
  . . .
  meshAnim.updateAnimation( delta *1000 );
  . . .
}
```

And the result for this specific collada file looks like this:

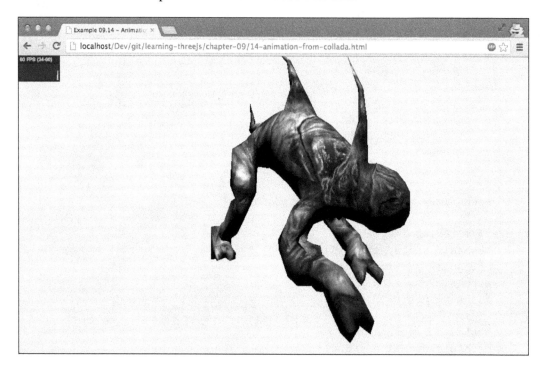

For collada files that contain bones, you can use the approach that was explained in the section on *Animating with bones*.

As a last example of an external model, that also uses morph targets, we'll look at the MD2 file format.

Animation loaded from a Quake model

The MD2 format was created to model Quake characters. Even though the newer engines use a different format, you can still find a lot of interesting models in the MD2 format. To use files in this format, we first have to convert them to the Three.js JavaScript format. You can do this online using the following site:

```
http://oos.moxiecode.com/js_webgl/md2_converter/
```

After conversion you'll get a JavaScript file in the Three.js format, which you can load and render using the `MorphAnimMesh` class. Since we've already seen how to do this in the previous sections, we'll skip the code where the model is loaded. One interesting thing though, is happening in the code. Instead of playing the complete animation, we provide the name of the animation that needs to be played:

```
mesh.playAnimation('crattack', 10);
```

The reason is that an MD2 file usually contains a number of different character animations. Luckily, though, Three.js provides functionality to determine the available animations and play them using the `playAnimation` function. The first thing we need to do is tell Three.js to parse the animations:

```
mesh.parseAnimations();
```

This results in a list of names for the animations that can be played using the `playAnimation` function. In our example you can select the name of the animation from the menu on the top right. The available animations are determined like this:

```
mesh.parseAnimations();

var animLabels = [];
for (var key in mesh.geometry.animations) {
  if (key === 'length' ||
    !mesh.geometry.animations.hasOwnProperty(key))
      continue;
  animLabels.push(key);
}

gui.add(controls,'animations',animLabels).onChange(function(e) {
  mesh.playAnimation(controls.animations,controls.fps);
});
```

Whenever an animation from the menu is selected the `mesh.playAnimation` function is called, with the specified animation name. The example that demonstrates this can be found here: `15-animation-from-md2.html`. Refer to the following screenshot:

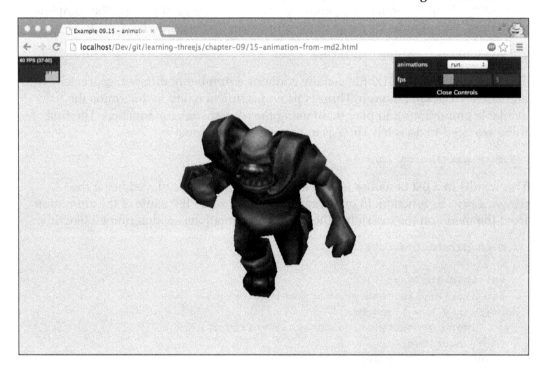

Summary

In this chapter we've looked at different ways you can animate your scene. We started with some basic animation tricks, moved on to camera movement and control and ended with animation models using morph targets and skeleton/bones animations. The most important things to remember from this chapter are:

- Once you have the `render` loop in place, adding animations is very easy. Just change a property of the mesh and the next rendering step Three.js will render the updated mesh.

- Three.js comes with a lot of different camera controls. Even though they do somewhat look the same, they are useful for different purposes. If you can't find one that exactly fits your needs, look at the code on how to configure it, or use it as a base for your own version.

- If you want a camera control that only allows you to look around while moving through a scene you can use the `PathControl`.

- There are two main forms of animating models. Using morph targets or using skeleton animation. When you use morph targets you morph your model from one keyframe to the other to create an animation. When you use skeleton animation you animate the model by moving the bones. Based on the bones' movement, Three.js will update the vertices attached to that bone.

- When loading models, a good place to start is just printing out the model to the console. Depending on the editor you might need to manually create new models, update materials, or fix other small issues.

- Three.js has two great helper meshes for working with morph targets and skeletons. For morph targets use the `MorphAnimMesh` class and for skeleton animations use the `SkinnedMesh` class.

In previous chapters we've already looked at the various materials you can use to skin your objects. For instance, we've seen how you can change the color, shininess, and opacity of these materials. What we haven't discussed in detail yet, however, is how you can use external images (also called textures) together with these materials. With textures you can easily create objects that look like they are made of wood, metal, stone, and much more. In the following chapter we'll explore all the different aspects of textures and how they are used in Three.js.

10
Loading and Working with Textures

In *Chapter 4*, *Working with Three.js Materials*, we've introduced you to the various materials that are available in Three.js. In that chapter, however, we didn't talk about applying textures to meshes yet. In this chapter, we'll look at that subject. More specifically in this chapter, we'll discuss the following topics:

- Loading textures in Three.js and applying them to a mesh
- Using bump and normal maps to apply depth and detail to a mesh
- Creating fake shadows using a light map
- Adding detailed reflection to a material using an environment map
- Using a specular map to set the 'shininess' of specific parts of the mesh
- Fine tuning the mapping with customizing the UV mapping of a mesh
- Using the HTML5 canvas and video element as input for a texture

These previous subjects all have to do with loading and displaying textures. Additionally, in this chapter, we'll also have a quick look at how you can create your own custom shaders by creating a vertex and a fragment shader. We start, however, with the most basic example, where we show you how to load and apply a texture.

Using textures in materials

There are different ways textures are used in Three.js. You can use them to define the colors of the mesh, but you can also use them to define shininess, bumps ,and reflections. The first example we look at, though, is the most basic approach where we use a texture to define the colors of the individual pixels of a mesh.

Loading a texture and applying it to mesh

The most basic usage of a texture is when it's set as a map on a material. When you use this material, together with geometry to create a mesh, the mesh will be colored, based on the supplied texture.

Loading a texture and using it on a mesh can be done in the following manner:

```
function createMesh(geom, imageFile) {
  var texture = THREE.ImageUtils.loadTexture
    ("../assets/textures/general/" + imageFile)

  var mat = new THREE.MeshPhongMaterial();
  mat.map = texture;

  var mesh = new THREE.Mesh(geom, mat);
  return mesh;
}
```

In this code sample we use the THREE.ImageUtils.loadTexture function to load an image file from a specific location. You can use PNG, GIF, or JPEG images as an input for a texture. Note that loading textures is done asynchronously. In our scenario this isn't an issue since we have a render loop, where we render the scene around 60 times per second. If you want to wait until a texture is loaded you could use the following approach:

```
texture = THREE.ImageUtils.loadTexture('texture.png', {},
  0020function() { renderer.render(scene); });
```

In this example we supply a callback function to loadTexture. This callback is called when the texture is loaded. In our examples, we don't use the callback and rely on the render loop to eventually show the texture when it's loaded.

You can use pretty much every image you'd like as texture. For best results, however, use a square texture whose dimensions are a power of 2. So dimensions such as 256 x 256, 512 x 512, 1024 x 1024, and so on work the best.

Since the pixels of a texture (also called **texels**) usually don't map one-to-one on the pixels of the face, the texture needs to be magnified or minified. For this purpose, WebGL and Three.js, offers a couple of different options. You specify how the texture is magnified by setting the magFilter property, and how it is minified with the minFilter property. These properties can be set to the following two basic values:

Name	Description
THREE.NearestFilter	This filter uses the color of the nearest texel that it can find. When used for magnification, this will result in blockiness, and when used for minification the result will lose much detail.
THREE.LinearFilter	This filter is more advanced and uses the color value of the four neighboring texels to determine the correct color. You'll still lose much detail in minification, but the magnificatio006E will be much more smooth, and less blocky.

Besides these basic values, we can also use a mipmap. A **mipmap** is a set of texture images, each half the size of the previous one. These are created when you load the texture and allow for much smoother filtering. So when you've got a square texture (as a power of 2) you can use a couple of additional approaches for better filtering. The properties can be set using the following values:

Name	Description
THREE. NearestMipMapNearestFilter	This property selects the mipmap that best maps the required resolution and applies the nearest filter principle that we discussed in the previous table. Magnification is still blocky, but minification looks much better.
THREE. NearestMipMapLinearFilter	This property selects not a single mipmap but the two nearest mipmap levels. On both these levels a nearest filter is applied to get two intermediate results. These two results are passed through a linear filter to get the final result.
THREE. LinearMipMapNearestFilter	This property selects the mipmap that best maps the required resolution and applies the linear filter principle we discussed in the previous table.
THREE. LinearMipMapLinearFilter	This property selects not a single mipmap, but the two nearest mipmap levels. On both these levels a linear filter is applied to get two intermediate results. These two results are passed through a linear filter to get the final result.

If you don't specify the `magFilter` and `minFilter` properties explicitly, Three. js uses the `THREE.LinearFilter` for the `magFilter` property and the `THREE. LinearMipMapLinearFilter` for the `minFilter` property. In our examples we'll just use these default properties. An example for the basic texture can be found here: `01-basic-texture.html`.

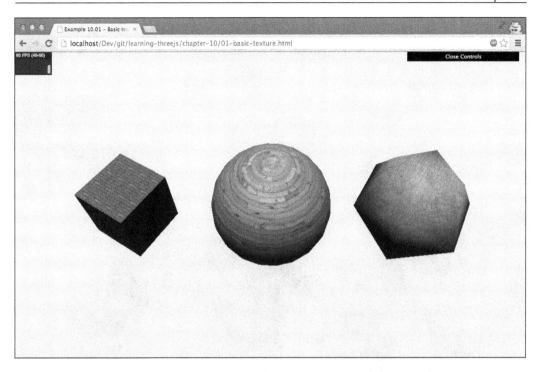

In this example we load a couple of textures (using the code you saw earlier) and apply them to various shapes. In these examples you can see that the textures nicely wrap around the shapes. When you create geometries in Three.js it makes sure that any texture that is used is applied correctly. This is done by something called **UV mapping** (more on this later in this chapter). With UV Mapping we tell the renderer which part of a texture should be applied to a specific face. The easiest example for this is the cube. The UV mapping for one of the faces looks like this: `(0,1),(0,0),(1,0),(1,1)`. This means that we use the complete texture (UV values range from 0 to 1) for this face.

In this example we've used the texture to define the color of the pixels of our mesh. We can also use textures for other purposes. The following two examples are used to define how shading is applied to a material. You use this to create bumps and wrinkles on the surface of the mesh.

Using a bump map to create wrinkles

A **bump map** is used to add more depth to a material. You can see this in action the best way by opening up the following example: `02-bump-map.html`. Refer to the following screenshot:

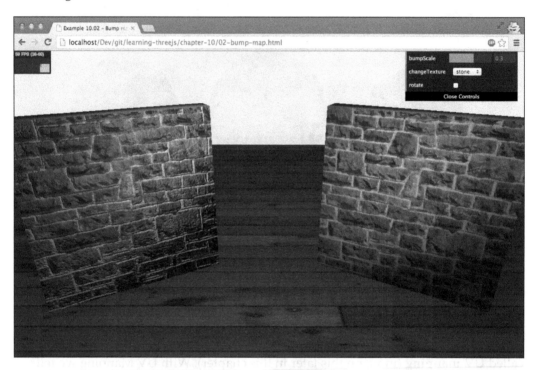

In this example you can see that the left wall looks much more detailed and seems to have much more depth, when you compare it with the wall on the right. This is done by setting an additional texture, a so-called bump map, on the material:

```
function createMesh(geom, imageFile, bump) {
  var texture = THREE.ImageUtils.loadTexture(
    "../assets/textures/general/" + imageFile)
  var mat = new THREE.MeshPhongMaterial();
  mat.map = texture;

  var bump = THREE.ImageUtils.loadTexture(
    "../assets/textures/general/" + bump)
  mat.bumpMap = bump;
```

```
mat.bumpScale = 0.2;


var mesh = new THREE.Mesh(geom, mat);
return mesh;
}
```

You can see in this code that besides setting the `map` property we also set the `bumpMap` property to a texture. Additionally, with the `bumpScale` property, we can set the height (or depth if set to a negative value) of the bumps. The textures used in this example are shown here:

The bump map is a grey scale image, but you can also use a color image. The intensity of the pixel defines the height of the bump. A bump map only contains the relative height of a pixel. It doesn't say anything about the direction of the slope. So the level of detail and perception of depth you can reach with a bump map is limited. For more details you can use a normal map.

Using more detailed bumps and wrinkles with a normal map

In a normal map, the height (displacement) is not stored, but the direction of the normal for each picture is stored. Without going into too much detail, with normal maps you can create very detailed looking models that still only use a small number of vertices and faces. For instance, have a look at the following example: `03-normal-map.html`.

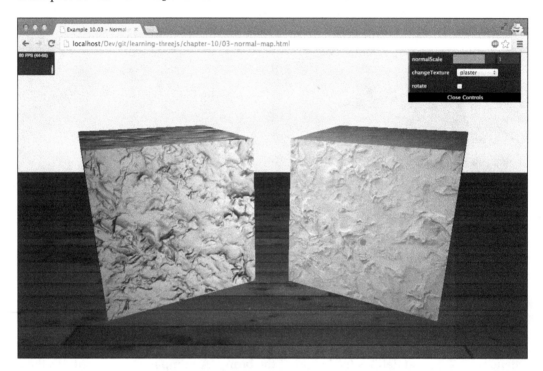

In this image you can see a very detailed plastered cube towards the left. The light source moves around the cubes, and you can see that the texture responds naturally to the light source. This provides a very realistic-looking model, and only requires a very simple model and a couple of textures. The following code fragment shows how to use a normal map from Three.js:

```
function createMesh(geom, imageFile, normal) {
  var t = THREE.ImageUtils.loadTexture
    ("../assets/textures/general/" + imageFile);
  var m = THREE.ImageUtils.loadTexture
    ("../assets/textures/general/" + normal);
  var mat2 = new THREE.MeshPhongMaterial({
```

```
    map: t,
    normalMap: m
  });
  var mesh = new THREE.Mesh(geom, mat2);
  return mesh;
}
```

The same approach is used here, as was done for the bump map. This time, though, we set the `normalMap` property to the normal texture. We can also define how pronounced the bumps look by setting the `normalScale` property: `mat.normalScale.set(1,1)`. With these two properties you can scale along the x and y axis. Best approach, though, is to keep these values the same for the best effect. Note that once again when these values are below zero, the heights inverse. The following screenshot shows both the texture (on the left) and the normal map (on the right).

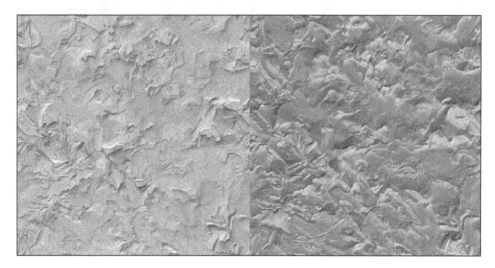

The problem with normal maps, however, is that they aren't very easy to create. You need to use specialized tools, such as Blender or Photoshop. They can use high resolution renderings or textures as input and create normal maps from them.

When modeling characters using a normal map is a good way to add lots of details to a low-polygon model. The following example shows how this is done.

Creating fake shadows using a light map

In the previous examples, we used specific maps to create real-looking shadows that react to the lighting in the room. There is an alternative option to create fake shadows. In this section we'll use a light map. A **light map** is a prerendered shadow that you can use to create the illusion of a real shadow. The following screenshot, from example 04-light-map.html, shows how this looks:

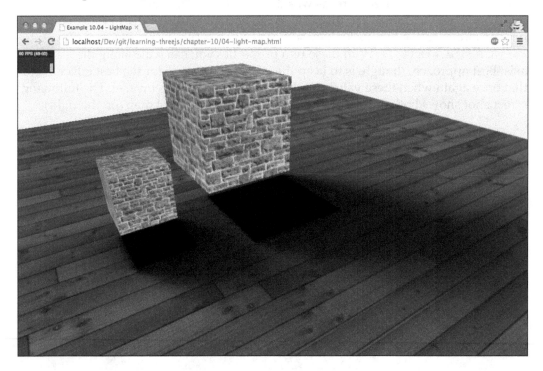

If you look at the previous example it shows a couple of very nice shadows, which seem to be cast by the two cubes. These shadows, however, are based on a light map texture that looks as follows:

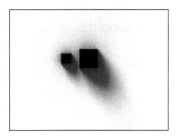

As you can see, the shadows as specified in the light map, are also shown as the shadows on the ground plane, creating the illusion of real shadows. You can use this technique to create high-resolution shadows, without incurring a heavy rendering penalty. This, of course, only works for static scenes. Using a light map is pretty much the same as using other textures with a couple of small differences.

```
var lm = THREE.ImageUtils.loadTexture(
    '../assets/textures/lightmap/lm-1.png');
var wood = THREE.ImageUtils.loadTexture(
    '../assets/textures/general/floor-wood.jpg');
var groundMaterial = new THREE.MeshBasicMaterial(
    {lightMap: lm, map: wood});
groundGeom.faceVertexUvs[1] = groundGeom.faceVertexUvs[0];
```

To apply a light map, we just need to set the `lightMap` property of the material to the light map we just showed. There is, however, an additional required step to get the light map to show up. We need to explicitly define the UV mapping (what part of the texture is shown on a face) for the light map. This needs to be done so you can apply and map the light map independently of the other textures. In our example, we just use the basic UV mapping, automatically created by Three.js when we created the ground plane. More information and background of why an explicit UV mapping is required can be found here: `http://stackoverflow.com/questions/15137695/three-js-lightmap-causes-an-error-webglrenderingcontext-gl-error-gl-invalid-op`

When the shadow map is positioned correctly, we need to place the cubes in the correct location, and we've got the example we just showed you.

Three.js provides another texture that you can use to fake advanced 3D effects. In the next section, we'll look at using environment maps for fake reflections.

Creating fake reflections using an environment map

Calculating environment reflections is very CPU-intensive and usually requires a ray tracer approach. If you want to use reflections in Three.js, you can still do that, but you'll have to fake it. You can fake it by creating a texture of the environment the object is in, and apply this to the specific object. First we'll show you the result we're aiming for (see `05-env-map-static.html`, also shown in the following screenshot):

In this screenshot you can see the sphere and cube reflect the environment. If you move your mouse around, you can also see that the reflection corresponds with the camera angle in relation to the city environment you see. To create this example we perform the following steps:

1. **Create a CubeMap object**: The first thing we need to do is create a `CubeMap` object. A cubeMap is a set of six textures that can be applied to each side of a cube.

2. **Create a cube with this Cubemap**: The cube created with the `CubeMap` object is the environment you see when you move the camera around. It gives the illusion that you're standing in an environment where you can look around. In reality you're inside a cube with textures rendered on the inside to give an illusion of space.

3. **Apply the CubeMap as a texture**: The same `CubeMap` object we used to simulate the environment can be used as a texture on the meshes. Three.js will make sure it looks like a reflection of the environment.

Creating a `CubeMap` object is pretty easy, once you've got the source material. What you need is six images that together make up a complete environment. So you need the following pictures: looking forward (`posz`), looking backward (`negz`), looking up (`posy`), looking down (`negy`), looking right (`posx`), and looking left (`negx`). Three.js will patch these together to create a seamless environment map. There are a couple of sites where you can download these pictures. The ones used in this example are from `http://www.humus.name/index.php?page=Textures`.

Once you've got the pictures, you can load them as shown in the following code fragment:

```
function createCubeMap() {

  var path = "../assets/textures/cubemap/parliament/";
  var format = '.jpg';
  var urls = [
    path + 'posx' + format, path + 'negx' + format,
    path + 'posy' + format, path + 'negy' + format,
    path + 'posz' + format, path + 'negz' + format
  ];

  var textureCube = THREE.ImageUtils.loadTextureCube( urls );
  return textureCube;
}
```

We again use the `THREE.ImageUtils` JavaScript object, but this time we pass in an array of textures to create the `CubeMap` object and use the `loadTextureCube` function. With this `CubeMap` object we first create a cube:

```
var textureCube = createCubeMap();
var shader = THREE.ShaderLib[ "cube" ];
shader.uniforms[ "tCube" ].value = textureCube;
var material = new THREE.ShaderMaterial( {
  fragmentShader: shader.fragmentShader,
  vertexShader: shader.vertexShader,
  uniforms: shader.uniforms,
  depthWrite: false,
  side: THREE.BackSide
});
cubeMesh = new THREE.Mesh(
  new THREE.CubeGeometry(100, 100, 100), material);
```

Three.js provides a specific shader that we can use with the THREE.ShaderMaterial class to create an environment based on the CubeMap object (var shader = THREE.ShaderLib["cube"];). We configure this shader with our CubeMap, create a mesh, and add it to the scene. This mesh, if seen from the inside, represents the fake environment we're standing in.

This same CubeMap instance can be applied to the meshes we want to render to create the fake reflection:

```
var sphere1 = createMesh(
  new THREE.SphereGeometry(10, 15, 15), "plaster.jpg");
sphere1.material.envMap = textureCube;
sphere1.rotation.y = -0.5;
sphere1.position.x = 12;
sphere1.position.y = 5;
scene.add(sphere1);

var sphere2 = createMesh(new THREE.CubeGeometry(10, 15, 15),
  "plaster.jpg","plaster-normal.jpg");
sphere2.material.envMap = textureCube;
sphere2.rotation.y = 0.5;
sphere2.position.x = -12;
sphere2.position.y = 5;
scene.add(sphere2);
```

As you can see, we set the envMap property of the material to the cubeMap object we created, the result is a scene where it looks like we're standing in a wide, outdoors environment, where the meshes reflect this environment. If you use the sliders you can set the reflectivity property of the material, and, as the name implies, this determines how much of the environment is reflected by the material. Besides reflection, Three.js also allows you to use a CubeMap instance for refraction (glass-like objects):

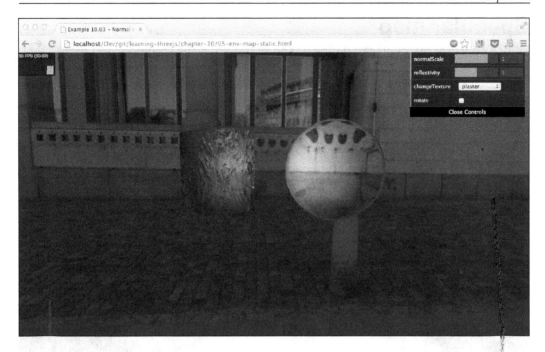

To get this effect we just need to change the loading of the textures to this:

```
var textureCube = THREE.ImageUtils.loadTextureCube(
    urls, new THREE.CubeRefractionMapping());
```

And you can control the `refraction` ratio with the `refraction` property on the material, just like with the `reflection` property. In this example we've used a static environment map for the meshes. In other words we only saw the environment reflection and not the other meshes in this environment. In the following example we'll show you how you can create a reflection that also shows the other objects in the scene.

The last of the basic material we'll look at is the specular map.

Specular map

With a **specular map** you can define a map that defines the shininess and the highlight color of a material. For instance, in the following screenshot, we've used a specular map together with a normal map to render a globe. You can see this example if you open `06-specular-map.html` in your browser. The result of this is also shown in the following screenshot:

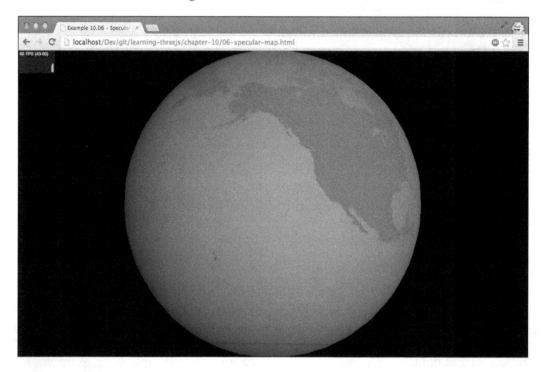

In this screenshot you can see that the oceans are highlighted and reflect light. The continents, on the other hand, are very dark and don't reflect (much) light. For this effect we didn't use any specific normal textures, but only a normal map to show heights and the following specular map to highlight the oceans:

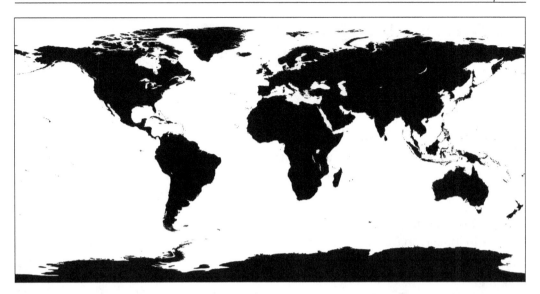

Basically what happens is that the higher the value of the pixel (from black to white) the shinier the surface will appear. A specular map is usually used together with the `specular` property that you can use to determine the color of the reflection. In this case it is set to red:

```
var specularTexture=THREE.ImageUtils.loadTexture(
  "../assets/textures/planets/EarthSpec.png");
var normalTexture=THREE.ImageUtils.loadTexture(
  "../assets/textures/planets/EarthNormal.png");

var planetMaterial = new THREE.MeshPhongMaterial();
planetMaterial.specularMap = specularTexture;
planetMaterial.specular = new THREE.Color( 0xff0000 );
planetMaterial.shininess = 1;

planetMaterial.normalMap = normalTexture;
```

Also note that the best effects are usually realized with a low shininess, but depending on the lighting, the specular map you use, you might need to experiment to get the desired effect.

Advanced usage of textures

In the previous section, we've seen some basic texture usages. Three.js also provides options for more advanced texture usage. In this section we'll look at a couple of options that Three.js provides.

Custom UV mapping

We'll start of with a deeper look at UV mappings. We explained earlier that with UV mapping you can specify what part of a texture is shown on a specific face. When you create a geometry in Three.js, these mappings will also be automatically created based on the type of geometry you created. In most cases you don't really need to change this default UV mapping. A good way to understand how UV mappings work is to look at an example from Blender:

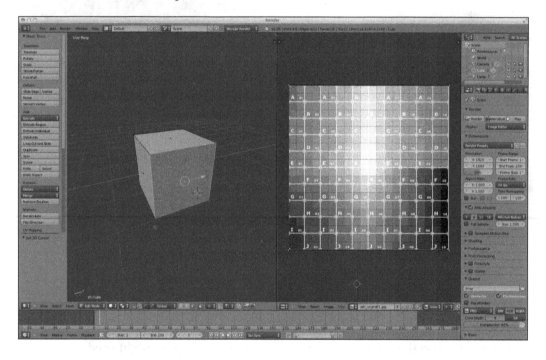

In this example you see two windows. The window on the left contains a cube geometry. The window on the right is the UV mapping, where we've loaded an example texture to show how the mapping is. In this example we've selected a single face for the window on the left and the window on the right shows the UV mapping for this face. As you can see each vertex of the face is positioned in one of the corners of the UV mapping on the right (the small circles). This means that the complete texture will be used for that face. All the other faces of this cube are mapped in the same manner, so the result will show a cube where each face shows the complete texture; see `07-uv-mapping.html` also shown in the following screenshot:

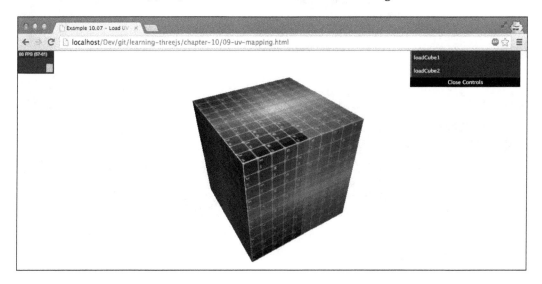

This is the default for a cube in Blender (also in Three.js). Let's change the UV mapping and see how this changes the way the texture is applied. Instead of showing the complete texture on each side, we let each face show only a part of the texture.

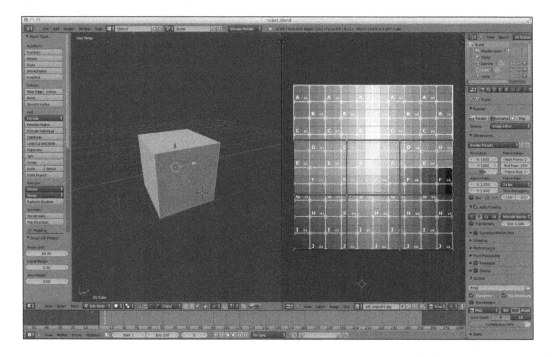

If we now show this in Three.js, you can see that the texture is applied differently.

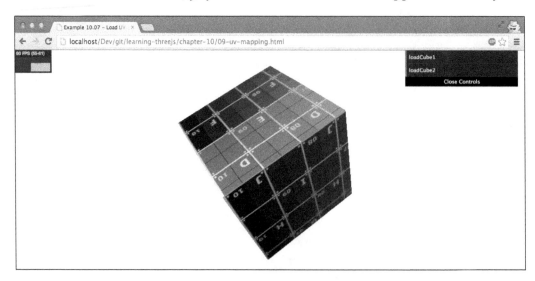

Customizing UV mappings is normally done from programs such as Blender, especially when the models become more complex. The most important part to remember here is that UV mappings run in two dimensions u and v, from 0 to 1. To customize the UV mapping you need to define, for each face, what part of the texture should be shown. You do this by defining the u and v coordinates for each of the vertices that make up the face.

Next, we'll look at how textures can be repeated, which is done by some internal UV mapping tricks.

Repeat wrapping

When you apply a texture to a geometry created by Three.js, Three.js will try to apply the texture as optimaly as possible. For instance, for cubes this means each side will show the complete texture, and for spheres the complete texture is wrapped around the sphere. There are, however, situations where you don't want the texture to spread around a complete face or the complete geometry, but have the texture repeat itself. Three.js provides detailed functionality that allows you to control this. An example where you can play around with the repeat properties is provided in this example: 08-repeat-wrapping.html

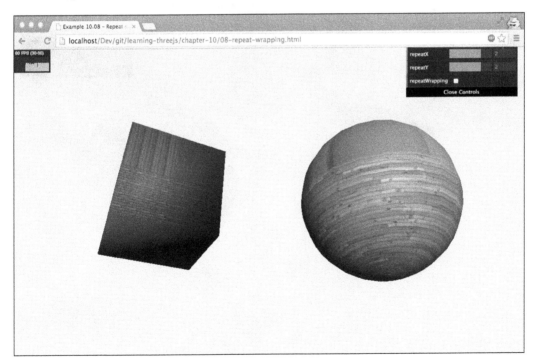

In this example you can set the property that controls how a texture repeats itself.

Before this property has the desired effect, you need to make sure you set the wrapping of the texture to THREE.RepeatWrapping as shown in the following code snippet:

```
cube.material.map.wrapS = THREE.RepeatWrapping;
cube.material.map.wrapT = THREE.RepeatWrapping;
```

The wrapS property defines how you want the texture to behave along its x-axis and the wrapT property defines how the texture should behave along its y-axis. Three.js provides two options for this, which are as follows:

- THREE.RepeatWrapping allows the texture to repeat itself.
- THREE.ClampToEdgeWrapping is a default setting. With THREE.ClampToEdgeWrapping the last pixel of the texture is stretched out to fill the remaining space

If you disable the **repeatWrapping** menu option, the THREE.ClampToEdgeWrapping option is used.

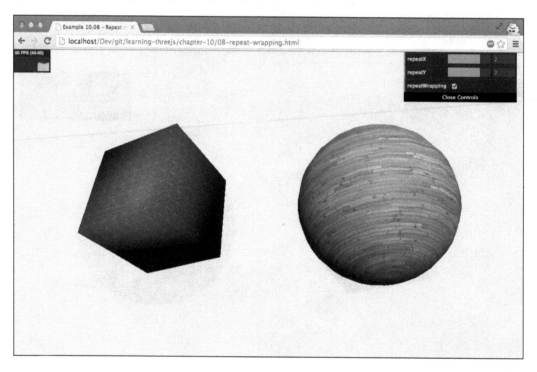

If we use `THREE.RepeatWrapping` we can set the `repeat` property as shown in the following code fragment:

```
cube.material.map.repeat.set(repeatX, repeatY);
```

The `repeatX` variable defines how often the texture is repeated along its x-axis and the `repeatY` variable defines the same for the y-axis. If these values are set to `1`, the texture won't repeat itself; if set to a higher value, you'll see that the texture will start repeating. You can also use values less than 1. In that case you can see that you'll zoom in on the texture. If you set the repeat value to a negative value, the texture will be mirrored.

When you change the repeat property, Three.js will automatically update the textures and render with this new setting. If you change from `THREE.RepeatWrapping` to `THREE.ClampToEdgeWrapping` you need to explicitly update the texture:

```
cube.material.map.needsUpdate = true;
```

So far we've only used static images for our textures. Three.js, however, also has the option to use the HTML5 canvas as a texture.

Rendering to canvas and using it as a texture

In this section we're going to look at two different examples. First we're going to look at how you can use the canvas to create a simple texture and apply it to a mesh, and after that we'll go one step further and create a canvas that can be used as a bump map using a randomly generated pattern.

Using canvas as a texture

In the first example we will use the `literally` library (from `http://literallycanvas.com/`) to create an interactive canvas that you can draw on, see the lower left corner in the following screenshot. You can view this example here: `09-canvas-texture`.

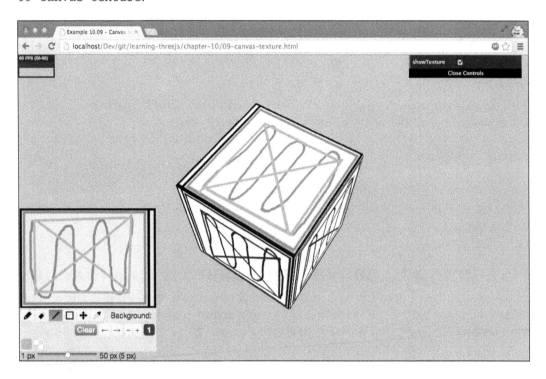

Anything you draw on this canvas is directly rendered on the cube as a texture. Accomplishing this in Three.js is really simple, and only takes a couple of steps. The first thing we need to do is create a canvas element and, for this specific example, configure it to be used with the `literally` library:

```
<div class="fs-container">
<div id="canvas-output" style="float:left">
</div>
</div>
...
var canvas = document.createElement("canvas");
$('#canvas-output')[0].appendChild(canvas);
$('#canvas-output').literallycanvas(
  {imageURLPrefix: '../libs/literally/img'});
```

Nothing to fancy here. We just create a `canvas` element from JavaScript and add it to a specific `div` element. With the `literallycanvas` call we can create the drawing tools that you can use to directly draw on the canvas. Next we need to create a texture that uses the canvas drawing as its input:

```
function createMesh(geom) {

    var canvasMap = new THREE.Texture(canvas);
    var mat = new THREE.MeshPhongMaterial();
    mat.map = canvasMap;
    var mesh = new THREE.Mesh(geom,mat);

    return mesh;
}
```

As the code shows, the only thing you need to do to is pass by reference the canvas element when you create a new texture: `new THREE.Texture(canvas)`. This will create a texture that uses the canvas as its material. All that is left is to update the material whenever we render so the last version of the canvas drawing is shown on the cube:

```
function render() {
    stats.update();

    cube.rotation.y += 0.01;
    cube.rotation.x += 0.01;

    cube.material.map.needsUpdate = true;
    requestAnimationFrame(render);
    webGLRenderer.render(scene, camera);
}
```

To inform Three.js that we want to update the texture, we just set the `needsUpdate` property of the texture to `true`. In this example we've used the canvas as input for the most simple of textures. We can of course use this same idea for all the different types of maps we've seen so far. In the next example we'll use it as a bump map.

Using canvas as a bump map

As we've seen earlier in this chapter we can create a simple wrinkled texture with a bump map. The higher the intensity of a pixel in this map, the higher the wrinkle. Since a bump map is just a simple black and white image, nothing keeps us from creating this on a canvas and using that canvas as an input for the bump map.

In the following example, we use a canvas to generate a random gray scale image and we use that image as an input for the bump map we apply to the cube. See example `09-canvas-texture-bumpmap.html`:

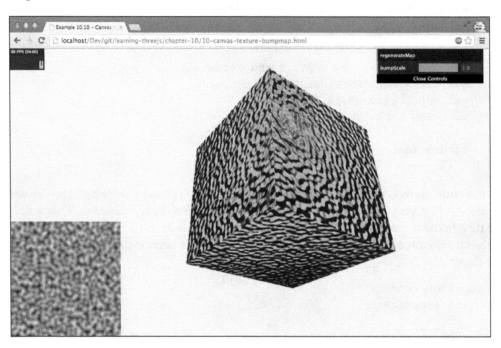

The JavaScript code required for this is not that different from the previous example we explained. We need to create a canvas element and fill this canvas with some random noise. For the noise, we use **Perlin noise**. Perlin noise (`http://en.wikipedia.org/wiki/Perlin_noise`) generates a very natural looking random texture, as you can see in the preceding screenshot. We use the Perlin noise function from `https://github.com/wwwtyro/perlin.js` for this like so:

```
var ctx = canvas.getContext("2d");
function fillWithPerlin(perlin, ctx) {

  for (var x = 0; x < 512; x++) {
    for (var y = 0; y < 512; y++) {
      var base = new THREE.Color(0xffffff);
      var value = perlin.noise(x / 10, y / 10, 0);
      base.multiplyScalar(value);
      ctx.fillStyle = "#" + base.getHexString();
      ctx.fillRect(x, y, 1, 1);
    }
  }
}
```

We use the `perlin.noise` function to create a value from 0 to 1 based on the x and y coordinate of the canvas. This value is used to draw a single pixel on the canvas. Doing this for all the pixels creates the random map you can also see in the lower left corner of the previous screenshot. This map can then easily be used as a bump map:

```
var bumpMap = new THREE.Texture(canvas);

var mat = new THREE.MeshPhongMaterial();
mat.color = new THREE.Color(0x77ff77);
mat.bumpMap = bumpMap;
bumpMap.needsUpdate = true;

var mesh = new THREE.Mesh(geom, mat);
return mesh;
```

The final input we use for the texture is another HTML element: the HTML5 video element.

Using the output from a video as a texture

If you've read the previous paragraph on rendering to canvas, you might have thought about rendering video to canvas and using that as input for a texture. That is an option, but Three.js (through WebGL) already has direct support to use the HTML5 video element: `11-video-texture.html`. Refer to the following screenshot:

Using video as input for a texture is, just like using canvas, very easy. First off, we need to have a video element to play the video:

```
<video  id="video"
  style="display: none;
  position: absolute; left: 15px; top: 75px;"
  src="../assets/movies/Big_Buck_Bunny_small.ogv"
  controls="true" autoplay="true">
</video>
```

Just a basic HTML5 video element that we set to play automatically. Next we can configure Three.js to use this video as an input for a texture:

```
var video   = document.getElementById('video');
texture = new THREE.Texture(video);
texture.minFilter = THREE.LinearFilter;
texture.magFilter = THREE.LinearFilter;
texture.generateMipmaps = false;
```

Since our video isn't square we need to make sure we disable the mipmap generation on the material. We also set some simple high-performance filters (see the section *Loading a texture and applying it to mesh,* in this chapter), since the material changes very often. All that is left to do now is create a mesh and set the texture. In this example, we've used the `MeshFaceMaterial` together with `MeshBasicMaterial`:

```
var materialArray = [];
materialArray.push(new THREE.MeshBasicMaterial(
  {color: 0x0051ba}));
materialArray.push(new THREE.MeshBasicMaterial(
  {color: 0x0051ba}));
materialArray.push(new THREE.MeshBasicMaterial(
  {color: 0x0051ba}));
materialArray.push(new THREE.MeshBasicMaterial(
  {color: 0x0051ba}));
materialArray.push(new THREE.MeshBasicMaterial(
  {map: texture }));
materialArray.push(new THREE.MeshBasicMaterial(
  {color: 0xff51ba}));

var faceMaterial = new THREE.MeshFaceMaterial(materialArray);
var mesh = new THREE.Mesh(geom, faceMaterial);
```

All that is left to do is to make sure that in our `render` loop we update the texture:

```
if ( video.readyState === video.HAVE_ENOUGH_DATA ) {
  if (texture) texture.needsUpdate = true;
}
```

In this example we just rendered the video to one side of the cube, but since this is a normal texture, we could do anything we want with it. We could, for instance, divide it along the sides of a cube using a custom UV mapping or we could even use video input as input for a bump map.

Summary

Hence we complete this chapter on textures. As you've seen, there are lots of different kinds of textures available in Three.js each with their different uses. The most important steps to remember when working with textures are the following:

- You can use any image in PNG, JPG, or GIF format as a texture. Loading these images is done asynchronously, so remember to either use a rendering loop, or add a callback when you load the texture.

- You'll get the best result when you use a square texture whose size is a power of 2 (for example, 256x256, 512x512, and 1024x1024). The reason is that scaling such textures can be done using mipmaps which provide better results.

- You can use textures to create great-looking objects from low poly models. Using bump maps and normal maps allows you to create fake detailed depth and shadows on simple models.

- In the standard way, Three.js doesn't support reflections out of the box aren't supported. You can however easily fake reflections by using an environment map.

- If you want a direct control over a surface's shininess, you can use a specular map.

- You can configure textures to be repeated by setting the `repeat` property on the texture. Remember to also change the wrapping for the material from `ClampToEdgeWrapping` to `RepeatWrapping`.

- With Three.js, it is also easy to create dynamic textures using either the HTML5 canvas element or the video element. Just define a texture with these elements as their input and set the `needsUpdate` property to `true` whenever you want the texture to be updated.

With this chapter out of the way we've pretty much covered all the important concepts of Three.js. We haven't however, looked at an interesting feature Three.js offers called **post processing**. With post processing you can add effect to your scene after it is rendered. You could, for instance, blur or colorize your scene, or add a TV-like effect using scan lines. In the next chapter we'll look at post processing and how you can apply it to your scene.

11

Custom Shaders and Render Post Processing

We're getting to the end of the book, and in this chapter we'll look at the one main feature of the Three.js library that we haven't touched upon: **render post processing**. Besides this subject in the chapter, we'll also introduce you to how you can create custom shaders. The main points that we'll discuss in this chapter are the following:

- Setting up a Three.js library for post processing
- The basic post processing passes provided by Three.js, such as `BloomPass` and `FilmPass`
- Applying effects to a part of the scene by using masks
- Using the `TexturePass` to store the rendered results
- Using the `ShaderPass` to add even more basic post processing effects, such as sepia filters, mirror effects, and color adjustments
- Using the `ShaderPass` for various blurring effects and more advanced filters
- Creating a custom post processing effect by writing a simple shader

In *Chapter 1, Creating Your First 3D Scene with Three.js*, we set up a `render` loop that we've used throughout the book to render and animate our scene. For post processing, we need to make a couple of changes to this setup to allow the Three.js library to post process the final rendering. In the first section we'll look at how to do this.

Setting up the post processing

To set up the Three.js library for post processing, we need to make a couple of changes in our current setup by taking the following steps:

1. Create an `EffectComposer` object that we can use to add the post processing passes.

2. Configure this object so that it'll render our scene and apply any additional post processing steps.

3. In the `render` loop, use the `EffectComposer` to render the scene, apply the passes, and show the output.

As always, we have an example that you can use to experiment with and adopt for your own uses. The first example for this chapter can be accessed in the file `01-basic-effect-composer.html`. You can use the menu in the top-right corner to modify the properties of the post processing steps used in this example, as shown in the following screenshot:

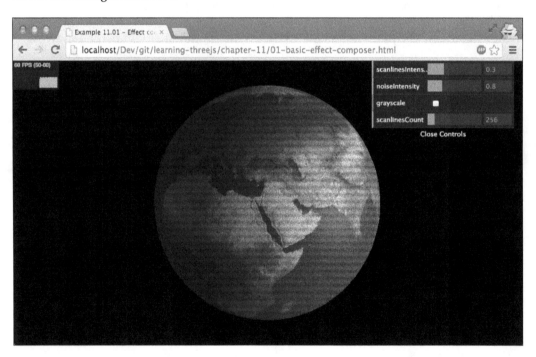

Creating the EffectComposer object

Let's first look at the additional JavaScript files that you need to include. These files can be found in the Three.js distribution in the `examples/js/postprocessing` and `examples/js/shaders` folders.

The minimal set is shown in the following code snippet:

```
<script type="text/javascript"
        src="../libs/postprocessing/EffectComposer.js"></script>
<script type="text/javascript"
        src="../libs/postprocessing/MaskPass.js"></script>
<script type="text/javascript"
        src="../libs/postprocessing/RenderPass.js"></script>
<script type="text/javascript"
        src="../libs/shaders/CopyShader.js"></script>
<script type="text/javascript"
        src="../libs/postprocessing/ShaderPass.js"></script>
```

The `EffectComposer.js` file provides the `EffectComposer` object that allows us to add the post processing steps. The `MaskPass.js`, `ShaderPass.js`, and `CopyShader.js` files are used internally by the `EffectComposer`, and the `RenderPass.js` file allows us to add a rendering pass to our `EffectComposer` object. Without that pass, our scene wouldn't be rendered at all.

For this example, we will add two additional JavaScript files to add a film-like effect to our scene, as follows:

```
<script type="text/javascript"
        src="../libs/postprocessing/FilmPass.js"></script>
<script type="text/javascript"
        src="../libs/shaders/FilmShader.js"></script>
```

The first thing that we need to do is create an `EffectComposer` object. You can do this by passing in a `WebGLRenderer` to its constructor as shown:

```
var composer = new THREE.EffectComposer(webGLRenderer);
```

Next, we will add various passes to this composer.

Configuring the EffectComposer object for post processing

Each pass is executed in the sequence that it is added to the `EffectComposer`. The first pass that we will add is a `RenderPass`. The following pass will render our scene, but doesn't output it to the screen:

```
var renderPass = new THREE.RenderPass(scene, camera);
composer.addPass(renderPass);
```

To create a `RenderPass`, we will pass in the scene that we want to render, and the camera that we want to use. With the `addPass()` function, we will add this `RenderPass` to the `EffectComposer`. The next step is to add another pass that will output its result to the screen. Not all of the available passes allow this (more on that later), but the `FilmPass` that is used in this example allows us to output the result of its pass to the screen. To add a `FilmPass`, we first need to create it, and then add it to the composer. The resulting code will look like the following code snippet:

```
var renderPass = new THREE.RenderPass(scene,camera);
var effectFilm = new THREE.FilmPass(0.8, 0.325, 256, false);
effectFilm.renderToScreen=true;

var composer = new THREE.EffectComposer(webGLRenderer);
composer.addPass(renderPass);
composer.addPass(effectFilm);
```

As you can see, we have created a `FilmPass` and set the `renderToScreen` property to `true`. This pass is added after the `RenderPass`, so that when this composer is used we can see the output.

Updating the render loop

Now, we just need to make a small modification to our `render` loop in order to use the composer instead of the `WebGLRenderer`:

```
var clock = new THREE.Clock();
function render() {
    stats.update();

    var delta = clock.getDelta();
    orbitControls.update(delta);

    sphere.rotation.y += 0.002;

    requestAnimationFrame(render);
    composer.render(delta);
}
```

Here, we have removed webGLRenderer.render(scene, camera); and replaced it with composer.render(delta);. This will call the render() function on our EffectComposer and, since we had set the renderToScreen of the FilmPass to true, the result from the FilmPass is shown on the screen.

With this basic setup, we'll look at the available post processing passes in the later couple of sections.

Post processing passes

The Three.js library comes with a number of post processing passes that you can use directly with an EffectComposer object. The following table gives an overview of the passes that are available. Note that it's best to play around with the examples in this chapter to see the result of these passes and understand what is happening.

Pass name	Description
BloomPass	An effect that makes the light areas bleed into the darker areas. It simulates an effect where the camera is overwhelmed by the extremely bright light.
DotScreenPass	This applies a layer of black dots across the screen that represents the original image.
FilmPass	This pass simulates a TV screen by applying scanlines and distortions.
MaskPass	This allows you to apply a mask to the current image. The subsequent passes are only applied to the masked area.
RenderPass	This pass renders a scene based on the supplied scene and camera.
SavePass	When this pass is executed, it makes a copy of the current rendering step that you can use later. This pass isn't that useful in practice and we won't use it in any of our examples.
ShaderPass	This allows you to pass in custom shaders for the advanced or custom post processing passes.
TexturePass	This pass stores the current state of the composer in a texture that you can use as input for the other EffectComposer instances.

Let's start with a number of simple passes.

Simple post processing passes

For the simple passes, we'll look at what we can do with the `FilmPass`, the `BloomPass`, and the `DotScreenPass`. For these passes, example `02-post-processing-simple-passes.html` is available; it allows you to experiment with these passes and see how they affect the original output, as shown in the following screenshot:

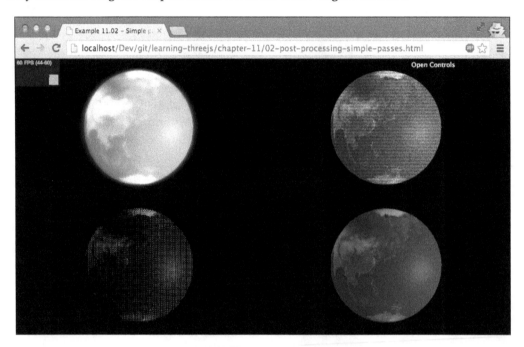

In this example, we have shown four scenes at the same time, and in each scene a different post processing pass is added. The one in the top-right corner shows the `FilmPass`, the top-left shows the `BloomPass`, the bottom-left shows the `DotScreenPass`, and the bottom-right shows the original render.

In this example we have also used a `ShaderPass` and `TexturePass` to reuse the output from the original rendering as input for the other three scenes. So before we look at the individual passes, let's look at these two passes first:

```
var renderPass = new THREE.RenderPass(scene, camera);
var effectCopy = new THREE.ShaderPass(THREE.CopyShader);
effectCopy.renderToScreen = true;

var composer = new THREE.EffectComposer(webGLRenderer);
composer.addPass(renderPass);
composer.addPass(effectCopy);

var renderScene = new THREE.TexturePass(composer.renderTarget2);
```

In this piece of code, we have set up an `EffectComposer` that will output the default scene (the one at the bottom-right corner). This composer has two passes: the `RenderPass`, which renders the scene, and the `ShaderPass`. If we configure the `ShaderPass` with a `CopyShader`, it will render the output, without any further post processing, to the screen if we set the `renderToScreen` property to `true`. If you've looked at the example, you can see that we have shown the same scene four times, but with a different effect applied. We could render the scene from scratch by using a `RenderPass` four times, but that would be a bit of a waste since we can just reuse the output from this first composer. To do this, we will create a `TexturePass` and pass in the `composer.renderTarget2` value. We can now use the `renderScene` variable as input for our other composers, without having to render the scene from scratch. Let's revisit the `FilmPass` first and see how we can use the `TexturePass` as input.

Using the FilmPass to create a TV-like effect

We've already looked at how to create a `FilmPass` in the first section of this chapter; let's now see how to use this effect together with the `TexturePass` from the previous section. This is shown in the code snippet that follows:

```
var effectFilm = new THREE.FilmPass(0.8, 0.325, 256, false);
effectFilm.renderToScreen=true;

var composer4 = new THREE.EffectComposer(webGLRenderer);
composer4.addPass(renderScene);
composer4.addPass(effectFilm);
```

The only step that you need to take to use the `TexturePass` is to add it as the first pass in your composer. We can add the `FilmPass` next, and the effect is applied. The `FilmPass` itself takes four parameters as shown:

Property	Description
noiseIntensity	This property allows you to control how grainy the scene is.
scanlinesIntensity	The `FilmPass` adds a number of scanlines to the scene. With this property, you can define how prominent these scanlines are.
scanlinesCount	The number of scanlines that are shown can be controlled with this property.
grayscale	If set to `true`, the output will be converted to a gray scale.

There are actually two ways in which you can pass these parameters. In this example we have passed them in as arguments to the constructor, but you can also set them directly, as in the following code snippet:

```
effectFilm.uniforms.grayscale.value = controls.grayscale;
effectFilm.uniforms.nIntensity.value = controls.noiseIntensity;
effectFilm.uniforms.sIntensity.value =
                    controls.scanlinesIntensity;
effectFilm.uniforms.sCount.value = controls.scanlinesCount;
```

In this approach we will use the `uniforms` property. It is used to communicate directly with WebGL. In the section where we will talk about creating a custom shader (later in this chapter), we'll go a bit deeper into `uniforms`; for now all that you need to know is that you can now directly update the configuration of post processing passes and shaders and directly see the results.

Adding a bloom effect to the scene with the BloomPass

The effect you see in the upper-left corner is called the **bloom effect**. When you apply the bloom effect, the bright areas of a scene will be made more prominent and bleed into the darker areas. The code to create a `BloomPass` is shown as follows:

```
var bloomPass = new THREE.BloomPass(3, 25, 5, 256);
var composer3 = new THREE.EffectComposer(webGLRenderer);
composer3.addPass(renderScene);
composer3.addPass(bloomPass);
composer3.addPass(effectCopy);
```

If you compare this with the `EffectComposer` that we used with the `FilmPass`, you'll notice that we add an additional pass here, the `effectCopy`. This step, which we had also used for the normal output, doesn't add any special effect, but just copies the output from the last pass to the screen. We need to add this step, since the `BloomPass` can't render directly to the screen. The following table lists the properties that you can set on the `BloomPass`:

Property	Description
Strength	This defines the strength of the bloom effect. The higher it is, the more brighter the bright areas are, and the more they bleed to the darker areas.
kernelSize	This property controls the offset of the bloom effect.
sigma	With the `sigma` property, you can control the sharpness of the bloom effect. The higher the value, the more blurred the bloom effect.
Resolution	This defines the preciseness of the bloom effect that is created. If you make this too low, the result will look blocky.

A better way to understand these properties is to just experiment with them by using the previously mentioned example: `02-post-processing-simple-passes.html`. In the following screenshot, you can see what the bloom effect looks like. This example uses a high `kernelSize`, a high `sigma`, and a low `Strength`.

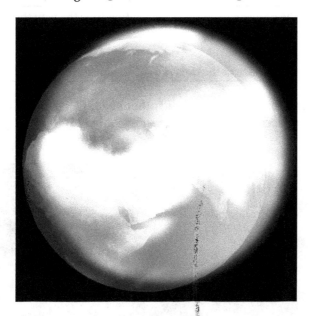

The last of the simple effects that we will have a look at is the `DotScreenPass`.

Outputting the scene as a set of dots with the DotScreenPass

Using the `DotScreenPass` is very similar to the `BloomPass` that we just saw; look at the following code snippet:

```
var dotScreenPass = new THREE.DotScreenPass();
var composer1 = new THREE.EffectComposer(webGLRenderer);
composer1.addPass(renderScene);
composer1.addPass(dotScreenPass);
composer1.addPass(effectCopy);
```

With this effect, we will once again have to add the `effectCopy` to output the result to the screen. The `DotScreenPass` can also be configured with a number of properties:

Property	Description
center	With the `center` property, you can fine-tune the way the dots are offset.
angle	The dots are aligned in a certain manner. With the `angle` property, you can change this alignment.
scale	This sets the size of the dots to use. The lower the `scale`, the larger the dots.

As for this shader, the same applies as the other shaders; it's much easier to get the right settings with experimentation. In the screenshot that follows, you can see the result of a `DotScreenPass` by using a high `scale` setting:

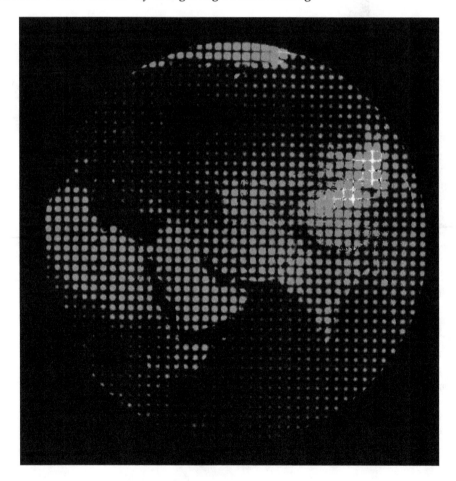

Showing the output of multiple renderers on the same screen

This section doesn't go into the details of how to use the post processing effects, but explains how to get the output of all the four EffectComposer instances on the same screen. First, let's look at the render loop that is used for this example:

```
function render() {
    stats.update();

    var delta = clock.getDelta();
    orbitControls.update(delta);

    sphere.rotation.y += 0.002;

    requestAnimationFrame(render);

    webGLRenderer.autoClear = false;
    webGLRenderer.clear();

    webGLRenderer.setViewport(0, 0,
                2 * halfWidth, 2 * halfHeight);
    composer.render(delta);

    webGLRenderer.setViewport(0, 0,
            halfWidth, halfHeight);
    composer1.render(delta);

    webGLRenderer.setViewport(halfWidth, 0,
            halfWidth, halfHeight);
    composer2.render(delta);

    webGLRenderer.setViewport(0, halfHeight,
            halfWidth, halfHeight);
    composer3.render(delta);

    webGLRenderer.setViewport(halfWidth, halfHeight,
            halfWidth, halfHeight);
    composer4.render(delta);
}
```

The first thing to notice here is that we have set the `webGLRenderer.autoClear` property to `false` and will now explicitly call the `clear()` function. If we don't do this each time we call the `render()` function on a composer, the previously rendered scenes will be cleared. With this approach, we will only clear everything at the beginning of our `render` loop.

To avoid all our composers rendering in the same space, we set the viewport of the `webGLRenderer`, which is used by our composers, to a part of the screen. This function takes four arguments: `x`, `y`, `width`, and `height`. As you can see in the code sample, we have used this function to divide the screen into four areas and make the composers render to their individual area.

 You can also use this approach with multiple scenes, cameras, and `WebGLRenderer` instances if you want.

So far we've only chained a couple of simple passes. In the next example, we'll configure a more complex `EffectComposer` and use masks to apply effects to a part of the screen.

Advanced EffectComposer flows by using masks

In the previous examples, we applied the post processing passes to the complete screen. The Three.js library, however, also has the ability to apply passes only to a specific area. In this section we're going to take the following steps:

1. Create a scene to serve as the background image.
2. Create a scene containing a sphere that looks like Earth.
3. Create a scene containing a sphere that looks like Mars.
4. Create an `EffectComposer` object that renders these three scenes into a single image.
5. Apply a colorify effect to the sphere rendered as Mars.
6. Apply a sepia effect to the sphere rendered as Earth.

This might sound complex, but is surprisingly easy to accomplish. First, let's look at the result that we're aiming for, in the following screenshot. It is shown in example `03-post-processing-masks.html`:

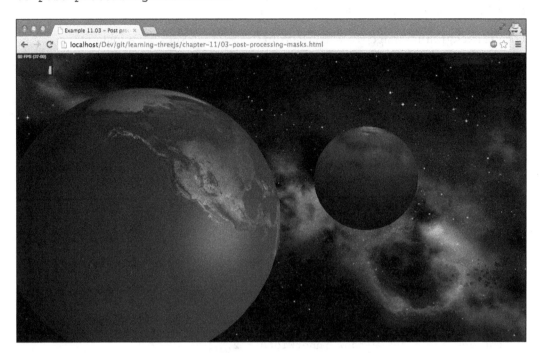

The first thing that we need to set up are the various scenes that we'll be rendering, as follows:

```
var sceneEarth = new THREE.Scene();
var sceneMars = new THREE.Scene();
var sceneBG = new THREE.Scene();
```

To create the Earth and Mars spheres, we will just create spheres with the correct material and textures, and add them to their specific scenes, as shown in the code snippet that follows:

```
var sphere = createEarthMesh(
                    new THREE.SphereGeometry(10, 40, 40));
sphere.position.x = -10;
var sphere2 = createMarshMesh(
                    new THREE.SphereGeometry(5, 40, 40));
sphere2.position.x = 10;
sceneEarth.add(sphere);
sceneMars.add(sphere2);
```

We also need to add some lights to the scene, just like for a normal scene, but we won't see that here. The only thing to remember is that the same light can't be added to different scenes, so you need to create separate lights for both the scenes. That's all the setup we need to do for these two scenes.

For the background image we will create an `OrthographicCamera` instance as shown. Remember from *Chapter 2, Working with the Basic Components That Make Up a Three.js Scene*, that the sizes of objects in the orthographic projection don't depend on the distance from the camera.

```
var cameraBG = new THREE.OrthographicCamera(
          -window.innerWidth,
           window.innerWidth,
           window.innerHeight,
          -window.innerHeight, -10000, 10000);
cameraBG.position.z = 50;

var materialColor = new THREE.MeshBasicMaterial(
    { map: THREE.ImageUtils.loadTexture(
       "../assets/textures/starry-deep-outer-space-galaxy.jpg"),
       depthTest: false });
var bgPlane = new THREE.Mesh(new THREE.PlaneGeometry(1, 1),
                           materialColor);
bgPlane.position.z = -100;
bgPlane.scale.set(window.innerWidth * 2,
                  window.innerHeight * 2, 1);
sceneBG.add(bgPlane);
```

We won't go into much detail for this part, but we have to take a couple of steps to create a background image. First, we will create a material from our background image, and we apply it to a simple `plane`. Next we will add this `plane` to the scene, and scale it to fill the screen completely. So when we render the scene with this camera, our background image is shown, stretched to the width of the screen.

We've now got our three scenes, and we can start to set up our passes and the `EffectComposer` object. Let's start by looking at the complete chain of passes, after which we'll look at the individual passes:

```
var composer = new THREE.EffectComposer(webGLRenderer);
composer.renderTarget1.stencilBuffer = true;
composer.renderTarget2.stencilBuffer = true;

composer.addPass(bgPass);
composer.addPass(renderPass);
```

```
composer.addPass(renderPass2);

composer.addPass(marsMask);
composer.addPass(effectColorify1);
composer.addPass(clearMask);

composer.addPass(earthMask);
composer.addPass(effectSepia);
composer.addPass(clearMask);

composer.addPass(effectCopy);
```

To work with masks, we need to create the `EffectComposer` object in a different manner. In this case we need to create a new `WebGLRenderTarget` object and set the `stencilBuffer` property of the internally used render targets to `true`. Let's look at the first three passes that are added first. These three passes render the background, the Earth scene, and the Mars scene, as shown:

```
var bgPass = new THREE.RenderPass(sceneBG, cameraBG);
var renderPass = new THREE.RenderPass(sceneEarth, camera);
renderPass.clear = false;
var renderPass2 = new THREE.RenderPass(sceneMars, camera);
renderPass2.clear = false;
```

Nothing new here, except that we have set the `clear` property of two of these passes to `false`. If we don't do this, we'll only see the output from `renderPass2`, since it will clear everything before it starts rendering. If you look back at the code for the `EffectComposer`, you'll see that the next three passes are the `marsMask`, `effectColorify`, and `clearMask`. First, we'll look at how these three passes are defined:

```
var marsMask = new THREE.MaskPass(sceneMars, camera );
var clearMask = new THREE.ClearMaskPass();
var effectColorify = new THREE.ShaderPass(THREE.ColorifyShader );
effectColorify.uniforms['color'].value.setRGB(0.5, 0.5, 1);
```

The first of these three passes is a `MaskPass`. When creating a `MaskPass`, you will pass in a scene and a camera, just like you did for a `RenderPass`. The `MaskPass` will render the scene internally, but instead of showing this on the screen, it will use this information to create a mask. When this `MaskPass` is added to an `EffectComposer`, all of the subsequent passes will only be applied to the mask defined by the `MaskPass`, until a `ClearMaskPass` is encountered. In this example, it means that the `effectColorify` pass, which adds a blue glow, is only applied to the objects rendered in `sceneMars`.

We will use the same approach to apply a sepia filter on the Earth object. We will first create a mask based on the Earth scene and use this mask in the EffectComposer. After the MaskPass, we add the effect that we want to apply (effectSepia in this case), and once we're done we add the ClearMaskPass to remove the mask. The last step for this specific EffectComposer is one that we've already seen. We need to copy the final result to the screen, and once again use the effectCopy pass for that.

There is one additional property that's interesting when working with a MaskPass and that's the inverse property. If this property is set to true, the mask is inversed. In other words, the effect is applied to everything but the scene passed into the MaskPass.

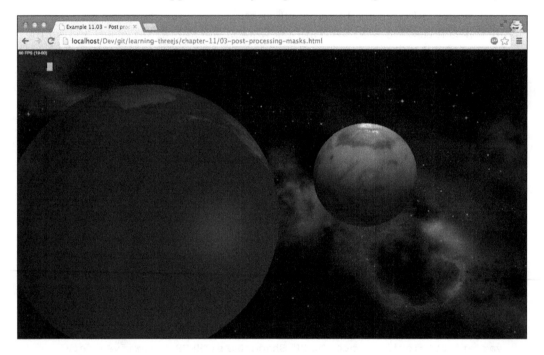

So far we've used the standard passes provided by the Three.js library for our effects. Three.js also provides a ShaderPass that can be used for custom effects and comes with a large number of shaders that you can use and experiment with.

Using the ShaderPass for custom effects

With the `ShaderPass` we can apply a large number of additional effects to our scene by passing in a custom shader. This section is divided into three parts. First we'll look at the following set of simple shaders:

Name	Description
MirrorShader	This creates a mirror effect for a part of the screen.
HueSaturationShader	This allows you to change the hue and saturation of the colors.
VignetteShader	This applies a vignette effect. This effect shows dark borders around the center of the image.
ColorCorrectionShader	With this shader you can change the color distribution.
RGBShiftShader	This shader separates the red, green, and blue components of a color.
BrightnessContrastShader	This changes the brightness and contrast of an image.
ColorifyShader	This applies a color overlay to the screen.
SepiaShader	This creates a sepia-like effect on the screen.

Next, we'll look at shaders that provide a couple of blur-related effects:

Name	Description
HorizontalBlurShader and VerticalBlurShader	These apply a blur effect to the complete scene.
HorizontalTiltShiftShader and VerticalTiltShiftShader	These recreate the tilt shift effect. With the tilt shift effect, it is possible to create a scene that looks like a miniature by making sure that only part of the image is sharp.
TriangleBlurShader	This applies a blur effect by using a triangle-based approach.

And finally, we'll look at a couple of shaders that provide advanced effects:

Name	Description
BleachBypassShader	This creates a bleach bypass effect. With this effect, a silver-like overlay will be applied to the image.
EdgeShader	This shader can be used to detect the sharp edges in an image and highlight them.
FXAAShader	This shader applies an antialiasing effect during the post processing phase. Use this if applying antialiasing during rendering is too expensive.

Name	Description
FocusShader	A simple shader that results in a sharply-rendered center area, and blurring along its borders.

We won't go into detail for all the shaders, since if you've seen how one works, you pretty much know how the others work. In the following sections, we'll highlight a couple of interesting ones. You can experiment with the other ones by using the interactive examples provided for each section.

We will start with a couple of the simple ones.

Simple shaders

To experiment with the basic shaders, we've created an example where you can play around with the shaders and see the effect directly in the scene. You can refer to the 04-shaderpass-simple.html example, as seen in the following screenshot:.

With the menu in the top-right corner, you can select the specific shader that you want to apply, and with the various drop-down menus you can set the properties of the shader that you've selected. For instance, the following screenshot shows the `RGBShiftShader` in action:

When you change one of the properties of a shader, the result is updated directly. For this example we will set the changed value directly on the shader. For instance, when the values for the `RGBShiftShader` change, we will update the shader, like in the following code snippet:

```
this.changeRGBShifter = function() {
  rgbShift.uniforms.amount.value = controls.rgbAmount;
  rgbShift.uniforms.angle.value = controls.angle;
}
```

Let's look at a couple of other shaders. The following screenshot shows the result of the VignetteShader:

The MirrorShader has the following effect:

That's enough for the simple shaders. As you can see, they are very versatile and can create very interesting-looking effects. In this example we applied a single shader each time, but you can add as many ShaderPass steps to the EffectComposer as you like.

Blurring shaders

In this section we won't dive into the code, we'll just show you the results from the various blur shaders. You can experiment with these by using the 05-shaderpass-blur.html example, as shown:

The earlier screenshot shows the `HorizontalBlurShader` and the `VerticalBlurShader`. You can see that the effect is a blurred scene. Besides these two blur effects, the Three.js library provides an additional shader that blurs an image, the `TriangleShader`, which is shown in the screenshot that follows:

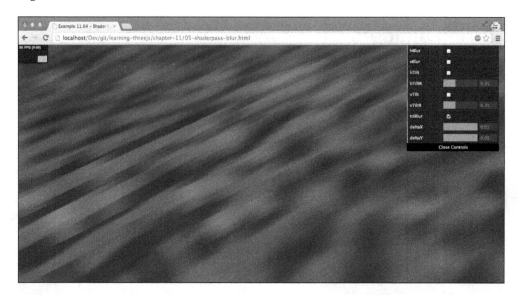

The last blur-like effect is provided by the `HorizontalTiltShiftShader` and the `VerticalTiltShiftShader`. This shader doesn't blur the complete scene, but only a small area. It provides an effect called as **tilt shift**. This is often used to create miniature-like scenes from normal photos. The following screenshot shows this effect:

Advanced shaders

For the advanced shaders, we'll do the same as we did for the previous blur ones. We'll just show you the output of the shaders; for details on how to configure them, look at example 06-shaderpass-advanced.html, as shown in the following screenshot:

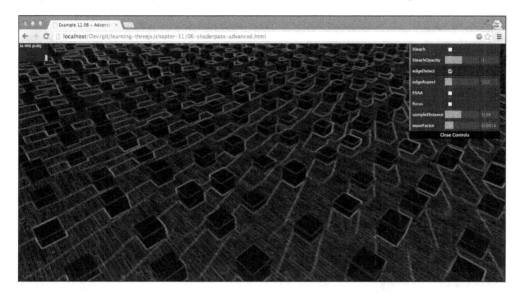

The earlier example shows the EdgeShader. With this shader you can detect the edges of the objects in your scene. In the screenshot that follows, you can see the result from the FocusShader, which only renders the center of the screen in focus:

So far we've only used shaders that are provided by the Three.js library. It is, however, also very easy to create shaders yourself.

Creating custom post processing shaders

In this section you'll learn how to create a custom shader that you can use in post processing. We'll create two different shaders. The first one will convert the current image into a grayscale image, and the second one will convert the image to an 8-bit image by reducing the number of colors that are available.

Creating the vertex and fragment shaders is a very broad subject. In this section, we will only touch the surface of what can be done by these shaders and how they work. For more in-depth information, you can find the WebGL specification at http://www.khronos. org/webgl/. An additional good resource full of examples is shadertoy: https://www.shadertoy.com/

Custom grayscale shader

To create a custom shader for the Three.js library (and also for the other WebGL libraries), you need to implement two components: a vertexShader and a fragmentShader. The vertexShader can be used to change the position of individual vertices and the fragmentShader is used to determine the color of individual pixels. For a post processing shader, we only need to implement a fragmentShader, and we can keep the default vertexShader provided by the Three.js library. An important point to make, though, before looking at the code, is that GPUs usually support multiple shader pipelines. This means that in the vertexShader step on the GPU, multiple shaders can run in parallel, and the same goes for the fragmentShader step.

Let's start by looking at the complete source code for the shader that applies a grayscale effect to our image (custom-shader.js):

```
THREE.CustomGrayScaleShader = {

    uniforms: {

        "tDiffuse": { type: "t", value: null },
        "rPower":   { type: "f", value: 0.2126 },
        "gPower":   { type: "f", value: 0.7152 },
```

```
        "bPower":  { type: "f", value: 0.0722 }

    },

    vertexShader: [
        "varying vec2 vUv;",
        "void main() {",
        "vUv = uv;",
        "gl_Position = projectionMatrix * modelViewMatrix
                      * vec4( position, 1.0 );",
        "}"
    ].join("\n"),

    fragmentShader: [

        "uniform float rPower;",
        "uniform float gPower;",
        "uniform float bPower;",
        "uniform sampler2D tDiffuse;",

        "varying vec2 vUv;",

        "void main() {",
        "vec4 texel = texture2D( tDiffuse, vUv );",
        "float gray = texel.r*rPower +
                      texel.g*gPower + texel.b*bPower;",
        "gl_FragColor = vec4( vec3(gray), texel.w );",
        "}"
    ].join("\n")
};
```

As you can see from the code, this isn't JavaScript. When you write shaders, you will write them in the OpenGL Shading Language (GLSL), which looks a lot like the C programming language. More information on GLSL can be found at: http://www.khronos.org/opengles/sdk/docs/manglsl/

Let's first look at this vertex shader:

```
"varying vec2 vUv;",
        "void main() {",
        "vUv = uv;",
        "gl_Position = projectionMatrix * modelViewMatrix
                      * vec4( position, 1.0 );",
        "}"
```

For post processing, this shader doesn't really need to do anything. The given code is the standard way in which the Three.js library implements a `vertexShader`. It uses the `projectionMatrix`, which is the projection from the camera, together with the `modelViewMatrix`, which maps each vertex of an object to the coordinates of the scene, to determine where to render an object on the screen.

For post-processing, the only interesting thing in this piece of code is that the `uv` value, which indicates the Texel (a pixel from a texture) to read from a texture, is passed on to the `fragmentShader` by using the `varying vec2 vUv` variable. We will use the `vUv` value to get the correct pixel to work on in the `fragmentShader`. Let's look at the `fragmentShader` and see what the code is doing. We will start with the variable declaration:

```
"uniform float rPower;",
"uniform float gPower;",
"uniform float bPower;",
"uniform sampler2D tDiffuse;",

"varying vec2 vUv;",
```

Here, we can see four uniforms. The `uniforms` are those values that are passed in from JavaScript to the shader. In this case we will pass in three floats, identified by the type `f` (which is used to determine the ratio of the color to include in the final grayscale image), and a texture (`tDiffuse`) is passed in, identified by the type `t`. This texture contains the image from the previous pass by the `EffectComposer`. Three.js makes sure that it gets passed correctly to this shader, and we can set the other uniforms from JavaScript ourselves. Before we can use these uniforms from JavaScript, we have to define which uniforms are available for this shader. This is done as shown, at the top of the shader file:

```
uniforms: {

    "tDiffuse": { type: "t", value: null },
    "rPower":   { type: "f", value: 0.2126 },
    "gPower":   { type: "f", value: 0.7152 },
    "bPower":   { type: "f", value: 0.0722 }

},
```

At this point we can receive the configuration parameters from the Three.js library and have received the image that we want to modify. Let's look at the code that will convert each pixel to a gray pixel:

```
"void main() {",
"vec4 texel = texture2D( tDiffuse, vUv );",
"float gray = texel.r*rPower +
             texel.g*gPower + texel.b*bPower;",
"gl_FragColor = vec4( vec3(gray), texel.w );"
```

What happens here is that we get the correct pixel from the passed in texture. We do this by using the `texture2D()` function, where we will pass in our current image (`tDiffuse`) and the location of the pixel (`vUv`) that we want to analyze. The result is a Texel that contains a `color` and an `opacity` (`texel.w`).

Next, we will use the `r`, `g`, and `b` properties of this Texel to calculate a gray value. This gray value is set to the `gl_FragColor` variable, which is eventually shown on the screen. With that, we've got our own custom shader. This shader works just like the other shaders. First, we will need to set up an `EffectComposer`, as shown:

```
var renderPass = new THREE.RenderPass(scene, camera);

var effectCopy = new THREE.ShaderPass(THREE.CopyShader);
effectCopy.renderToScreen = true;

var shaderPass = new THREE.ShaderPass(THREE.CustomGrayScaleShader);

var composer = new THREE.EffectComposer(webGLRenderer);
composer.addPass(renderPass);
composer.addPass(shaderPass);
composer.addPass(effectCopy);
```

Then we have to call the `composer.render(delta)` function in the `render` loop. If we want to change the properties of this shader at runtime, we can just update the uniforms that we've defined, as follows:

```
shaderPass.enabled = controls.grayScale;
shaderPass.uniforms.rPower.value = controls.rPower;
shaderPass.uniforms.gPower.value = controls.gPower;
shaderPass.uniforms.bPower.value = controls.bPower;
```

And the result will look like the following screenshot (example `07-shaderpass-custom.html`):

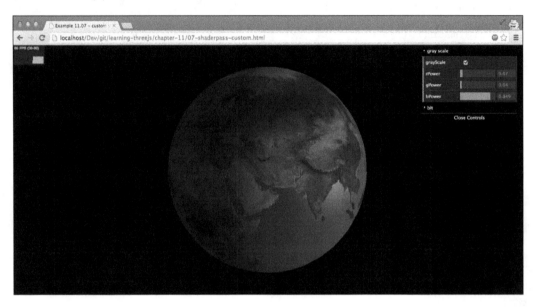

Let's create another custom shader. This time we'll reduce the 32-bit output to a lower bit count.

Creating a custom bit shader

Normally, the colors are represented as 24-bit values, which give us about 16 million different colors. In the early days of computing, this wasn't possible and colors were often represented in 8-bit or 16-bit colors. With this shader, we'll automatically transform our 24-bit output to a color depth of 8 bits (or anything that you want).

We'll skip the `vertexShader`, since it hasn't changed in regard to our earlier example, and directly list the `uniforms` and the `fragmentShader`, as shown in the following code snippet:

```
uniforms: {

        "tDiffuse": { type: "t", value: null },
        "bitSize":  { type: "i", value: 4 }

}
```

The `fragmentShader` itself, defined as shown:

```
fragmentShader: [

    "uniform int bitSize;",

    "uniform sampler2D tDiffuse;",

    "varying vec2 vUv;",

    "void main() {",

    "vec4 texel = texture2D( tDiffuse, vUv );",
    "float n = pow(float(bitSize),2.0);",
    "float newR = floor(texel.r*n)/n;",
    "float newG = floor(texel.g*n)/n;",
    "float newB = floor(texel.b*n)/n;",

    "gl_FragColor = vec4(newR, newG, newB, texel.w );",

    "}"

].join("\n")
```

We will define two uniforms that can be used to configure this shader. The first one is the one that the Three.js library uses to pass to the current screen, and the second one is the one defined by us, as an integer (`type: "i"`), and serves as the color depth that we want to render the result in. The code itself is very straightforward. The steps are as follows:

1. We will first get the `texel` from the texture, `tDiffuse`, based on the passed in `vUv`.

2. We will then calculate the amount of colors that we may have based on the `bitSize` property by calculating 2 to the power of `bitSize` (`pow(float(bitSize),2.0)`).

3. Next, we will calculate the new value of the color of the `texel` by multiplying the value with `n`, rounding it off (`floor(texel.r*n)`), and dividing it again by `n`.

4. The result is set to `gl_FragColor` (red, green, and blue values, and the opacity) and shown on the screen.

You can view the result for this custom shader in the same example as our previous custom shader: 07-shaderpass-custom.html.

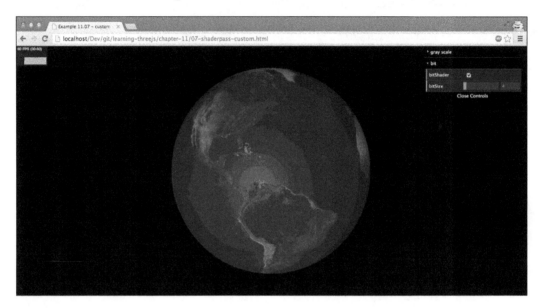

That's it for the chapter on post processing.

Summary

We've talked about a lot of different post processing options in this chapter. As you've already seen, creating the EffectComposer instances and chaining the passes together is actually very easy. The main subjects to remember from this chapter are the following:

- Not all the passes output to the screen. If you want to output to the screen you can always use a ShaderPass with a CopyShader.

- The sequence in which you add the passes to a composer is important. The effects are applied in that sequence.

- If you want to reuse the result from a specific EffectComposer, you can do so by using a TexturePass.

- When you have more than one RenderPass in your EffectComposer object, make sure to set the clear property to false. If not, you'll only see the output from the last RenderPass.

- If you only want to apply an effect to a specific object, you can use `MaskPass`. When you're done with mask, clear the mask with the `ClearMaskPass`.

- Besides the standard passes provided by the Three.js library, there are also a large number of standard shaders available. You can use these together with a `ShaderPass`.

- Creating custom shaders for post processing is very easy by using the standard approach from the Three.js library. You only need to create a `fragmentshader`.

So far we've pretty much covered everything that there is to know about Three.js. For the next chapter, the last one, we'll look at a library called Physijs, one that you can use to extend Three.js with physics, such as collisions, gravity, and constraints.

12
Adding Physics to Your Scene with Physijs

In this final chapter we'll look at another library that you can use to extend the basic functionality of Three.js. The library we'll discuss in this chapter is called **Physijs**. Physijs is a library that allows you to introduce physics into your 3D scene. By physics, we mean that our objects are subject to gravity — they can collide with each other, can be moved by applying impulse, and can be constrained in their movement through hinges and sliders. This library makes use of another well known physics engine named ammo.js.

In this chapter we'll look at how Physijs allows you to do the following:

- Create a Physijs scene where your objects are subject to gravity and can collide with each other
- Show how to change the friction and restitution (bounciness) of the objects in the scene
- Explain the various shapes supported by Physijs and how to use them
- How to create compound shapes by combining simple shapes together
- Show how a `height` field allows you to simulate a complex shape
- Limit the movement of an object by applying a point, hinge, slider, cone twist, and the `degree of freedom` constraint

First thing we need to do, is create a Three.js scene that can be used with Physijs. We'll do that in our first example.

Creating a basic Three.js scene ready for Physijs

Setting up a Three.js scene for Physijs is very simple and only takes a couple of steps. First thing we need to do is include the correct JavaScript file, which you can get from the GitHub repository available at `http://chandlerprall.github.io/Physijs/`.

```
<script type="text/javascript" src="../libs/physi.js"></script>
```

Simulating a scene is rather CPU intensive. If we do this on the `render` thread, it could seriously affect the frame rate of our scene. To compensate for that Physijs does its calculations in a background thread. This background thread is provided through the **Web workers** specification that is implemented by most modern browsers. With this specification, you can run CPU-intensive tasks in a separate thread, thus without affecting the rendering. More information on web workers can be found at the following site: `http://www.whatwg.org/specs/web-apps/current-work/multipage/workers.html`

For Physijs, this means we have to configure the JavaScript file that contains this worker task and also tell Physijs where it can find the `ammo.js` file needed to simulate our scene. The reason we need to include the `ammo.js` file is that Physijs is a wrapper around `ammo.js` to make it easy to use. ammo.js (which you can find here: `https://github.com/kripken/ammo.js/`) is the library that implements the physics engine, Physijs just provides an easy-to-use interface to this physics library. Since Physijs is just a wrapper, we can also use other physics engines along with Physijs. On the Physijs repository you can also find a branch that uses Cannon.js, a different physics engine.

We do this by setting the following two properties:

```
Physijs.scripts.worker = '../libs/physijs_worker.js';
Physijs.scripts.ammo = '../libs/ammo.js';
```

The first property points to the worker tasks that we want to execute, and the second property to the ammo.js library that is used internally. The next step we need to do is create a scene. Physijs provides a wrapper around Three.js normal scene, so in your code you do the following to create a scene:

```
var scene = new Physijs.Scene();
scene.setGravity(new THREE.Vector3(0, -10, 0));
```

This creates a new scene where physics are applied, and we set the gravity. In this case we set the gravity on the y-axis to be -10. In other words, objects fall straight down. You can set, or change at runtime, the gravity for the various axes to any value you see fit, and the scene will respond accordingly.

Before we can start simulating the physics in the scene we need to add some objects. For this we can use the normal way Three.js specifies objects, but we have to wrap them inside a specific Physijs object.

```
var stoneGeom = new THREE.CubeGeometry(0.6,6,2);
var stone = new Physijs.BoxMesh(stoneGeom,
  new THREE.MeshPhongMaterial({color: 0xff0000}));
scene.add(stone);
```

In this example we create a simple CubeGeometry. Instead of creating a THREE.Mesh object we create a Physijs.BoxMesh object. This BoxMesh object tells Physijs to treat the geometry as a box when simulating and detecting collisions. Physijs provides a number of meshes you can use for various shapes. More on this later in this chapter.

Now that the BoxMesh object has been added to the scene we've got all the ingredients for the first Physijs scene. All that is left to do is tell Phyijs.js to simulate the physics and update the position and rotation of the objects in our scene. We can do this by calling the simulate method on the scene we just created. So for this we change our basic render loop to this:

```
render = function() {
  requestAnimationFrame(render);
  renderer.render(scene, camera);
  scene.simulate();
}
```

And with that final step, we've got our basic setup for a Physijs scene. If we run this example, though, we wouldn't see much. We would just see a single cube in the middle of the screen, which starts falling down as soon as the scene renders. So let's look at an example, which is a bit more complex, where we'll simulate domino stones falling down.

For this example we're going to create the following scene:

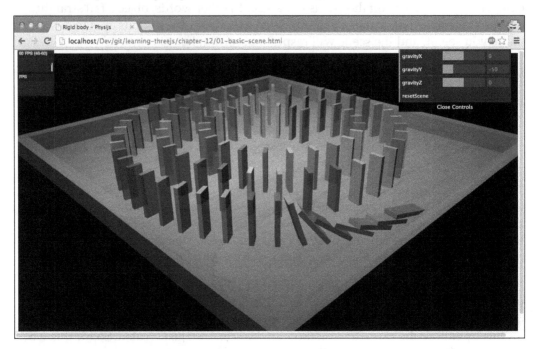

If you open this example, `01-basic-scene.html` in your browser you'll see a set of domino stones that start falling down as soon as the scene is loaded. The first one will tip over the second one, and so on. The complete physics of this scene is managed by Physijs. The only thing we did to start this animation is tip over the first domino. Creating this scene is actually very easy and only takes a couple of steps:

1. Define a Physijs scene.
2. Define the ground area that holds the stone.
3. Place the stones.
4. Tip over the first stone.

Let's skip this first step, since we've already seen how to do this, and go directly to the second part where we define the ground. This `ground` shape is constructed out of a couple of cubes that are grouped together:

```
function createGround() {
  var ground_material = Physijs.createMaterial(
    new THREE.MeshPhongMaterial({ map: THREE.ImageUtils.loadTexture(
      '../assets/textures/general/wood-2.jpg' )}),0.9,0.3);

  var ground = new Physijs.BoxMesh(
```

```
    new THREE.CubeGeometry(60, 1, 60), ground_material, 0);

  var borderLeft = new Physijs.BoxMesh(
    new THREE.CubeGeometry(2, 3, 60), ground_material, 0);
  borderLeft.position.x=-31;
  borderLeft.position.y=2;
  ground.add(borderLeft);

  var borderRight = new Physijs.BoxMesh(
    new THREE.CubeGeometry(2, 3, 60), ground_material, 0);
  borderRight.position.x=31;
  borderRight.position.y=2;
  ground.add(borderRight);

  var borderBottom = new Physijs.BoxMesh(
    new THREE.CubeGeometry(64, 3, 2), ground_material, 0);
  borderBottom.position.z=30;
  borderBottom.position.y=2;
  ground.add(borderBottom);

  var borderTop = new Physijs.BoxMesh(
    new THREE.CubeGeometry(64, 3, 2), ground_material, 0);
  borderTop.position.z=-30;
  borderTop.position.y=2;
  ground.add(borderTop);

  scene.add(ground);
}
```

This code isn't very complicated. First we create a simple cube that serves as the ground plane, and next we add a couple of borders to prevent objects falling off this ground plane. We add these borders to the ground object to create a compound object. This is an object that is treated by Physijs as a single object. More on compound objects, further in this chapter. There are a couple of other new things in this code fragment that we'll explain in more depth in the following sections. The first one is the ground_material that we create. We use the Physijs. createMaterial function to create this material. This function wraps a standard Three.js material, but allows us to set the friction and the restitution (bounciness) properties of the material. More on this in the next section. Another new aspect is the final parameter we add to the Physijs.BoxMesh constructor. For all the BoxMesh objects we create we add 0 as the final parameter. With this parameter we set the weight of the object. We do this to prevent the ground from being subject to the gravity in the scene.

Now that we've got the ground, we can put the dominos down. For this we create simple `Three.CubeGeometry` instances that we wrap inside a `BoxMesh` object and place them at a specific position on the ground mesh.

```
var stoneGeom = new THREE.CubeGeometry(0.6,6,2);
var stone = new Physijs.BoxMesh(stoneGeom, Physijs.createMaterial(new
THREE.MeshPhongMaterial(
  {
    color: scale(Math.random()).hex(),
    transparent:true, opacity:0.8
  }))));
stone.position=point.clone();
stone.lookAt(scene.position);
stone.__dirtyRotation = true;
stone.position.y=3.5;
scene.add(stone);
```

We don't show the code where the position of each domino is calculated (see the source code of the example for this), this code just shows how the dominos are positioned. What you can see here is that we once again create a `BoxMesh` object that wraps a `CubeGeometry`. To make sure the dominos are aligned correctly we use the `lookAt` function to set their correct rotation. If we don't do this, they'll all face the same way, and won't fall down. We have to make sure that after we manually update the rotation (or the position) of a Physijs wrapped object; we have to tell Physijs that something has changed. For the rotation we can do this with the `__dirtyRotation` property and for the position we set the `__dirtyPosition` to true.

Now all that is left to do is tip the first domino. We do this by just setting the rotation around the x-axis to `0.2`, which tips it slightly. The gravity in the scene will do the rest and completely tip over the first domino.

```
stones[0].rotation.x=0.2;
stones[0].__dirtyRotation = true;
```

This completes the first example that already shows a lot of features from Physijs. If you want to play around with the gravity you can change it through the menu on the top-right of the scene. The change to the gravity is applied when you click on the **resetScene** button.

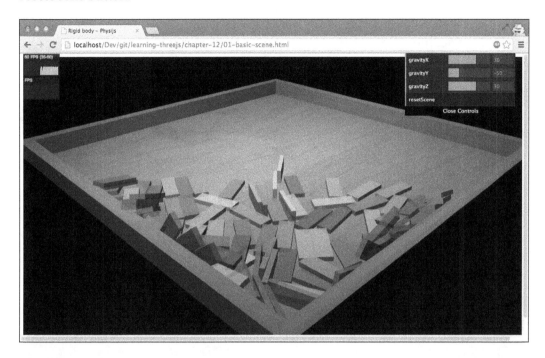

In the next section we'll have a closer look at how the Physijs material properties affect the objects.

Material properties

Let's begin with an explanation of the example. When you open up example `02-material-properties.html` you'll see an empty box somewhat similar to the previous example. This box is rotating up and down around its x-axis. In the menu at the top right you've got a couple of sliders that can be used to change a couple of Physijs properties. These properties apply to the cubes and to the spheres that you can add with the **addCubes** and **addSpheres** buttons. When you click on the **addSpheres** button, five spheres will be added to the scene and when you click on the **addCubes** button, five cubes will be added, as shown in the following screenshot:

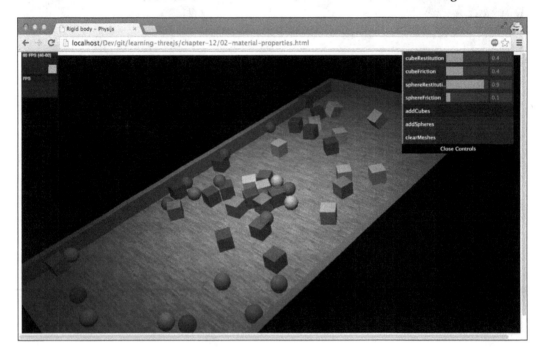

This example allows you to play around with the `restitution` and `friction` properties that you can set when you create a `Physijs` material. If, for example, you set the **cubeFriction** all the way to 1 and add a couple of cubes, you'll see that, even though the ground is moving, the cubes barely move. If you set the **cubeFriction** to 0, you'll notice the cubes shifting around as soon as the ground stops being level, as shown in the following screenshot:

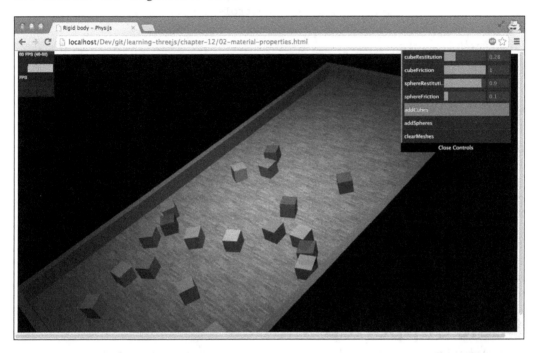

The other property that you can set in this example is the `restitution` property. The `restitution` property defines how much of the energy that an object possesses is restituted when it collides. In other words a high restitution creates a bouncy object, a low restitution results in an object that stops immediately when it hits another object. A good way to demonstrate this is by using spheres, setting the restitution to 1 and clicking on the **addSpheres** button a couple of times. This will create a lot of bouncy spheres that bounce everywhere.

Before we move on to the next section let's look at a bit of code used in this example:

```
box = new Physijs.SphereMesh(
  new THREE.SphereGeometry( 2, 20 ),
  Physijs.createMaterial(
    new THREE.MeshPhongMaterial(
      {color: colorSphere, opacity: 0.8, transparent: true}),
        controls.sphereFriction, controls.sphereRestitution));

box.position.set(
  Math.random() * 50 -25,
  20 + Math.random() * 5,
  Math.random() * 50 -25);
scene.add( box );
```

This is the code that gets executed when we add spheres to the scene. This time we use a different Physijs mesh: the `SphereMesh`. We're creating a `SphereGeometry` and the best match from the set of meshes provided is, logically, the `SphereMesh` (more on this in the next section). When we create this `SphereMesh` we pass in our geometry and use the `Physijs.createMaterial` to create a Physijs specific material. We do this, so that we can set the friction and restitution properties for this object.

So far we've seen the `BoxMesh` and the `SphereMesh`. In the next section we'll explain and show all the types of meshes provided by Physijs that you can use to wrap your geometries.

Basic supported shapes

Physijs provides a number of shapes you can use to wrap your geometries. In this section we'll walk you through all the available Physijs meshes and demonstrate these meshes through an example. Remember that all you have to do to use these meshes is replace the `THREE.Mesh` constructor with one of these meshes.

The following table provides an overview of the meshes that are available in Physijs:

Name	Description
Physijs.PlaneMesh	This mesh can be used to create a zero-thickness plane. You could also use a `BoxMesh` object for this along with a `THREE.CubeGeometry` property with a low height.
Physijs.BoxMesh	If you have geometries that look like a cube, use this mesh. For instance, this is a good match for the `THREE.CubeGeometry` property.
Physijs.SphereMesh	For spherical shapes use this geometry. This geometry is a good match for the `THREE.SphereGeometry` property.

Name	Description
Physijs.CylinderMesh	With the THREE.Cylinder property you can create various cylindrical shapes. Physijs provides multiple meshes depending on the shape of the cylinder. The Physijs.CylinderMesh should be used for a normal cylinder having a same top and bottom radius.
Physijs.ConeMesh	If you specify the top radius as 0 and use a positive value for the bottom radius, you can use the THREE.Cylinder property to create a cone. If you want to apply physics to such an object the best fit from Physijs is the ConeMesh class.
Physijs.CapsuleMesh	A capsule is just like a THREE.Cylinder property, but with a rounded top and bottom. We'll show you how to create a capsule in Three.js, further down in this section.
Physijs.ConvexMesh	A Physijs.ConvexMesh is a rough shape you can use for more complex objects. It creates a convex (just like the THREE.ConvexGeometry property) to approximate the shape of complex objects.
Physijs.ConcaveMesh	While the ConvexMesh is a rough shape, a ConcaveMesh is a more detailed representation of your complex geometry. Note that the performance penalty of using a ConcaveMesh is very high. Usually it is better to either create separate geometries with their own specific Physijs mesh, or group them together (like we do with the floors shown in the previous examples).
Physijs.HeightfieldMesh	This mesh is a very specialized one. With this mesh you can create a height field from a THREE.PlaneGeometry property. Look at example 03-shapes.html for an example of this mesh.

We'll quickly walk you through these shapes using 03-shapes.html as a reference. We don't explain Physijs.ConcaveMesh any further since its usage is very limited.

Before we look at the example, we'll first have a quick look at Physijs.PlaneMesh. This mesh creates a simple plane, based on THREE.PlaneGeometry:

```
var plane = new Physijs.PlaneMesh(
  new THREE.PlaneGeometry(5,5,10,10),
  material
);


scene.add( plane );
```

In this function you can see that we just pass in a simple THREE.PlaneGeometry to create this mesh. If you add this to the scene you'll notice something strange. The mesh you just created doesn't respond to gravity. The reason is that a Physijs. PlaneMesh object has a fixed weight of 0, so it won't respond to gravity or is moved by collisions with other objects. Besides this mesh, all the other meshes respond to gravity and collisions, as you'd expect.

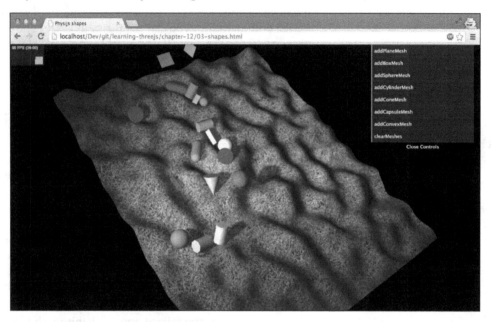

The preceding screenshot shows example 03-shapes.html. In this example we've created a random height field (more on that later) and have a menu on the top right, which you can use to drop objects of various shapes. If you play around with this example, you'll see how different shapes respond differently to the height map and in collisions with other objects.

Let's look at the construction of some of these shapes:

```
new Physijs.SphereMesh(new THREE.SphereGeometry(3,20),mat);
new Physijs.BoxMesh(new THREE.CubeGeometry(4,2,6),mat);
new Physijs.CylinderMesh(new THREE.CylinderGeometry(2,2,6),mat);
new Physijs.ConeMesh(new THREE.CylinderGeometry(0,3,7,20,10),mat);
```

Nothing special here, we create a geometry and use the best-matching mesh from Physijs to create the object we add to the scene. But what if we want to use the Physijs.CapsuleMesh. Three.js doesn't contain a capsule-like geometry, so we have to create one ourselves:

```
var cyl = new THREE.CylinderGeometry(2,2,6 );
```

```
var top = new THREE.SphereGeometry(2);
var bot = new THREE.SphereGeometry(2);

// create normal meshes
var topMesh = new THREE.Mesh(top);
var botMesh = new THREE.Mesh(bot);
topMesh.position.y=3;
botMesh.position.y=-3;

// merge to create a capsule
THREE.GeometryUtils.merge(cyl,topMesh);
THREE.GeometryUtils.merge(cyl,botMesh);

// create a physijs capsule mesh
var capsule = new Physijs.CapsuleMesh(
  cyl,
  getMaterial()
);
```

A `Phyijs.CapsuleMesh` looks like a cylinder, but has a rounded top and bottom. We can easily recreate this in Three.js by creating a cylinder (`cyl`) and two spheres (`top` and `bot`) and merging them together using the `THREE.GeometryUtils.merge()` function.

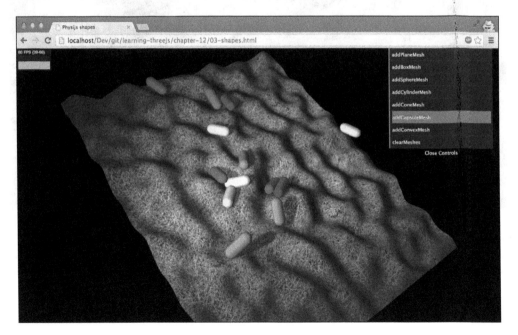

Before we look at the `height` map let's look at the last of the shapes you can add to this example: the `Physijs.ConvexMesh`. A convex is the minimal shape that wraps all the vertices of a geometry. The resulting shape will only have angles smaller than 180 degrees. You could use this mesh for complex shapes such as a torus knot:

```
var convex = new Physijs.ConvexMesh(
    new THREE.TorusKnotGeometry(0.5,0.3,64,8,2,3,10),
    material);
```

In this case, for physics simulation and collisions, the convex of the torus knot will be used. This is a very good way to apply physics and detect collisions for complex objects, while still minimizing the performance impact.

The last mesh to discuss from Physijs is the `Physijs.HeightMap`.

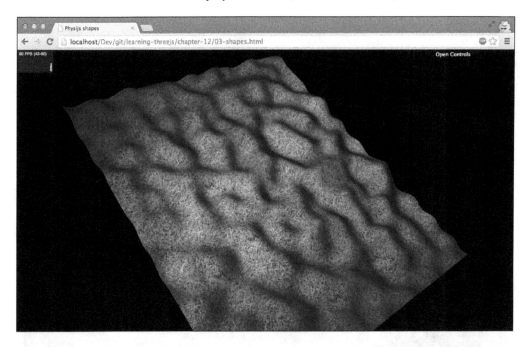

With a height map, you can very easily create a terrain that contains bumps and shallows. By using the `Physijs.Heightmap` class we make sure all the objects respond correctly to the height differences of this terrain. Let's look at the code required for this:

```
var date = new Date();
var pn = new Perlin('rnd' + date.getTime());

function createHeightMap(pn) {

    var ground_material = Physijs.createMaterial(
```

```
new THREE.MeshLambertMaterial({
    map: THREE.ImageUtils.loadTexture(
      '../assets/textures/ground/grasslight-big.jpg')
  }),
  0.3, // high friction
  0.8 // low restitution
);

var ground_geometry = new THREE.PlaneGeometry(120, 100, 100, 100);
for (var i = 0; i < ground_geometry.vertices.length; i++) {
  var vertex = ground_geometry.vertices[i];
  var value = pn.noise(vertex.x / 10, vertex.y / 10, 0);
  vertex.z = value * 10;
}
ground_geometry.computeFaceNormals();
ground_geometry.computeVertexNormals();

var ground = new Physijs.HeightfieldMesh(
  ground_geometry,
  ground_material,
  0, // mass
  100,
  100
);
ground.rotation.x = Math.PI / -2;
ground.rotation.y = 0.4;
ground.receiveShadow = true;

return ground;
}
```

In this code fragment we take a couple of steps to create the height map that
you can see in the example. First off, we create the Physijs material and a simple
`PlaneGeometry` object. To create a bumpy terrain from the `PlaneGeometry` object,
we walk through each of the vertices of this geometry and randomly set the
z-property. For this we use a Perlin noise generator, just like we used in *Chapter 10,
Loading and Working with Textures*, in the section *Using canvas as a bump map*, to create
a bump map. We need to call `computeFaceNormals` and `computeVertexNormals`
functions to make sure the texture, lighting, and shadows are rendered correctly.
At this point we've got a `PlaneGeometry` object that contains the correct
height information. With this `PlaneGeometry` object we can create a `Physijs.`
`HeightFieldMesh` property. The last two parameters for the constructor take the
number of horizontal and vertical segments of the `PlaneGeometry` object and should
match the last two properties used to construct the `PlaneGeometry` object. Finally we
rotate the `HeightFieldMesh` instance to the position we want and can add it to the
scene. All other Physijs objects will now interact correctly with this height map.

Using constraints to limit movement of objects

So far we've seen some basic physics in action. We've seen how the various shapes respond to gravity, friction, and restitution, and affect collisions. Physijs also provides advanced constructs that allow you to limit the movement of your objects. In Physijs these objects are called constraints. The following table gives an overview of the constraints that are available in Physijs:

Constraint	Description
PointConstraint	This constraint allows you to fix the position of one object to the position of another object. If one object moves, the other will move with it, keeping the distance and orientation between them the same.
HingeConstraint	The hinge constraint allows you to limit the movement of an object as if it were on a hinge, like a door.
SliderConstraint	This constraint, as the name implies, allows you to limit the movement of an object to a single axis. For instance, a sliding door.
ConeTwistConstraint	With this constraint you can limit the rotation and the movement of one object to another. This constraint functions like a ball-and-socket joint. For instance, the way your arm moves in your shoulder socket.
DOFConstraint	The degree of freedom constraint allows you to specify the limit of movement around any of the three axes and it allows you to set the minimum and maximum angle that is allowed. This is the most versatile of the constraints available.

The easiest way to understand these constraints is to see them in action, and play around with them. For this we've provided an example where all these constraints are used together: 04-physijs-constraints.js.

Refer to the following screenshot:

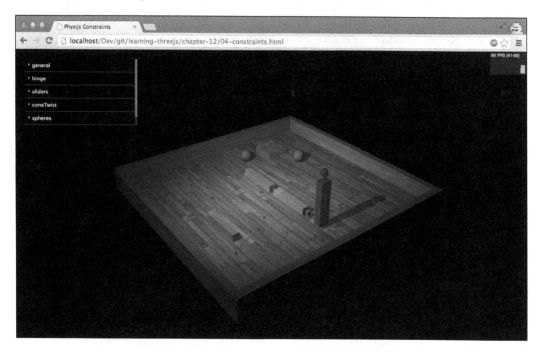

Based on this example we'll walk you through four of these five constraints. For the DOFConstraint we've created a separate example. The first one we look at is the PointConstraint.

Using PointConstraint to limit movement between two points

If you open the example you'll see two red spheres. These two spheres are connected to each other using a PointConstraint object. With the menu on the top left, you can move the sliders around. As soon as one of the sliders hits one of the red spheres, you'll see that both of them move in the same manner, and they keep the distance between them the same, while still complying with weight, gravity, friction, and other physics.

The PointConstraint in this example was created like this:

```
function createPointToPoint() {
  var obj1 = new THREE.SphereGeometry(2);
  var obj2 = new THREE.SphereGeometry(2);

  var objectOne = new
```

```
          Physijs.SphereMesh(obj1,Physijs.createMaterial(
            new THREE.MeshPhongMaterial({color: 0xff4444, transparent:
              true, opacity:0.7}),0,0));
    objectOne.position.z=-18; objectOne.position.x=-10;
    objectOne.position.y=2;
    scene.add(objectOne);

    var objectTwo = new
          Physijs.SphereMesh(obj2,Physijs.createMaterial(
            new THREE.MeshPhongMaterial({color: 0xff4444, transparent:
              true, opacity:0.7}),0,0));
    objectTwo.position.z=-5; objectTwo.position.x=-20;
    objectTwo.position.y=2;
    scene.add(objectTwo);

    var constraint = new Physijs.PointConstraint(objectOne,
        objectTwo, objectTwo.position);
    scene.addConstraint(constraint);
  }
```

Here you can see that we create objects using a Physijs specific mesh
(a `SphereMesh` instance in this case), and add them to the scene. We use
the `Physijs.PointConstraint` constructor to create the constraint. This
constraint takes three parameters:

- The first two objects define which objects you want to connect to each other.
  In this case we connect two spheres to one another.

- The third object defines at what position the constraint is bound. For
  instance, if you bind the first object to a very large other object, you can set
  this position, for instance, to the right side of that object. Usually if you just
  want to connect two objects together, a good choice is to just set it to the
  position of the second object.

If you don't want to fix an object to another one, but to a static position in the scene
you can omit the second parameter. In that case the first object keeps the same
distance to the position you specified, while complying with gravity and other
physics of course.

Once the constraint is created we can enable it by adding it to the scene with
the `addConstraint` function. As you start experimenting with constraints,
you'll likely run into some strange issues. To make debugging easier you can
pass in `true` to the `addConstraint` function. If you do this, the constraint point
and orientation is shown in the scene. This can help you get the rotation and
position of your constraint correctly.

Creating door-like constraints with a HingeConstraint

The `HingeConstraint` class, as the name tells you, allows you to create an object that behaves like a hinge. It rotates around a specific axis, limiting the movement to a specific angle. In our example the `HingeConstraint` object is shown with two flippers at the center of the scene. These flippers are constrained to the small brown cubes and can rotate around them. If you want to play around with these hinges, you can enable them by checking the `enableMotor` checkbox in the **hinge** menu. This will accelerate the flippers to the velocity specified in the **general** menu. A negative velocity will move the hinges down and a positive velocity will move them up.

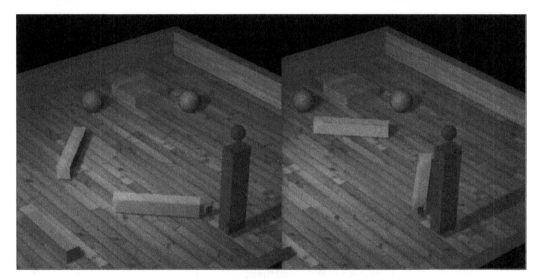

Let's look a bit closer at how we created one of these flippers.

```
var constraint = new Physijs.HingeConstraint(
    flipperLeft, flipperLeftPivot, flipperLeftPivot.position,
    new THREE.Vector3(0,1,0));
scene.addConstraint(constraint);
constraint.setLimits(-2.2, -0.6, 0.1, 0);
```

This constraint takes four parameters. Let's look at each one in a bit more detail:

Parameter	Description
mesh_a	The first object passed into the function is the object that is to be constrained. In this example the first object is the white cube that serves as the flipper. This is the object that is constrained in its movements.

Parameter	Description
mesh_b	The second object defines to which object mesh_a is constrained. In this example mesh a is constrained to the small brown cube. If we move this mesh around, mesh_a would follow it around, still keeping the HingeConstraint in place. You'll see that all constraints have this option. You could, for instance, use this if you've created a car that moves around, and want to create a constraint for opening a door. If this second parameter is omitted the hinge will be constrained to the scene (and never move around).
position	The point where the constraint is applied to. In this case the hinge point around which mesh_a rotates. If you've specified mesh_b, this hinge point will move around with the position and rotation of mesh_b.
axis	The axis around which the hinge should rotate. In this example we've set the hinge horizontally (0,1,0).

Adding a HingeConstraint object to the scene, works in the same way as we've seen with PointConstraint. You use the addConstraint method, specify the constraint to add, and optionally add true to show the exact location and orientation of the constraint for debug purposes. For a HingeConstraint object, however, we need to set the properties of the constraint. We do this with the setLimits function.

This function takes the following four parameters:

Parameter	Description
low	This property specifies the minimum angle of motion in radians.
high	This property specifies the maximum angle of motion in radians.
bias_factor	This property defines the rate with which the constraint corrects itself after an error in position. For instance, when the hinge is pushed out of its constraints by a different object, it will move itself to its correct position. The higher this value, the faster it will correct its position. Best to keep it below 0.5.
relaxation_factor	This property defines the rate at which the velocity is changed by the constraint. If this is set to a high value, the object will bounce when it reaches its minimum or maximum angle of motion.

You can change these properties at run time if you want. If you add a `HingeConstraint` with these properties, you won't see much movement yet. The mesh will only move when hit by another object, or based on gravity. This constraint, as many others, however, can also be moved by an internal motor. This is what you see when you check the `enableMotor` checkbox in the **hinge** submenu from our example. The following code is used to enable this motor:

```
constraint.enableAngularMotor( controls.velocity,
    controls.acceleration );
```

This will speed up the mesh (in our case the flipper) to the specified velocity using the provided acceleration. If we want to move the flipper the other way, we just specify a negative velocity. If we didn't have any limits, this would cause our flipper to rotate, as long as our motor keeps running. To disable a motor we can just call:

```
flipperLeftConstraint.disableMotor();
```

Now the mesh will slow down, based on friction, collisions, gravity, and other physics.

Limiting movement to a single axis with a SliderConstraint

The next constraint is the `SliderConstraint`. With this constraint you can limit the movement of an object to any one of its axes.

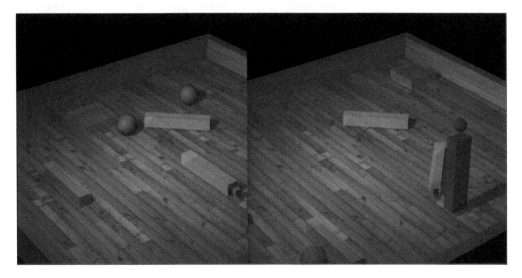

The sliders in example `04-constraints.html` can be controlled from the **sliders** submenu. With the **SlidersLeft** button, the sliders will move to the left (their lower limit), and with the **SlidersRight** button, they will move to the right (their upper limit). Creating these constraints from code is very easy:

```
var constraint = new Physijs.SliderConstraint(
  sliderMesh,
  new THREE.Vector3(0, 2, 0),
  new THREE.Vector3(0, 1, 0));

scene.addConstraint(constraint);
constraint.setLimits(-10, 10, 0, 0);
constraint.setRestitution(0.1, 0.1);
```

As you can see from the code, this constraint takes three parameters (or four if you want to constrain an object to another object). The following table explains the arguments for this constraint:

Parameter	Description
mesh_a	The first object passed into the function is the object that is to be constrained. In this example the first object is the green cube that serves as the slider. This is the object that will be constrained in its movements.
mesh_b	The second object defines to which object mesh_a is constrained. This is an optional argument and omitted in this example. If omitted, the mesh will be constrained to the scene. If it is specified, the slider will move around when this mesh moves around or its orientation changes.
position	The point where the constraint is applied to. This is especially important when you constrain mesh_a to mesh_b.
axis	The axis on which mesh_a will slide. Note that this is relative to the orientation of mesh_b if that one is specified. In the current version of Physijs, there seems to be a strange offset to this axis when using a linear motor with linear limits. What works for this version is the following. If you want to slide along: • the x-axis: new THREE.Vector3(0,1,0) • the y-axis: new THREE.Vector3(0,0,Math.PI/2) • the z-axis: new THREE.Vector3(Math.PI/2,0,0)

After you've created the constraint and added it to the scene using `scene.addConstraint` you can set the limits for this constraint to specify how far the slider may slide: `constraint.setLimits(-10, 10, 0, 0)`. You can set the following limits on the `SliderConstraint`:

Parameter	Description
`linear_lower`	This property specifies the lower linear limit of the object.
`linear_upper`	This property specifies the upper linear limit of the object.
`angular_lower`	This property specifies the lower angular limit of the object.
`angular_higher`	This property specifies the upper angular limit of the object.

And finally you can set the restitution (the bounce) that'll occur when you hit one these limits. You do this with `constraint.setRestitution(res_linear, res_angular)`, where the first parameter sets the amount of bounce when you hit the linear limit, and the second one sets the amount of bounce when you hit the angular limit.

Now the complete constraint has been configured and we can wait until collisions occur that slide the object around or use a motor. For the `SlideConstraint` we've got two options, we can use an angular motor to accelerate along the axis we specified, and complying with the angular limits we set or use a linear motor to accelerate along the axis we specified and complying with the linear limits. In this example we've used a linear motor. For use of an angular motor look at the `DOFConstraint` explained further down in this chapter.

Creating a ball joint-like constraint with the ConeTwist Constraint

With the `ConeTwistConstraint`, it is possible to create a constraint where the movement is limited to a set of angles. We can specify what the minimum and maximum angles are from one object to the other for the x, y, and z-axis.

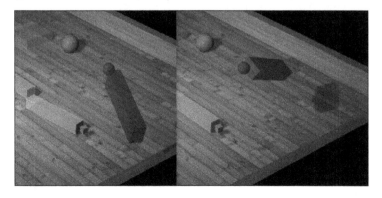

The easiest way to understand the ConeTwistConstraint is by looking at the code required to create one:

```
var baseMesh = new THREE.SphereGeometry(1);
var armMesh = new THREE.CubeGeometry(2, 12, 3);

var objectOne = new
  Physijs.BoxMesh(baseMesh, Physijs.createMaterial(
    new THREE.MeshPhongMaterial({color: 0x4444ff,
      transparent: true, opacity:0.7}), 0, 0), 0);
objectOne.position.z = 0;
objectOne.position.x = 20;
objectOne.position.y = 15.5;
objectOne.castShadow = true;
scene.add(objectOne);

var objectTwo = new
  Physijs.SphereMesh(armMesh, Physijs.createMaterial(
    new THREE.MeshPhongMaterial({color: 0x4444ff,
      transparent: true, opacity:0.7}), 0, 0), 10);
objectTwo.position.z = 0;
objectTwo.position.x = 20;
objectTwo.position.y = 7.5;
scene.add(objectTwo);
objectTwo.castShadow = true;

var constraint = new Physijs.ConeTwistConstraint(
  objectOne, objectTwo, objectOne.position);

scene.addConstraint(constraint);

constraint.setLimit(0.5*Math.PI, 0.5*Math.PI, 0.5*Math.PI);
constraint.setMaxMotorImpulse(1);
constraint.setMotorTarget(new THREE.Vector3(0, 0, 0));
```

In this piece of JavaScript, you'll probably already recognize a number of concepts we've discussed earlier. We start with creating the objects that we connect to each other with the constraint: `objectOne` (a sphere) and `objectTwo` (a box). We position these objects so that `objectTwo` hangs below `objectOne`. Now we can create the `ConeTwistConstraint`. The arguments this constraint takes aren't anything new if you've already looked at the other constraints. The first parameter is the object to constrain and the second parameter is the object to which the first object is constrained and the last parameter is the location where the constraint is constructed (in this case it's the point around which `objectOne` rotates). After adding the constraint to the scene we can set its limits with the `setLimit` function. This function takes three radian values that specify the maximum angle for each of the axes.

Just like with most of the other constraints, we can move `objectOne` by using the motor provided by the constraint. For the `ConeTwistConstraint` object we set the `MaxMotorImpulse` property (how much force the motor can apply) and we set the target angles the motor should move `objectOne` to. In this example we move it to its resting position directly below the sphere. In the example you can play around with this example by setting this target value. The following screenshot shows the output of the example `04-constraints.html`:

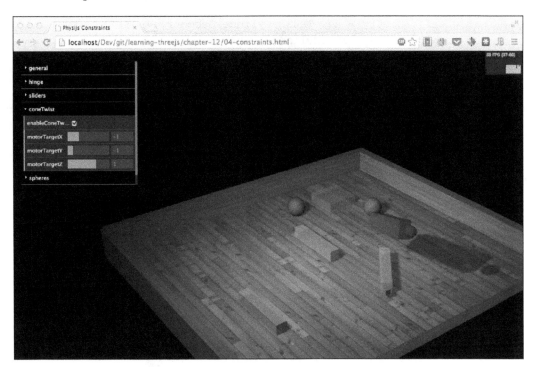

The last constraint we look at is also the most versatile: the `DOFConstraint`.

Creating detailed control with the DOFConstraint

The DOFConstraint, also called the degree of freedom constraint, allows you to exactly control an object's linear and angular movement. We'll show how to use this constraint by creating an example where you can drive around a simple car-like shape. This shape consists of a single rectangle that serves as the body and four spheres that serve as the wheels. Let's start by creating the wheels:

```
function createWheel(position) {
  var wheel_material = Physijs.createMaterial(
    new THREE.MeshLambertMaterial({
      color: 0x444444,
      opacity: 0.9,
      transparent: true
    }),
    1.0, // high friction
    0.5 // medium restitution
  );

  var wheel_geometry = new THREE.CylinderGeometry(4, 4, 2, 10);
  var wheel = new Physijs.CylinderMesh(
    wheel_geometry,
    wheel_material,
    100
  );

  wheel.rotation.x = Math.PI / 2;
  wheel.castShadow = true;
  wheel.position = position;
  return wheel;
}
```

In this piece of code we just create a simple `CylinderGeometry` and a `CylinderMesh` that can be used as the wheels for our car as shown in the following screenshot:

Next we need to create the body of the car and add everything to the scene:

```
var car = {};
var car_material = Physijs.createMaterial(
  new THREE.MeshLambertMaterial({
    color: 0xff4444,
    opacity: 0.9,  transparent: true
  }),   0.5, 0.5
);

var geom = new THREE.CubeGeometry(15, 4, 4);
var body = new Physijs.BoxMesh(geom, car_material, 500);
body.position.set(5, 5, 5);
body.castShadow = true;
scene.add(body);

var fr = createWheel(new THREE.Vector3(0, 4, 10));
```

```
var fl = createWheel(new THREE.Vector3(0, 4, 0));
var rr = createWheel(new THREE.Vector3(10, 4, 10));
var rl = createWheel(new THREE.Vector3(10, 4, 0));

scene.add(fr);
scene.add(fl);
scene.add(rr);
scene.add(rl);
```

So far we've just created the separated components that will have to make up our car. To tie everything together we're going to create constraints. Each wheel will be constrained to the body object:

```
var frConstraint = new Physijs.DOFConstraint(fr,body,
  new THREE.Vector3(0,4,8));
scene.addConstraint(frConstraint);
var flConstraint = new Physijs.DOFConstraint (fl,body,
  new THREE.Vector3(0,4,2));
scene.addConstraint(flConstraint);
var rrConstraint = new Physijs.DOFConstraint (rr,body,
  new THREE.Vector3(10,4,8));
scene.addConstraint(rrConstraint);
var rlConstraint = new Physijs.DOFConstraint (rl,body,
  new THREE.Vector3(10,4,2));
scene.addConstraint(rlConstraint);
```

Each wheel (the first argument) has its own constraint and the position (the second argument) defines where the wheel is attached to the body of the car. If we ran the code with this configuration we'd see that the four wheels hold up the body of the car. We need to do two more things to get the car moving: we need to set up the constraints for the wheels (the axis along which they can move) and we need to configure the correct motors. First we set up the constraints for the two front wheels, what we want for these front wheels is to just be able to rotate along the z-axis so they can power the car, and they shouldn't be allowed to move along the other axis. We can code the constraints as follows:

```
frConstraint.setAngularLowerLimit({ x: 0, y: 0, z: 0 });
frConstraint.setAngularUpperLimit({ x: 0, y: 0, z: 0 });
flConstraint.setAngularLowerLimit({ x: 0, y: 0, z: 0 });
flConstraint.setAngularUpperLimit({ x: 0, y: 0, z: 0 });
```

At first glance this might seem weird. By setting the lower and upper limits to the same value, we make sure that no rotation is possible in the specified direction. This would also mean that the wheels can't rotate around their z-axis. The reason we specify it like this is that when you enable a motor for a specific axis, these limits are ignored. So setting limits on the z-axis at this point doesn't have any effect for our front wheels.

We're going to steer with our rear wheels and to make sure they don't fall over, we need to fix the x-axis. With the following code, we fix the x-axis (set upper and lower to 0), fix the y-axis so these wheels are already initially turned, and we disable any limit on the z-axis, as follows:

```
rrConstraint.setAngularLowerLimit({ x: 0, y: 0.5, z: 0.1 });
rrConstraint.setAngularUpperLimit({ x: 0, y: 0.5, z: 0 });
rlConstraint.setAngularLowerLimit({ x: 0, y: 0.5, z: 0.1 });
rlConstraint.setAngularUpperLimit({ x: 0, y: 0.5, z: 0 });
```

As you can see, to disable the limits we have to set the lower limit of that specific axis higher than the upper limit. This will allow free rotation around that axis. If we don't set this for the z-axis these two wheels will just be dragged along. In this case they'll turn together with the other wheels because of the friction with the ground.

All that is left to do is set up the motors for the front wheels:

```
flConstraint.configureAngularMotor(2, 0.1, 0, -2, 1500);
frConstraint.configureAngularMotor(2, 0.1, 0, -2, 1500);
```

Since there are three axes, we can create a motor for we need to specify the axis the motor works on: 0 is for the x-axis, 1 is for the y-axis, and 2 is for the z-axis. The second and third arguments define the angular limits for the motor. Here we once again set the lower limit (0.1) higher than the upper limit (0) to allow free rotation. The third argument specifies the velocity we want to reach, and the last argument specifies the force this motor can apply. If this last one is too little, the car won't move, if it's too high the rear wheels will lift off from the ground.

And enable them:

```
flConstraint.enableAngularMotor(2);
frConstraint.enableAngularMotor(2);
```

If you open up example 05-dof-constraint.html you can play around with the various constraints and motors and drive the car around as shown in the following screenshot:

Summary

In this last chapter we've explored how you can extend the basic 3D functionality from Three.js by adding physics. For this we've used the Physijs library, which allows you to add gravity, collisions, constraints, and much more. The most important things to remember when working with this library are the following:

- To use Physijs you need to change the scene you instantiate and specify the gravity you want to use. You also need to change the render loop to include a simulate step that tells Physijs to calculate the position and rotation of all the objects in the scene.

- Only geometries wrapped in their Physijs counterpart will be subject to the physics. In most cases you can just change the THREE.Mesh definition with the Physijs variant.

- You can specify how an object interacts with other objects by using Physijs material. On this material you can set the friction for the object and the restitution.

- Beware to use the correct Physijs mesh when creating meshes from your geometries. Collisions are based on the Physijs mesh in combination with the underlying geometry, not just on the geometry.

- When you've added an object to the scene, Physijs will be responsible for the object's position and rotation. If these are modified outside of Physijs you need to set the __dirtyRotation or __dirtyPosition properties to true.

- Avoid using ConcaveMesh when you've got complex shapes. This object is very bad for the performance of your scene.

- Constraints are a very powerful way to add interactivity and physics to your scene. Using constraints, however, isn't always very straightforward. You can see the exact behavior of the constraint by providing true as an additional parameter to the addConstraint function.

- Often the best way to get started with a constraint is by using a working example and configuring and changing it to your liking.

That's it for this book on Three.js. In these chapters we've covered a lot of different subjects and explored pretty much everything that Three.js has to offer. In the first couple of chapters we explained the core concepts and ideas behind Three.js, after that we looked at the available lights and seen how materials affect how an object is rendered. After the basics, we explored the various geometries that Three.js has to offer, and how you can combine geometries to create new ones.

In the second part of the book we looked at some more advanced subjects. You've learned how to create particle systems, how to load models from external sources, and create animations. And finally, in these last couple of chapters we've looked at advanced textures you can use in skinning and post-processing effects that can be applied after the scene is rendered. We end the book with this chapter on physics, which, besides explaining how you can add physics to your Three.js scene, also shows the active community of projects surrounding Three.js, which you can use to add even more functionality to an already great library.

I hope you've enjoyed reading this book, and playing around with the examples, as much as I have writing it!

Index

Symbols

3D file format
geometry, importing from 224
3D object
rendering 19, 21
viewing 19, 21
3D text
creating 167
custom font, adding 170
rendering 170
rendering, TextGeometry used 167, 168

A

add(color) function 70
addColors(color1, color2) function 70
addConstraint function 356, 358
add() function 41, 46, 208
addPass() function 310
addScalar(s) function 70
advanced EffectComposer object
creating, MaskPass used 318-322
advanced geometry
about 153
amount property 159
bevelEnabled property 159
bevelSegments property 159
bevelSize property 159
bevelThickness property 159
ConvexGeometry 154, 155
curveSegments property 159
ExtrudeGeometry 158-160
extrudeMaterial property 160
extrudePath property 159
LatheGeometry 156, 157
material property 160

ParametricGeometry 164-167
steps property 159
TubeGeometry 160-162
advanced materials
about 110
MeshLambertMaterial 110, 111
MeshPhongMaterial 112, 113
ShaderMaterial 114-121
advanced properties, materials
about 94, 96
alphaTest 96
depthTest 96
depthWrite 96
polygonOffset 96
polygonOffsetFactor 96
polygonOffsetUnits 96
advanced shaders
about 323, 329, 330
BleachBypassShader 323
EdgeShader 323
FocusShader 324
FXAAShader 323
alignment property 202
alphaTest property 96
AmbientLight 66-69
ambient property 110, 112
ammo.js 339
URL 340
amount property 159
angle property 75, 316
animation
about 238-240
bones, used 263-266
creating, blender used 266-270
creating, by setting morphTargetInfluence
property 262, 263

creating, external models used 266
defining, morph target used 257, 258
defining, skeletal animation used 258
loading, from collada model 270-272
loading, from MD2 model 272, 273
loading, prerequisites 261
objects, selecting 240-242
skinning, used 263-266
with MorphAnimMesh 259, 261
archive
  downloading, to get source code 14
  extracting, to get source code 14
arc property 144
AreaLight 66, 84-86
ASCII effect
  about 33, 34
  using 33, 34
aspect property 60
axes object 19, 23
axis parameter 358, 360

B

ball
  bouncing 30, 31
basic lights
  about 66
  AmbientLight 66-69
  DirectionalLight 66, 80, 82
  PointLight 66, 71-74
  SpotLight 66, 75-80
basic properties, materials 94, 95
  ID 94
  name 94
  needsUpdate 95
  opacity 94
  overdraw 95
  side 95
  transparent 95
  visible 95
bevelEnabled property 159, 169
bevelSegments property 159, 169
bevelSize property 159, 169
bevelThickness property 159, 169
billboarding 199
binary operation
  used, for combining mesh 171-173

bitstream vera sans mono font 171
BleachBypassShader 323
blenddst property 95
blendequation property 96
Blender
  about 218, 266
  model, exporting from 221-223
  model, loading from 221-223
  Three.js exporter, installing in 219, 220
  URL 218
  URL, for downloading 219
  used, for creating animation 266-270
blending attribute 89, 188
blending property, materials
  about 94-96
  blenddst 95
  blendequation 96
  blending 95
  blendsrc 95
blending property 95, 103, 187, 201
blendsrc property 95
bloom effect
  about 314
  adding, BloomPass used 314, 315
BloomPass 311
  kernelSize property 314
  property 314
  Resolution property 314
  sigma property 314
  Strength property 314
  used, for adding bloom effect 314, 315
blurring shaders
  about 323, 327, 328
  HorizontalBlurShader 323
  HorizontalTiltShiftShader 323
  TriangleBlurShader 323
  VerticalBlurShader 323
  VerticalTiltShiftShader 323
bones
  used, for animation 263-266
bottom property 62
BoxMesh 348
BrightnessContrastShader 323
browsers, Three.js
  running on 9
bump map 301
  about 282

used, for creating wrinkles 282, 283
bumpMap property 283

C

callback function 232
camera
    about 37, 245
    controls 245
    focusing, on specific point 62, 63
    using 57
camera object 19, 22
camera, types
    orthographic camera 57
    perspective camera 57
canvas
    rendering 299
    using, as bump map 301-303
    using, as texture 299-301
CanvasRenderer
    HTML5 canvas, using with 188, 189
CapsuleMesh 349
castShadow property 75
center property 316
chain() function 244
children property 46
Chrome Frame
    URL 9
CircleGeometry 130-132
    property 131
clear() function 318
clear property 321
clone() function 50, 51, 71
closed property 162
Collada file format
    about 212
    loading 228, 229
collada model
    about 266
    animation, loading from 270-272
color attribute 89, 188
ColorCorrectionShader 323
ColorifyShader 323
color property 72, 84, 97, 122, 186, 201
components, Three.js scene
    about 37
    camera 37

lights 37
objects 38
ConcaveMesh 349
ConeMesh 349
ConeTwistConstraint 354
    about 361, 363
    used, for creating ball joint-like constraint
        361, 363
constraints, Physijs
    about 354, 355
    ConeTwistConstraint 354, 361, 363
    DOFConstraint 354, 364-367
    HingeConstraint 354, 357-359
    PointConstraint 354-356
    SliderConstraint 354, 359-361
    used, for controlling movement of
        object 354, 355
controls, camera 245
    FirstPersonControls 245, 250-252
    FlyControls 245, 248, 249
    OrbitControls 245, 252-254
    PathControls 245, 254-256
    RollControls 245, 250
    TrackBallControls 245-248
convertGammaToLinear() function 70
convertLinearToGamma() function 70
ConvexGeometry 154, 155
ConvexMesh 349
copy(color) function 70
copyGammaToLinear(color) function 70
copyLinearToGamma(color) function 70
createParticles function 189
createParticleSystem() function 206
createSystem function 197
CTM file format 212
    loading 229, 231
cube
    animating 30
CubeGeometry
    about 138, 139
    property 138
cube object 19
curveSegments property 159, 169
custom bit shader
    creating 334-336
custom effects
    ShaderPass, using 323, 324

custom font
  adding, to 3D text 170
custom grayscale shader 330-334
custom shader
  creating 330
  custom bit shader 334-336
  custom grayscale shader 330-334
CylinderGeometry
  about 142, 143
  property 142
CylinderMesh 349

D

dashSize property 124
dat.GUI library
  about 32, 33
  URL 32
  using 32
debug property 162
degree of freedom constraint. *See*
      DOFConstraint
depth property 138
depthSegments property 139
depthTest property 96, 202
depthWrite property 96, 198, 202
detail property 148
DirectionalLight
  about 66, 80, 82
  property 81
distance argument 88
distance property 72, 74
DOFConstraint 354
  about 364-367
  used, for creating detailed control 364-367
DotScreenPass 311
  angle property 316
  center property 316
  property 316
  scale property 316
  using 315
draw function 189

E

easing 242
easing() function 242
EdgeShader 323

EffectComposer object
  configuring 310
  creating 309
  render loop, updating 310, 311
emissive property 110, 112
environment map
  used, for creating fake reflections 288-291
envMap property 290
exponent property 75
external models
  used, for creating animation 266
ExtrudeGeometry 158-160
extrudeMaterial property 160, 169
extrudePath property 159, 169
extruding
  from SVG 162-164

F

face 47
faces property 148
fake reflections
  creating, environment map used 288-291
fake shadows
  creating, light map used 286, 287
far property 44, 61, 62, 101
field of view. *See* fov
file format
  supported, by Three.js 212, 213
FilmPass
  about 311
  grayscale property 313
  noiseIntensity property 313
  property 313
  scanlinesCount property 313
  scanlinesIntensity property 313
  using, to create TV-like effect 313, 314
FirstPersonControls 245, 250-252
FlyControls 245, 248, 249
FocusShader 324
fog effect
  adding, to Three.js scene 44
fog property 44, 46, 98, 114, 122, 187, 201
font property 168, 170
fov property 60
fragmentShader 115, 330
friction property 346-348

function property 166
FXAAShader 323

G

gapSize property 124
generateSprite() function 206
geometry
  about 127, 128
  advanced geometry 153
  functions 47-52
  grouping and merging 207
  importing, from 3D file format 224
  importing, from MTL file format 224-227
  importing, from OBJ file format 224-227
  loading, from external resource 212, 213
  loading, in JSON file format 213-215
  property 47-52
  saving, in JSON file format 213-215
  three-dimensional geometry 128
  two-dimensional geometry 128
geometry, grouping and merging 207
  multiple meshes, merging 210, 211
  objects, grouping together 208, 209
getChildByName(name) function 46
getDelta() function 246
getHex() function 70
getHexString() function 70
getHSV() function 70
getStyle() function 70
getTexture() function 192, 201
Git client
  URL 13
git command line tool 13
GitHub
  about 12
  URL 12
  used, for getting source code 13
Gosper curve
  URL 123
grayscale property 313
groundColor property 84

H

Head-Up display (HUD) 199
HeightfieldMesh 349
height property 129, 138, 142, 168

heightScale property 147
heightSegments property 129, 139, 140
helvetiker font 171
HemisphereLight
  about 66, 83, 84
  Color property 84
  groundColor property 84
  intensity property 84
HingeConstraint 354
  about 357, 359
  parameters 357
  used, for creating door-like
    constraints 357, 359
holes property 134
HorizontalBlurShader 323
HorizontalTiltShiftShader 323
HTML5 canvas
  particles, styling 187
  using, with CanvasRenderer 188, 189
  using, with WebGLRenderer class 190, 192
HTML skeleton page
  creating 16-18
HueSaturationShader 323

I

IcosahedronGeometry 149
ID property 94
iewebgl
  URL 9
init() function 256
installation, Three.js exporter
  in Blender 219, 220
intensity property 72, 73, 84
intersect function 171, 177, 178

J

JSON file format
  about 212
  geometry, loading in 213-215
  geometry, saving in 213-215
  scene, loading 216, 217
  scene, saving 216, 217

K

kernelSize property 314

L

LatheGeometry
about 156, 157
phiLength property 157
phiStart property 157
points property 157
property 157
segments property 157
left property 61
LensFlare 66, 87-91
lerp(color, alpha) function 71
light map
about 286
used, for creating fake shadows 286, 287
lightMap property 287
lights
about 37, 66
adding 24-26
basic lights 66
special lights 66
SpotLight 75
LineBasicMaterial
about 94, 122-124
color property 122
fog property 122
LineCap property 122
LineJoin property 122
linewidth property 122
vertexColors property 122
LineCap property 122
LineDashedMaterial
about 94, 124
dashSize property 124
gapSize property 124
scale property 124
LineJoin property 122
linewidth property 122
literally library
about 300
URL 300
load function 215
loadTexture() function 192, 278
lookAt() function 23, 245, 255

M

map property 186, 190, 192, 194, 201, 283

MaskPass 311
used, for creating advanced
EffectComposer object 318-322
material property 160, 169
material property, Physijs 346-348
materials
about 93, 94
adding 24-26
advanced materials 93, 94, 110
advanced properties 94, 96
basic properties 94, 95
blending properties 94-96
simple materials 93, 94, 97
Math.tan() function 77
MD2 model 266
animation, loading from 272, 273
mesh
combining, binary operation used 171-173
functions 52-56
property 52-56
texture, applying to 278-281
mesh_a parameter 357, 360
MeshBasicMaterial 93
about 97-99
color property 97
fog property 98
shading property 97
vertexColors property 97
wireframeLinecap property 97
wireframeLinejoin property 97
wireframeLinewidth property 97
wireframe property 97
mesh_b parameter 358, 360
mesh, Physijs
about 348, 349
BoxMesh 348
CapsuleMesh 349
ConcaveMesh 349
ConeMesh 349
ConvexMesh 349
CylinderMesh 349
HeightfieldMesh 349
PlaneMesh 348
SphereMesh 348
MeshDepthMaterial
about 93, 100-102
wireframeLinewidth property 100

wireframe property 100
MeshFaceMaterial 93, 107-109
MeshLambertMaterial
    about 93, 110, 111
    ambient property 110
    emissive property 110
MeshNormalMaterial 93
    about 104-107
    shading property 106
    wireframeLinewidth property 106
    wireframe property 106
MeshPhongMaterial 93
    about 112, 113
    ambient property 112
    emissive property 112
    shininess property 112
    specular property 112
mipmap 280
MirrorShader 323
model
    exporting, from Blender 221-223
    loading, from Blender 221-223
Mongoose
    about 15, 16
    URL, for downloading 15
morph animation 269
MorphAnimMesh
    animation with 259, 261
morph target
    used, for defining animation 257, 258
morphTargetInfluence property
    setting, to create animation 262, 263
MTL file format 212
    geometry, importing from 224-227
multiple meshes
    merging, into single mesh 210, 211
multiple renderers
    output, displaying 317, 318
multiply(color) function 70
multiplyScalar(s) function 70

N

name property 94
near property 44, 60, 62, 101
needsUpdate property 95, 301
noiseIntensity property 313

normal map
    about 284, 285
    using 284, 285
normalMap property 285
Notepad++ 11
NPM-based approach 15

O

objects
    about 38
    grouping together 208, 209
    selecting 240-242
OBJ file format 212
    geometry, importing from 224-227
onlyShadow property 75
opacity attribute 188
opacity property 94, 187, 201
openCTM 212
openEnded property 143
OpenGL Shading Language (GLSL)
    about 331
    URL 331
OrbitControls 245, 252-254
orthographic camera
    about 57
    bottom property 62
    far property 62
    left property 61
    near property 62
    property 61
    right property 61
    top property 62
    vs, perspective camera 57-61
overdraw property 95
overrideMaterial property 46
    about 45
    using 45, 46

P

parameters, HingeConstraint
    axis 358
    mesh_a 357
    mesh_b 358
    position 358
parameters, PointConstraint 356

ParametricGeometry
about 164, 166, 167
function property 166
slices property 166
stacks property 166
useTris property 166
parse method 215
ParticleBasicMaterial object
properties, setting 186, 187
ParticleCanvasMaterial
attributes, setting 188
particles
about 181-183
creating 182-185
styling, texture used 192-198
styling, with HTML5 canvas 187
particle system
about 184
creating 185-187, 204-206
passes, post processing
about 311
BloomPass 311
DotScreenPass 311
FilmPass 311
MaskPass 311
RenderPass 311
SavePass 311
ShaderPass 311
TexturePass 311
PathControls 245, 254-256
path property 161
PDB 231
PDB file format 213
loading 231-233
proteins, displaying 231-233
Perlin noise
about 302
URL 302
perlin.noise function 303
perspective camera
about 57
aspect property 60
far property 61
fov property 60
near property 60
property 60
vs, orthographic camera 57-61

phiLength property 140, 157
phiStart property 140, 157
physics 339
Physijs
about 339
constraints 354, 355
material property 346-348
mesh 348, 349
shapes, supported 348-353
Three.js scene, creating for 340-345
PlaneGeometry
about 128-130
property 129
PlaneMesh 348
plane object 19
playAnimation function 273
PLY file format
about 213
particle system, creating 234, 235
working with 234, 235
PointConstraint
about 354
parameters 356
using 355, 356
PointLight
about 66, 71, 72, 74
color property 72
distance property 72
intensity property 72
position property 72
visible property 72
points property 157
polygonOffsetFactor property 96
polygonOffset property 96
polygonOffsetUnits property 96
PolyhedronGeometry
about 147, 148
IcosahedronGeometry 149
property 148
TetrahedronGeometry 149, 150
position parameter 358, 360
position property 52, 53, 55, 72
post processing
EffectComposer object, configuring 310
EffectComposer object, creating 309
passes 311
setting up 308

simple passes 312, 313
p property 146
program attribute 188
property, DirectionalLight 81
protein databank. *See* PDB
Python-based approach 15

Q

q property 147

R

radialSegments property 144, 146
radiusBottom property 142
radius property 131, 140, 144, 146, 148, 161
radiusSegments property 162
radiusTop property 142
reflection property 291
reflectivity property 290
refraction property 291
remove() function 41, 46
render() function 29, 30, 43, 238, 311, 318
render loop
    updating 310, 311
RenderPass 311
render post processing 307
renderScene() function 27
repeat wrapping 297-299
repository
    reference link 13
requestAnimationFrame() method 27-30
resolution property 314
restitution property 346-348
RGBShiftShader 323
right property 61
RollControls 245, 250
rotation property 30, 52, 55

S

SavePass 311
Scalable Vector Graphics. *See* SVG
scaleByViewport property 202
scale property 52, 55, 124, 316
scanlinesCount property 313
scanlinesIntensity property 313
scene.add() function 23

Scene.Add() function 43
Scene.children() function 43
Scene.getChildByName() function 43
Scene.Remove() function 43
segments property 131, 157, 161
segmentsX property 142
segmentsY property 143
SepiaShader 323
setHex(value) function 69
setHSL() method 123
setHSV(h,s,v) function 70
setInterval() function 27
setInterval() method 27
setLimits function
    about 358, 363
    bias_factor parameter 358
    high parameter 358
    low parameter 358
    relaxation_factor parameter 358
setMode() function 28
setRGB(r,g,b) function 70
setSize() function 22
setStyle(style) function 70
set(value) function 69
shader
    about 114
    advanced shaders 323
    blurring shaders 323
    creating, with ShaderMaterial 114-121
    simple shaders 323
ShaderMaterial
    about 93, 114-121
    fog property 114
    fragmentShader 115
    shader, creating with 114-121
    shading property 114
    vertexColors property 114
    vertexShader 115
    wireframeLinewidth property 114
    wireframe property 114
ShaderPass
    about 311
    using, for custom effects 323, 324
shadertoy
    URL 330
shading property 97, 106, 114
shadowBias property 75

shadowCameraFar property 75
shadowCameraFov property 75
shadowCameraNear property 75
shadowCameraVisible property 75
shadowDarkness property 75
shadowMapHeight property 75
shadowMapWidth property 75
shadows
  adding 24-26
ShapeGeometry 132-137
shapes, Physijs 348-353
shininess property 112
side property 95, 99
sigma property 314
simple materials
  about 97
  combining 102, 103
  LineDashedMaterial 122-124
  MeshBasicMaterial 97-99
  MeshDepthMaterial 97, 100-102
  MeshFaceMaterial 97, 107-109
  MeshNormalMaterial 97, 104-107
simple passes, post processing 312, 313
simple shaders
  about 323-326
  BrightnessContrastShader 323
  ColorCorrectionShader 323
  ColorifyShader 323
  HueSaturationShader 323
  MirrorShader 323
  RGBShiftShader 323
  SepiaShader 323
  VignetteShader 323
sizeAnnutation property 187, 201
size argument 88
size property 168, 186
skeletal animation
  about 269
  used, for defining animation 258
skinning
  used, in animation 263-266
slices property 166
SliderConstraint 354
  about 359-361
  axis parameter 360
  limits, setting 361
  mesh_a parameter 360

mesh_b parameter 360
position parameter 360
using 359-361
source code
  getting 12
  getting, by downloading archive 14
  getting, by extracting archive 14
  getting, GitHub used 13
  testing 14
source code, testing
  Mongoose 15, 16
  NPM-based approach 15
  Python-based approach 15
special lights
  about 66
  AreaLight 66, 84-86
  HemisphereLight 66, 83, 84
  LensFlare 66, 87-91
  using 83
specular map 292
specular property 112, 293
SphereGeometry
  about 139-141
  property 140
SphereMesh 348
sphere object 19
SpotLight
  about 66, 75-80
  angle property 75
  castShadow property 75
  exponent property 75
  onlyShadow property 75
  shadowBias property 75
  shadowCameraFar property 75
  shadowCameraFov property 75
  shadowCameraNear property 75
  shadowCameraVisible property 75
  shadowDarkness property 75
  shadowMapHeight property 75
  shadowMapWidth property 75
  target property 75
SpotLight() method 24, 26
sprite
  about 199-203
  creating 199-203
stacks property 166
stencilBuffer property 321

steps property 159, 169
STereoLithography. *See* STL
STL 212
STL file format 212
  loading 229, 231
Strength property 314
style property 168
Sublime Text Editor 11
  URL, for downloading 11
subtract function 171-176
SVG
  about 162-164
  extruding from 162-164

T

target property 75
TetrahedronGeometry 149, 150
texels 279
TextGeometry
  bevelEnabled property 169
  bevelSegments property 169
  bevelSize property 169
  bevelThickness property 169
  curveSegments property 169
  extrudeMaterial property 169
  extrudePath property 169
  font property 168
  height property 168
  material property 169
  size property 168
  steps property 169
  style property 168
  used, for rendering 3D text 167-170
  weight property 168
texture
  advanced usage 294
  applying, to mesh 278-281
  loading 278-281
  repeat wrapping 297-299
  used, for styling particles 192-198
  using 278
texture2D() function 333
texture argument 88
TexturePass 311
thetaLength property 131, 140
thetaStart property 131, 140

ThreeBSP
  about 171
  intersect function 171, 177, 178
  subtract function 171, 173-176
  union function 171, 179
  URL 171
THREE.Color() object
  about 69, 70
  add(color) function 70
  addColors(color1, color2) function 70
  addScalar(s) function 70
  clone() function 71
  convertGammaToLinear() function 70
  convertLinearToGamma() function 70
  copy(color) function 70
  copyGammaToLinear(color) function 70
  copyLinearToGamma(color) function 70
  getHex() function 70
  getHexString() function 70
  getHSV() function 70
  getStyle() function 70
  lerp(color, alpha) function 71
  multiply(color) function 70
  multiplyScalar(s) function 70
  setHex(value) function 69
  setHSV(h,s,v) function 70
  setRGB(r,g,b) function 70
  setStyle(style) function 70
  set(value) function 69
  using 69-71
three-dimensional geometry
  about 128, 137
  CubeGeometry 138, 139
  CylinderGeometry 142, 143
  PolyhedronGeometry 147, 148
  SphereGeometry 139-141
  TorusGeometry 144, 145
  TorusKnotGeometry 145
Three.js
  about 7
  animation 238-240
  camera 245
  features 7
  file format, supported by 212, 213
  geometry 127, 128
  lights 65, 66
  materials 93, 94

particles 181-184
running, on browsers 9
sprite 199-203
using, requisites 11, 12
versions 18
Three.js exporter
installing, in Blender 219, 220
Three.js, requisites
Notepad++ 11
Sublime Text Editor 11
WebStorm 11
Three.js scene
animating 27
ball, bouncing 30, 31
components 37
creating 19, 21, 37, 38
creating, for Physijs 340-345
cube, animating 30
fog effect, adding 44
function 46
functionality 38-43
lights, adding 24-26
loading 216, 217
materials, adding 24-26
property 46
saving 216, 217
shadows, adding 24-26
THREE.LensFlare object
blending argument 89
color argument 89
distance argument 88
size argument 88
texture argument 88
top property 62
TorusGeometry
about 144, 145
property 144
TorusKnotGeometry
about 145
property 146
TrackBallControls 245-248
translate() function 52, 56
translateX(amount) function 52
translateY(amount) function 52
translateZ(amount) function 52
transparent property 95, 103, 187, 188
traverse() function 43, 46

TriangleBlurShader 323
TubeGeometry
about 160, 161, 162
closed property 162
debug property 162
path property 161
radius property 161
radiusSegments property 162
segments property 161
tube property 144, 146
tubularSegments property 144, 146
tweening 242
Tween.js
about 242
animating with 242-244
URL 242
two-dimensional geometry
about 128
CircleGeometry 130-132
PlaneGeometry 128-130
ShapeGeometry 132-137
typeface.js
about 170
URL 170

U

UglifyJS 18
uniforms property 314
union function 171, 179
update method 266
useScreenCoordinates property 201, 203
useTris property 166
UV mapping
about 281, 294, 296, 297
customizing 294-297
uvOffset property 201, 202
uvScale property 201, 202

V

vertexColors property 97, 114, 122, 187
vertexShader 115, 330
VerticalBlurShader 323
VerticalTiltShiftShader 323
vertices 47
vertices property 148

video element
  using, as texture 303, 304
VignetteShader 323
visible property 72, 95
VTK file format
  about 213
  loading 229, 231

W

waypoints property 256
WebGL
  URL 330
WebGLRenderer class
  about 190
  HTML5 canvas, using with 190, 192

WebStorm 11
web workers
  about 340
  URL 340
weight property 168
width property 129, 138
widthSegments property 129, 139, 140
wireframeLinecap property 97
wireframeLinejoin property 97
wireframeLinewidth property 97, 100, 106,
    114
wireframe property 97, 100, 106, 114
wrapS property 298
wrapT property 298

Thank you for buying
Learning Three.js: The JavaScript
3D Library for WebGL

About Packt Publishing

Packt, pronounced 'packed', published its first book "*Mastering phpMyAdmin for Effective MySQL Management*" in April 2004 and subsequently continued to specialize in publishing highly focused books on specific technologies and solutions.

Our books and publications share the experiences of your fellow IT professionals in adapting and customizing today's systems, applications, and frameworks. Our solution based books give you the knowledge and power to customize the software and technologies you're using to get the job done. Packt books are more specific and less general than the IT books you have seen in the past. Our unique business model allows us to bring you more focused information, giving you more of what you need to know, and less of what you don't.

Packt is a modern, yet unique publishing company, which focuses on producing quality, cutting-edge books for communities of developers, administrators, and newbies alike. For more information, please visit our website: www.packtpub.com.

About Packt Open Source

In 2010, Packt launched two new brands, Packt Open Source and Packt Enterprise, in order to continue its focus on specialization. This book is part of the Packt Open Source brand, home to books published on software built around Open Source licences, and offering information to anybody from advanced developers to budding web designers. The Open Source brand also runs Packt's Open Source Royalty Scheme, by which Packt gives a royalty to each Open Source project about whose software a book is sold.

Writing for Packt

We welcome all inquiries from people who are interested in authoring. Book proposals should be sent to author@packtpub.com. If your book idea is still at an early stage and you would like to discuss it first before writing a formal book proposal, contact us; one of our commissioning editors will get in touch with you.

We're not just looking for published authors; if you have strong technical skills but no writing experience, our experienced editors can help you develop a writing career, or simply get some additional reward for your expertise.

Learning JavaScriptMVC

ISBN: 978-1-78216-020-5   Paperback: 124 pages

Learn to build well-structured JavaScript web applications using JavaScriptMVC

1. Install JavaScriptMVC in three different ways, including installing using Vagrant and Chef

2. Document your JavaScript codebase and generate searchable API documentation

3. Test your codebase and application as well as learning how to integrate tests with the continuous integration tool, Jenkins

Blender 3D Basics

ISBN: 978-1-84951-690-7   Paperback: 468 pages

The complete novice's guide to 3D modeling and animation

1. The best starter guide for complete newcomers to 3D modeling and animation

2. Easier learning curve than any other book on Blender

3. You will learn all the important foundation skills ready to apply to any 3D software

Please check **www.PacktPub.com** for information on our titles

Ext JS 4 Web Application Development Cookbook

ISBN: 978-1-84951-686-0   Paperback: 488 pages

Over 110 easy-to-follow recipes backed up with real-life examples, walking you through basic Ext JS features to advanced application design using Sencha's Ext JS

1. Learn how to build Rich Internet Applications with the latest version of the Ext JS framework in a cookbook style

2. From creating forms to theming your interface, you will learn the building blocks for developing the perfect web application

3. Easy to follow recipes step through practical and detailed examples which are all fully backed up with code, illustrations, and tips

HTML5 Enterprise Application Development

ISBN: 978-1-84968-568-9   Paperback: 332 pages

A step-by-step practical introduction to HTML5 through the building of a real-world application, including common development practices

1. Learn the most useful HTML5 features by developing a real-world application

2. Detailed solutions to most common problems presented in an enterprise application development

3. Discover the most up-to-date development tips, tendencies, and trending libraries and tools

Please check **www.PacktPub.com** for information on our titles

www.ingramcontent.com/pod-product-compliance
Lightning Source LLC
Chambersburg PA
CBHW062035050326
40690CB00016B/2951